Cultural Studies

Theorizing Politics, Politicizing Theory

VOLUME 13 NUMBER 1 JANUARY 1999

CW01566957

Editorial Statement

Cultural Studies continues to expand and flourish, in large part because the field keeps changing. Cultural studies scholars are addressing new questions and discourses, continuing to debate long-standing issues, and reinventing critical traditions. More and more universities have some formal cultural studies presence; the number of books and journals in the field is rapidly increasing. *Cultural Studies* welcomes these developments. We understand the expansion, reflexivity and internal critique of cultural studies to be both signs of its vitality and signature components of its status as a field. At the same time, cultural studies has been – and will no doubt continue to be – the subject of numerous attacks, launched from various perspectives and sites. These have to be taken seriously and answered, intellectually, institutionally and publicly. *Cultural Studies* hopes to provide a forum for response and strategic discussion.

    Cultural Studies assumes that the knowledge formations that make up the field are as historically and geographically contingent as are the determinations of any cultural practice or configuration and that the work produced within or at its permeable boundaries will be diverse. We hope not only to represent but to enhance this diversity. Consequently, we encourage submissions from various disciplinary, theoretical and geographical perspectives, and hope to reflect the wide-ranging articulations, both global and local, among historical, political, economic, cultural and everyday discourses. At the heart of these articulations are questions of community, identity, agency and change.

    We expect to publish work that is politically and strategically driven, empirically grounded, theoretically sophisticated, contextually defined and reflexive about its status, however critical, within the range of cultural studies. *Cultural Studies* is about theorizing politics and politicizing theory. How this is to be accomplished in any context remains, however, open to rigorous enquiry. As we look towards the future of the field and the journal, it is this enquiry that we especially hope to support.

Lawrence Grossberg
Della Pollock

January 1998

Contents

VOLUME 13   NUMBER 1   JANUARY 1999

Articles

Reviews

Stephen Muecke

TRAVELLING THE SUBTERRANEAN RIVER OF BLOOD: PHILOSOPHY AND MAGIC IN CULTURAL STUDIES

Abstract

This article argues for a philosophical and 'magical' turn in cultural studies in order to account for multidimensional aspects of rituals which work to reproduce cultures. It is suggested that those Western disciplines which have dominated understandings of Aboriginality in Australia are anthropology, history and literature and that they have done so with two important reifications: *the social* and *the word*. A philosophical rereading of a major interpreter of Aboriginal religion, W. E. H. Stanner, discovers a text dominated by the referent, enlightenment secularity, and a lack of self-reflexivity typical of his time. The more recent work of José Gil and Michael Taussig allows for immediate and performative body–country relations (examples are given from indigenous and state rituals which use the trope of blood). Powerful events in the indigenous and non-indigenous historical landscape are thus described in vernacular terms without recourse to the displacing categories of social system or text. The article concludes that national myths are established and maintained through rituals which attribute power to the dead in particular places, and that 'primitive' magico-religious forces are at the heart of nation-forming ceremonies in contemporary state society.

Keywords

Aborigines; sacred; philosophy; magic; nation

'Everything standing up alive.'
David Mowaljarlai, *c.*1928–1997.
In Memoriam

Lest we forget

CULTURE PERFORMS ITS MAGIC in ways structuralists could never have imagined. The forces bound up and then released in the events of our lives are multiply coded and inflected. Their most salient feature is not the *formal*, textual, transformations beloved of structuralists, and nor is the search for *meaning* the performers' sovereign aim – neither for the 'native' participants, nor for the researcher-performers. Signs, forces and bodies are all essential elements in the description of cultures which work to enhance life forms.

To demonstrate this thesis, already somewhat accepted among the loose ranks of those called poststructuralists but not yet worked up as an argument for the re-enchantment of cultural studies via magical and philosophical thought, I will discuss a couple of ceremonies.

A piece of music is played on a brass instrument by a lone man at dawn. It is a trace of rhythmic energy, an almost perfect sine-wave, emerging from a body and entering *every* sympathetic, permeable body in the listening host which in its life movement alternates inside and outside, self and other, sound and the whisper of breath. The sound swells, other forces come together and intensify into something which might be called an event, perhaps a ritual. Its performance is designed to ensure cultural growth, or at least to instil a structure of feeling. And as the final tone of the 'Last Post' fades on the breeze, there is hardly a dry eye at the Shrine of Remembrance (Garton, 1996: 8).[1] This 1920s war memorial is described by Greg Dening as 'harsh and heavy, like some pillbox standing in Flanders fields, it is all contradiction in architectural design, a ziggurat on top of a columned temple . . . through the ziggurat is carved a shaft. At the eleventh hour on the eleventh day of the eleventh month every year, the light of the sun beams through this shaft directly on the Unknown Soldier's tomb' (Dening, 1996: 225). Dening adds, wistfully, as he describes yet another kind of magic: 'Or it used to, before daylight saving. It is all done with mirrors now.' I am starting to think that if the older magic was more à la Stonehenge, cultural events were always 'done with mirrors', the necessary seductive illusion being part of their force.

The crowd gathered there re-creates the nation every time with this multiplicitous event: myth of origin, ceremony, music, bodies full of affect. The force of the myth lies not just in its meaning construction; it rather derives from the power of death as a vital force, this derivation as complex as the seeming necessity for music on this occasion and others like it, and it is also the transformation of the bodies of those present at this ritual. Michael Taussig talks of the 'magical harnessing of the dead for stately purpose' the state's 'attraction and repulsion, tied to the Nation, to more than a whiff of a certain sexuality reminiscent of the Law of the Father and, lest we forget, to the specter of death, human death in that soul-stirring insufficiency of Being' (Taussig, 1996: 3).

There is a vitalism, encapsulated in the epigraph from Aboriginal elder David Mowaljarlai, which can be read into the analysis of foundation myths and rituals as the condensation of positive forces in the transformation of bodies in space. Death is a positive force, to the extent that it makes gifts to the living, and in return the living must make sacrifice, which of course literally means 'make sacred'. There is no greater sacrifice, we are told, than the gift of one's life for the nation: the 'unknown soldier' stands for the universal and arbitrary grandeur of this gift. The state, relentlessly secular in its definition, remains none the less the highest form of the sacred-in-death ('the horror of the mute-absurd of the violence upon which all states are founded' (Taussig, 1996: 195)). Blood has been spilt. The political stakes for the sacredness of the state are high. The political question however, in a multiracial and multicultural nation, is *whose* dead will count on the rolls of honour? In Australia the quasi-magical *force* of Aboriginal cultures far outweighs the normal political calculations of numbers (now 2 per cent of the population) and representation, something the prime minister John Howard seems unable to understand or accept. Where is all this damn cultural force coming from? And so, the prime ministerial emotion concerning the stolen children will be one of anger not sorrow.[2]

Men of strange classes

When this mixed host reached the border of the Ilbalintja territory which is owned by Bangata-Panangka men, they decided to continue their further journey under the ground, lest they should trespass upon the ancient soil belonging to men of strange classes.

> They arose from Ititjankerama and continued their journey. They marched onward; they entered into the mulga thicket. Ntjipurara, the leader of the combined hosts, sat down with his legs crossed under him. The iliara seated themselves around him in circles. They all opened their veins. Thereupon a wondrous river of blood swallowed them all; it engulfed them deep in the ground; the blood rose to the top. Underneath the surface of the ground they continued their journey in the direction of Untjuiatjatua.

The host emerged from the ground when Unmatjera territory was reached, and continued to march on the surface.

(Strehlow, 1947: 143–4)

Strehlow wrote this account into a literary aesthetic; the original performance would no doubt be quite different from this written representation in its form and effect.

There are points of similarity between the 'Last Post' ritual and this other ceremony describing the spilling of blood for one's country. For me, the relationship is heuristic rather than culturally comparative. Travelling this trope of blood allows for metonymic associations: giving of life-forces for the communal good, creating this community in corporeal transformations hinged around death. In such rituals, mimetic effects *touch* the participants; the contagious magic uniting them seems not to be explicable in the distancing vocabulary of sign, structure or function, which is why I would argue that one needs to rethink the apparatuses for understanding. Call them academic disciplines.

Those Western disciplines which have dominated understandings of Aboriginality – where 'understanding' means in effect sanitizing the primitive, and drawing out its power without recognizing one's own primitivity – anthropology, history and literature, have done so with two important reifications: *society* and *the word*. For anthropology, man's relationship to land is defined through activities conceived of as *systematic* elements of community, tribe or group (the principal activity here is the description of pre-state communities). For history and literature, the same relationship is dominated by temporally unfolding representation (the text, and the activity is hermeneutics). Such understandings might become less monological by expansion into another discipline, philosophy, dealing as it does with the conceptual underpinnings of ways of life. Is 'philosophy' for this project riskier than cultural studies, does it have greater deconstructive power, i.e. does it, fiercely modernistic, turn and attack its own operative concepts as soon as they show signs of permanence? Is it riskier to talk of an 'Aboriginal philosophy' rather than an 'indigenous cultural studies'; does 'Aboriginal philosophy' (an English phrase deriving from Latin and Greek words) risk colonizing more 'authentic' Aboriginal traditions?

As a cultural studies person I have my philosophical prejudices. I would not be interested in finding 'systems of thought' in Aboriginal philosophy, nor cosmologies, nor logical systems. My prejudice would tend more towards the practical and ethical, towards 'philosophy as a way of life' (Hadot, 1995). Looking at various texts which give accounts of Aboriginal cultures, I would not be trying to boil them down to foundational principles, trying to establish 'models' for an Aboriginal philosophy, but rather seeing in a series of events the abstract potentials for Aboriginality, concrete exercises in Aboriginal-becoming, or ways of conducting oneself as an Aboriginal person.

This philosophy would then overlap a little with cultural studies, since it links up once again with historical and anthropological methods; historical, since a contemporary field of Aboriginal philosophy cannot ignore the massive upheaval of the colonialist process (the condition and the necessity for a contemporary Aboriginal philosophy); and anthropological because primitive and sacred rituals have not been displaced by modernism or science, and indeed, some have come to talk of a rearticulation in the 'modern sacred' (Gelder and Jacobs, 1998). The crucial relationship in much of Aboriginal Australian ritual, I would maintain, is between *body* and *country*, so I will give examples to suggest that 'society' and 'the word' are less significant operative concepts, or rather that they have been recently interposed between body and country.

History's poison blanket

The promise that was Aboriginal history has failed in some respects. Emerging some two decades ago, it has failed to deliver radical new understandings of history itself and of Australian history in particular. Was it such a gift to Aboriginal peoples that their history was brought into being as a pre-history to European settlement? That in the early 1980s '20,000 years' became a mantra of truth? Nevertheless, 'Captain Cook' histories of exploration and discovery have been displaced, and with that triumphalism deflated, history, anthropology and the law combined in a powerful way to create the conditions whereby the 'Mabo' judgement could become a reality and *terra nullius* denied.[3]

The first premise of my argument is that Aboriginal peoples, prior to invasion, had no history. This needs to be qualified in the light of the long-standing Hegelian assertion. There was no history in the sense of a set of texts setting out a linear chronology of events. There certainly was a sense of time, a sense of past events, and ways of connecting past events to ones taking place in the here and now. This historical attitude was not just produced as a set of texts, oral or written, it was produced rather more ritually or ceremonially.

The second premise of the argument is that Aboriginal peoples and the invaders had radically different philosophical orientations. Let us hazard that while Aboriginal peoples were obsessed with space, the Europeans were obsessed with time. There were both technological and philosophical aspects to the Europeans' obsession. The technological includes the need for the invention of chronometers to make the fixing of longitude possible in navigation; it also includes timetabling the working day, calendars and so on. The philosophical includes an obsession with the position of imperial activity at the end point of a linear forward-thrusting history. Agamben (1993: 91) would call these technological and philosophical positions an 'experience of time':

> Every culture is first and foremost a particular experience of time, and no new culture is possible without an alteration of this experience. The original task of a genuine revolution, therefore, is never merely to 'change the world', but also – and above all – to 'change time'.

So it may be true that time changed in Australia in the early 1980s. For some people this experience was ephemeral, for others it was deeply felt, but in any case the germ of a new Australian culture was born. Most of us remember the discovery of ancient human cremation at Lake Mungo, and at about the same time Henry Reynolds forged his reputation as a pioneering historian with the publication of *The Other Side of the Frontier*. '20,000 years' became an activist slogan which had the effect of stretching national time back into the distant past, crossing an intellectual frontier (just as the real 'bush' one was disappearing), indigenizing history, and creating new beginnings for the national story. This process has not gone all the way to completion; further steps could be taken, steps which broaden the process, and in some ways make it less the business of historians, and more the business of philosophers.

Dipesh Chakrabarty speaks philosophically, yet as a historian, when he listens to complex voices in subaltern pasts, murmuring in the background, as Marxist historians take a peasant revolt of the Santal people in nineteenth-century Bengal as an instance of a modern revolutionary consciousness at work. Flip to the archival documents and here are the peasants' *words*, clearly insisting that they were acting under the inspiration of their god Thakur. Their actions and their history have a supernatural dimension, which we moderns can nevertheless understand because 'we have a pre-theoretical, everyday understanding [of this dimension] because the supernatural, or the divine, as principles, have not disappeared from the life of the modern' (Chakrabarty, 1997: 27). He argues for the complexity of time to be written into historians' accounts, and for the peculiar contemporaneity of others to become part of understandings giving rise to 'forms of democracy that we cannot yet either completely understand or envisage' (p. 26).

The production of cross-cultural historical knowledge is not just an epistemological problem, concerning the foundations for knowledge (principles we can 'settle on' in order to work from them) but also an evolving temporal one *occurring* in rituals like 'writing a historical essay'. It is therefore crucial continually to contrast accounts of ways in which other peoples come to know things with ways in which European institutions organize knowledge rituals. For instance, T. G. H. Strehlow (1947: 125–6) reports an account of a promising pupil of Aranda knowledge about fifty years ago:

> The old men took me apart from the other young men of my own age at an early date. They showed me many gurra ceremonies which they withheld from the other members of my bandicoot clan because they were still too young. I remember their teachings well. I often had my veins opened to supply blood for the ceremonies. I dutifully paid large meat-offerings for the instruction that I had received. Some of the ceremonies were too secret to be shown even to ordinary men of the bandicoot clan. . . . My elders kept repeating these ceremonies time and again in my presence: they were afraid that I might forget them.

Now while university students don't come to seminars with 'large meat-offerings' or open their veins (the state bleeds them with tuition fees), it is more significant that the exhortation here is to remember the sacred text exactly, through excessive mimeticism, constant repetition. In university seminars the students are instead urged to put the text in their own words, to contribute, eventually, to the endless proliferation of commentary which is the European way of sacralizing texts, to renovate the classic text by making it 'mean something' in the contemporary context, coordinating the responses of other commentators, finding a new relevance for a theory by attaching it to a new object; in other words, dis*place*ment. So what is interesting for me in both cases is not core knowledge as such, but ways of practising knowledge repetitively, keeping it alive. If I were to risk a generalization, I would say Aboriginal philosophy is all about keeping things alive *in their place*.

We could therefore ask a question of ways of knowing a thing like Australian history. Which is more important, the existence of major historical texts on library shelves, or the way in which they get activated as social memory (Healy, 1997) through rituals like annual final year school examinations as rites of passage? Or, indeed, does the Gallipoli episode get reinforced as an Australian foundation myth more through the annual ritual of the ANZAC Day dawn services and the march, or through the books, films and school excursions?

Life, abundant life

The field of traditional anthropology which has come closest to a description of Aboriginal 'philosophy' is that of the study of religion, and in that field the work of W. E. H. Stanner touches on the problem of the relation between philosophy and religion. Earlier, in a famous speech in 1969 he established with the powerful evocation of the 'Great Australian Silence' the force of historical forgetting (Stanner, 1969; Rowlands, 1997), the repressed potential of which may be later released in that spasm of community feeling which is the sacred.[4] But the problematic of the sacred is not here his concern. Here he actually develops a description of a pan-Aboriginal philosophy, with statements like 'The known evidence suggests that Aboriginal religion was probably one of the least material-minded, and most life-minded, of any of which we have knowledge'(Stanner, 1984: 149).

He does not qualify 'material' here, but he is probably referring to the minimal physical necessities for transitory lifestyles, and a non-accumulative economy of exchanges where objects have cultural rather than inherent and arbitrary value. By 'life-minded' he means an

> intense, one could almost say obsessive, preoccupation with the signs, symbols, means, portents and evidences of vitality. The whole religious corpus vibrated with an expressed aspiration for life, abundant life. Vitality,

fertility and growth; the conservation, production, protection and rescue of life. . . . Vitalistic things obtruded throughout the myths and rites – water, blood, fat, hair, excrements; the sex organs, semen, sexuality in all its phases, the quickening of the womb; child spirits, mystical impregnation and reincarnation; the development of the body from birth to death; the transitions of the human spirit from before organic assumption until after physical dissolution; apparently animated phenomena such as green leaves, rain and the seasons, lightning, whirlwinds, shooting stars and the heavenly bodies; or things of unexplained origin, unusual appearance and giant size.

(Stanner, 1984: 149)

This text has a sympathetic libidinal economy – Stanner is getting excited about his tropes of listings, metaphors and climaxes. 'Aboriginal philosophy' is making connections happen in the mimetic and intersubjective sense of making things come to life, move, like his text quickening with poiesis. But elsewhere in his text his operative vocabulary centres around 'signs', 'symbols', 'symbol function' and 'symbolism', a thoroughgoing representationalism which I will argue takes him down the wrong track, i.e. significantly *away from* the 'religion' he is describing. At the time he was writing it was intellectually mandatory, it seems, to say that something stands for something else, or that a sign or symbol is a 'vehicle'. He defines 'symbol' as 'the patterns, structures and designs that connect arrangements or systems of vehicles and their elements' (Stanner, 1984: 167). A whole range of things are patterned in this way: iconic markings like 'zig-zags' and 'lines', semiotic things like 'silences' and 'facial expressions', ritualistic things like 'drawing of human blood', 'laying on of hands', etc. He gives an example of how a whole range of things can come together:

in certain initiatory rites a blood-smeared bullroarer is thrust between the loins of young men. Blood, bullroarer and loins are all symbolic of something else, but the significations may vary with context. In this case, evidently it is the pattern of structure or arrangement of the whole act that is 'the symbol'. But what is symbolized by it is not revealed directly or necessarily in the immediacy of the act itself.

(Stanner, 1984: 167–8)

He is searching for words, for an explanation, 'evidently it is the pattern of structure or arrangement', and now puts 'the symbol' in inverted commas, perhaps because it has become a multiplicity. 'Thrusting' no doubt signifies something else too for this mode of analysis.

Now, certain directions in poststructuralist thinking have given us grounds for doing a pretty solid critique of this sort of representationalism. One does not have to postulate another side to be revealed, away from the immediacy of the act. 'The presence of the sign is not an identity but an envelopment of difference, of a multiplicity of actions, materials and levels', says Brian Massumi in the 'Meaning is force' chapter in *A User's Guide to Capitalism and Schizophrenia* (1994: 10). 'Blood', 'loins', 'bullroarer' are not metaphorical displacements either; they are planes of consistency intersecting in this particular ritual, they contribute to a buildup of intensity which makes this ritual 'work' as it is in itself, to have the powerful effect of initiating someone.[5] Their significance is not elsewhere, as if thrusting *really* has to do with sex. Rather, thrusting is all over the place. Everything is thrusting, more or less, it just quickens in certain times and places. And it is movement going on here, not meaning; rapidity, not *logos*.

Stanner will later claim that one of the reasons there is no Aboriginal philosophy is that there is no tradition of intellectual detachment. True, there isn't an Aboriginal philosopher standing to one side observing this ceremony, stroking his beard and saying, 'Hum, yes, definite sexual symbolism going on here.' That's the anthropologist's job. And we would have to reverse the gaze and ask Stanner just how 'intellectually detached' he was about his *own* sacred rituals (seminars, advancements of science); just how seriously was he taking himself? Wittgenstein would no doubt have 'intellectual detachment' pegged as just one language game, perhaps the everyday version of negative theology. And we have to bear in mind that seriousness is not sustained in Aboriginal ceremony; there are significant periods of hilarity, lewd behaviour, clowning around, alternating with the most serious, life-transforming ritual. What's all that good fun supposed to 'mean', since anthropologists traditionally bracket it out? Later, Stanner's language performs his confusion (1984: 168):

> One studies symbolisms for the sake of the symbols, and the symbols for the sake of the symbolized. The things to which the symbols point are metaphysical objects, in patterns, structures and designs that, in religious study, are the true objects of inquiry.

So the real reason for all this symbolism is so that the 'true object' can become metaphysical! And his object of study has shifted. The contemplation of these (almost visual) patterns and designs will no doubt produce 'religious study', but not, I think, understandings of 'Aboriginal religion'. He goes on: 'In Aboriginal religions they form a highly involuted complex which anthropology is only beginning to break down' (p. 168).

If it is highly involuted, why not at least try to understand it *as such*, with an analysis for which the 'break down' is less obviously non-Aboriginal? He goes on:

> Whether such objects are 'real' is a question for philosophy, not for anthropology. It is sufficient that the Aborigines use symbols to conceptualize and express them, or features or aspects of them, in perceivable or inferrable ways. The symbols, by pointing to, stand for; by standing for they represent; by representing, they objectify; by objectifying they betoken ultimate

or metaphysical things, which they thus mediate to living men by means of images. The vehicles conveying the images attract to themselves the sentiments, thoughts and acts properly due to what they ultimately designate. The vehicles are not themselves 'the religion', though they have sometimes been confounded with it because of a failure to distinguish the symbols from what is symbolized. They are but the husk around a kernel; means of symbolizing something else; tools or instruments.

(Ibid.)

He is floundering around with a circular representationalist model where 'things' have to be objectified and made metaphysical, converted to images, and fed back into the ritual complex from which they originally emerged. The process he is describing is not an Aboriginal process of understanding, but the process of his own science's rationalizations of 'Aboriginal religion'. The Aboriginal people he is talking about did not, of course, have the specific vocabulary he is using, a vocabulary designed to separate meanings from acts. In any case, Stanner himself denies that any Aboriginal person could have conceived of the functions of representation because there was no 'tradition of intellectual detachment', no 'class of interpreters' (1984: 151). No hermeneutic tradition, so the ritual, like the initiation, has to be taken on its own terms: it means what it does via *immediate* relations between objects, things, feelings, words, music.

The work of José Gil can help us here. He advocates taking seriously the words tribal people use to describe things, and formulates a new approach in terms of forces:

to stop giving prime attention to the *meaning* of signs, to their representational contents, in order to focus instead on their *practical effects*. To give up trying to decode the significance hidden behind symbols, but to ask what forces they draw on or shore up, and through which mechanisms they are likely to trigger certain effects.

(1998: xii)

Michael Taussig also offers a political critique of anthropology's reduction to the symbolic, the function being to create understandable and exploitable 'traditions' out of the force and magic of the primitive:

How often we have been told that ritual's function brings spirit and matter into a divine unity as with the romantic understanding of the symbol (the understanding implicit in anthropological discourse). How often we have been told that rites, especially healing rites, recruit the passions in order to consolidate the cake of custom, sustaining the normality of the norm, the internalization of the convention (and so on).

(1987: 328)

Gil again:

> In other words, and we must stress this notion, it is not a question of study-ing *forces* (magical, religious, prestigious or whatever) according to their representational contents, but to grasp them in the way they function in their own right, that is, in the way they may differ from the signs and symbols that are attached to them.
>
> (1998: xii)

Now, Stanner has given us the words of an Aboriginal informant, or rather a kind of scenario which is instructive in a number of ways:

> Scholars familiar with Aborigines have usually had one impressive experi-ence in common: to be taken by Aboriginal friends to places in the wilds and there shown something – tree, rocky outcrop, cranny, pool – with for-mality, pride and love. Conversations follow rather like this: 'There is my Dreaming [place]. My father showed me this place when I was a little boy. His father showed him.' Perhaps a child stands near by, all eyes and ears. Here is a tradition being made continuous, as in the past, by overlapping life-spans. What had his father said? He said: 'Your Dreaming is there; you want to look after this place; you don't want to let it go [forget, be care-less about it] ; it is from the first [totemical] man.' The historical link is thus made: from the now old to the still young; from the living to the anciently dead; from the very first true man to next true man; from the oldest time to the here and now. (Down with a crash come the needless postulates of racial and collective unconscious.) What did the father do there? 'He used to come here every year with the old men, the wise men; they used to do something here [hit, rub, break off pieces, brush with green leaves, sing]; that way they made the [totem] come on, come back, jump up, spread out.' *How* did that happen? *What* is it that is in the place? 'We do not know. *Some-thing* is there. Like my spirit [soul, shadow, invisible counterpart]; like my Dreaming [naming the totem entity].' Will he think more? What else did his father say? That there was something in the Dreaming-place? The dark eyes turn and look intent, puzzled, searching. My father did not say. He said this: 'My boy, look! Your Dreaming is there; it is a big thing; you never let it go [pass it by]; all Dreamings [totem entities] come from there; your spirit is there.' Does the white man now understand? The blackfellow, earnest, friendly, makes a last effort. 'Old man, you listen! Something is there; we do not know what; *something*.' There is a struggle to find words, and perhaps a lapse into English. 'Like engine, like power, plenty of power, it does hard work; it *pushes*.'
>
> (Stanner, 1984: 165–6)

Let us take the informant at his own word. More important than the explanation (the *logos*) is the quasi-ritual (the approach to the place, the things one must do there, the 'way of life'). In any case there is a 'struggle to find words'. And most importantly, there is a *force* in this place ('it *pushes*'), not a meaning.

Stanner's argument about why there is an Aboriginal religion, but not a philosophy, is based on the need for stated 'axioms' to be non-ritual and non-mythic, i.e. 'scientific':

> There were no Aboriginal philosophers and one can thus speak of 'philosophy' only metaphorically. But there is ground for saying that they lived – and therefore thought – by axioms, which were 'objective' in that they related to a supposed nature of man and condition of human life. Myths presented the axioms in intuitive-contemplative aspect. Rites presented them in passionist-activist aspect. No Aboriginal put the axioms into words but the existence and efficacy of anything – including intuitional awareness and insights – do not depend on someone's formal affirmation of them in words. Myths would not be stories, and rites would not have an invariant structure, if axioms could not exist by other than formalized means. I shall try not to do more than state what I believe to have been the principle of Aboriginal philosophy in the metaphorical sense. I propose to call it a principle of assent to the disclosed terms of life.
>
> (Stanner, 1984: 152)

As he says elsewhere, 'Religious belief expressed a philosophy of assent to life's terms' (p. 145). It seems to me that the dominance of a certain kind of philosophy led early scholars of Aboriginal societies to opt for the category of 'religion' for these peoples. Even Stanner is not sure; since Aboriginal peoples had no gods as such there could be no theology. The problem is how to recognize the 'potencies' (p. 155) Aboriginal people understand, since Western categories flip between the theistic and the scientific.[6] To his credit, Stanner ends up saying that the 'Aboriginal religions must be described and analysed as significant in their own right, as expressions of human experience of life; as essays of passion, imagination and striving' (p. 155) which is a broad, almost philosophical definition, certainly one which is in tune with my interest in a 'philosophy as a way of life'. As I have argued elsewhere, the intersubjective element will mean that the *approach* to the problem is as significant as its attempted solution, the

> Aboriginal protocols and practices will have to become part of the philosophical apparatus, things one learns about obligations for exchange both within communities and in the so-called fieldwork situation which has been the terrain in which most Aboriginal knowledge has been elicited. Being a philosopher in an Aboriginal community will be a quite different thing from being a social scientist there. For instance, Paddy Roe said to me once

when I asked to work with him that 'things must go both ways'. When I asked what he meant he laughed and said could I start by loading that corrugated iron on the truck.

(Muecke, 1995: 177)

Exfoliations of the body

Legitimate occupancy of the country, currently much contested in Australia, is about what people's bodies can conceivably do there. For this, José Gil has created the term exfoliation, the ways in which the body opens into the spaces it can occupy or articulate with, and I can use it to 'read' (i.e. displace, move from there/then to here/now) the story about the subterranean river of blood. The body, he says, is a volume in a perpetual state of disintegration and reconstitution through exfoliations:

> The anatomical diversity of the body and its various articulations show us that the space of the body is in itself diversified. There is no sole space, but multiple spaces; no sole relation, but a multiplicity of relations. . . . The body 'lives' in space, but not like a sphere with a closed continuous surface. On the contrary, its movements, limbs and organs determine that it has singular relations with things in space, relations which are individually integrated for the decoder. These relations imply *exfoliations* of the space of the body which can be treated separately. Relations to a tree, a prey, a star, an enemy, a loved object, desired nourishment, set into train certain privileged organs inducing precise places of the body. Exfoliation is the essential way the body 'turns onto' things, onto objective space, onto living things. Here there is a type of communication which is always present, but only makes itself really visible in pathological or magical experiences. Nevertheless the ordinary experience of relations to things also implies this mode of communication. Being in space means to establish diverse relationships with the things that surround our bodies. Each set of relations is determined by the action of the body which accompanies an investment of desire in a particular being or particular object. Between the body (and the organs in use) and the thing, is established a connection which immediately effects the form and space of the body; between the one and the other a privileged spatial relation emerges which defines the space which unites them as 'near' or 'far,' resistant, thick, wavy, vertiginous, smooth, prickly. The use of these metaphors in order to characterise the space of communication simply shows that the body is a foundation for metaphorization; because a 'petrified space,' for example, speaks of nothing but the quality between the body and the objective space – something of the order of 'petrification' coming from things effecting the body; and something of

the order of the body (its capacity to qualify space, to transform it through affective investment) comes to effect things.

(Gil, 1998: 126–7)[7]

There are many examples of this in Aboriginal Australia. In some mythical accounts of metamorphosis, round stones are the 'petrified' eggs of a snake who is an ancestor figure. The body has become animal and then stone, or rather a transformative relationship between stone, human body and animal is set up which is flickering in perception. A perpetual transformative effect is the consequence of some 'blockage' in narrative or ritual, like Lot's Wife who was turned into a pillar of salt because she broke the law.

So many Aboriginal stories seem to culminate in metamorphoses, beings turning into trees, stars or tracks. But these are not everyday stories; they are magical stories underpinned by strong beliefs and rituals which intensify the (bodily) energies of the participants in the ceremony. A ritual performance is an event where codes (music, dance, myth, organization of space) which are normally, in everyday life, quite separate, are brought together and condensed so that actual transformations can be brought about on the bodies of the participants, or a single participant: an initiate to be made into a man and imbued with knowledge, a sick person to be cured. These bodies 'turn into' the body of the ancestor-snake, or the pain in the body is transformed into, for instance, a shard of quartz. Ritual exfoliations, therefore, are extraordinary compared to standard exfoliations of the body which involve the ability to walk down a path, sit in a chair, drive a car – the body exfoliates into these spaces; leaves or laminates of surfaces as extensions of organs are involved, not the unitary body driven by a total self-image or central motor. Aboriginal Australia might thus be constructed out of ritual exfoliations which relate individual and communitary bodies powerfully and magically to features of the country, just as the ANZAC and Remembrance Day rituals sanctify a particular national history.

The subterranean river of blood story is about the bodies of the participants collectively joining the flows of their life forces, their blood, to create a fluidity which dissolves all borders (between their individual bodies and the sacred ground, the ground made sacred). The exfoliation is almost absolute, but it retains these features: vitality, movement, transformation (the bodies return to normal when they re-emerge). The movement is into country (at a place which gives life, like a soak) and out of it again, like ceremonies which are culture made to 'move', 'stand up alive', and go down into the ground, 'quiet again' at the end. The force of the metaphor is also a powerful oneiric image of being moved, effortlessly, in a warm, fluid space, absolutely red when the light is shining through. As Gil (1998: 232) says for indigenous peoples:

The Earth is not limited by a border which has precise contours tailored to the needs of the military, administration, customs, taxation or politics.

The Earth is the magical territory perceived in the extension of the community body in relation to the ancestors.

In the subterranean river of blood story, blood is spilt in order to avert possible danger and conflict with other people; in yet other stories the sight of spurting blood from a leg wound is a sign that a debt has been adequately settled (Benterrak *et al.*, 1996: 141). Elsewhere, donations of this precious fluid fall into the domain of charity, for the moment, still for the collective good, not yet 'privatized', the aura of the sacred still isolating this substance from normal commodification.

In many Aboriginal accounts, the death of individuals is not so much about the demise of their bodies as about a return of their energy to the place of emanation where it rejoins the identity of that place. In this life-affirming philosophy death has a significant place: as in any philosophy people arrange things so that their beliefs about life and death become the effective means of their power.

In this article I have tried to show that the secular state finds in its foundation myths and rituals the same magico-religious forces observable in the rituals, and the cultural poiesis, of non-state societies. Accounting for the force of the cultural means accounting for the persistence of ritual in state societies, not to mention the persistence of other rituals in these multicultural societies.

> The history of the State in the West has been a long process of disengagement of political power from its religious roots, while at the same time seeking out a new sacred foundation for its authority. This would be an interminable task. Where is the transcendence of the secular State to be sited, if it is away from religious or divine sources? It seems that no modern State has satisfactorily resolved this question. But history is revealing; in the absence of being able to give itself a religious foundation, the State will transfer aspects of its sovereignty and authority towards the 'nation'; and the latter will be founded on the power of the dead.
>
> (Gil, 1998: 52–3)

The resurgence of the power of Aboriginal cultural formations in the context of Australia as nation in recent years emerges not just as a consequence of calculations about politics and justice, but also because of the resurgence of the power of Aboriginal rituals and of Aboriginality in rituals. This would be most significant in revisions of history and nationhood which would seek to pay homage to the Aboriginal dead. Making the unknown soldier in a shrine of remembrance Aboriginal would be the radical gesture which would honour all dead and those particular dead, change the site of our foundation myths to this country (rather than its current location in overseas wars) and create the possibility of seeing in Australia's Aboriginal wars the horror and violent legitimacy of sacrifice and gift.

Acknowledgement

Thanks to Dipesh Chakrabarty for useful discussion at an early stage of this article.

Notes

1   Stephen Garton wrote *The Cost of War* partly out of this feeling: 'I have no experience of war, nor any real knowledge of military history, but few things move me more deeply than remembrance ceremonies, and few pieces of music wrench the heart more than "The Last Post".'

2   In 1997 a major report was published on the forced separation of Aboriginal families by government agencies for most of this century. The Prime Minister, John Howard, created controversy by refusing to apologize for this injustice. See *Bringing them Home: Report of the National Inquiry into the Separation of Aboriginal and Torres Strait Islander Children from their Families* (Commissioner: Ronald Wilson), Sydney: Human Rights and Equal Opportunity Commission, 1997.

3   Named after Eddie Mabo from the Torres Strait Islands, this high court decision (Mabo *vs.* Queensland) recognized Aboriginal rights to land for the first time and effectively cancelled the legalistic fiction of *terra nullius* (empty land) at the time of colonization.

4   'The sacred is only a privileged moment of communal unity, a moment of the convulsive communication of what is ordinarily stifled' (Bataille, 1985: 242).

5   'The initiatory rites all rose to a tense crisis that brought about . . . a physical-moral-spiritual change in the initiates.' Rites of initiation existed as *disciplines*. They both *fashioned* the uncompleted man, and *transformed* him into a being of higher worth (Stanner, 1984: 151).

6   'A comparable difficulty affects our ability to grasp their jurisprudence, economy and polity. The categories and concepts are fatally pre-arranged. They are quite unsuited to the facts' (Stanner, 1984: 155).

7   Gil also notes: 'In certain stories, characters are petrified by a magic spell because they did not know how to translate the codes, for example they have not been able to go through an initiation procedure' (1998: 318, n 48).

References

Agamben, Giorgio (1993) *Infancy and History: The Destruction of Experience* (trans. Liz Heron), London: Verso.

Bataille, Georges (1985) 'The Sacred', in *Visions of Excess, Selected Writings 1927–1939* (trans. Alan Stoekl), Minneapolis: University of Minnesota Press.

Benterrak, Krim, Muecke, Stephen and Roe, Paddy (1996) *Reading the Country: Introduction to Nomadology*, Liverpool: University of Liverpool Press.

Chakrabarty, Dipesh (1997) 'Minority histories, subaltern pasts', *Humanities Research*, Winter: 17–32.

Dening, Greg (1996) 'Anzac Day', in *Performances*, Melbourne: Melbourne University Press.

Garton, Stephen (1996) *The Cost of War*, Melbourne: Oxford University Press.

Gelder, Ken and Jacobs, Jane M. (1998) *Uncanny Australia: Sacredness and Identity in a Postcolonial Nation*, Melbourne: Melbourne University Press.

Gil, José (1998) *Metamorphoses of the Body* (trans. Stephen Muecke), Minneapolis, University of Minnesota Press. *Theory out of Bounds*, 12.

Hadot, Pierre (1995) *Philosophy as a Way of Life: Spiritual Exercises from Socrates to Foucault*, ed. Arnold Davidson (trans. Michael Chase), Oxford: Blackwell.

Healy, Chris (1997) *From the Ruins of Colonialism: History as Social Memory,* Melbourne: Cambridge University Press.

Massumi, Brian (1994) *A User's Guide to Capitalism and Schizophrenia*, Boston, MA: MIT Press.

Muecke, Stephen (1995) 'Towards an Aboriginal philosophy of place', in Penny van Toorn and David English (eds) *Speaking Positions: Aboriginality, Gender and Ethnicity in Australian Cultural Studies*, Melbourne: Victoria University of Technology.

Reynolds, Henry (1981) *The Other Side of the Frontier,* Townsville: James Cook University Press.

Rowlands, Michael (1997) 'Memory, sacrifice and the nation', *New Formations*, 30.

Stanner, W. E. H. (1969) *After the Dreaming,* Boyer Lectures Series, Sydney: Australian Broadcasting Commission.

—— (1984) 'Religion, totemism and symbolism', [1965] in Max Charlesworth *et al.* (eds) *Religion in Aboriginal Australia: An Anthology,* St Lucia: University of Queensland Press.

Strehlow, T. G. H. (1947) *Aranda Traditions,* Melbourne: Melbourne University Press.

Taussig, Michael (1996) *The Magic of the State*, New York: Routledge.

—— (1987) *Shamanism, Colonialism and the Wild Man: A Study In Terror and Healing,* Chicago, Ill: Chicago University Press.

Myung Koo Kang

POSTMODERN CONSUMER CULTURE WITHOUT POSTMODERNITY: COPYING THE CRISIS OF SIGNIFICATION

Abstract

The purpose of this study was to interpret the meaning of the postmodern discourse produced by Korean television advertisements, by categorizing postmodern television advertisements and describing their representations and images of reality in detail. Considering the production process of Korean postmodern advertisements, the study raised a question: How can we interpret the phenomena of imitating and assimilating the style of advertisements from the reservoir of postmodern signifiers, while not taking into account the values, ideas and ways of thinking implicit in such advertisements?

There are two ways of interpretation. First, it would be an effect of structural dependence, in which postmodern consumer cultural forms are replicated and replace local products with mass-produced goods. The narratives of postmodern advertisements serve as the catalyst to introduce these advertisements and to teach the grammar of international advertising. Second, the assimilation of postmodern advertisements in Korean television means a newly emergent hybrid culture. Because the target of postmodern advertisements is the young consumer, the producers adopt postmodern tastes and styles, inserting and translating their roots into local forms. The study concluded that it may be more appropriate not to choose one of these interpretations as a single correct theory; it is better to look at the articulation of different forces and processes within a field of interconnections among mediascape, financescape and technoscape.

Keywords

advertising; South Korea; postmodern; consumer culture; signification; television

Introduction

DISCOURSES ON POSTMODERN social science and philosophy papers have proliferated in Korea since the end of the 1980s. By translating the works of Foucault, Derrida, Lyotard, Baudrillard and Jameson, some Korean intellectuals and artists have attempted to introduce Western debates such as Habermas vs. Lyotard, and Laclau and Mouffe vs. Geras and Mouzelis. With the collapse of the socialist regime in Soviet Russia and Eastern Europe, the so-called 'post' phenomenon has blossomed in the fields of philosophy, art, the social sciences, the humanities and social movements. In spite of the volume of papers debating the meaning and implications of postmodern discourse, there has been strong and persistent scepticism of the 'post' phenomena in Korea. There has been a healthy questioning both of the theoretical and practical efficacy of the movement and of its relevance to political and cultural changes.

Much of the debate and discussion of postmodern culture in Korean society is limited to simple introductions and summaries of the 'canonical' Western texts. Little productive discussion and evaluation is devoted to the analysis of postmodern culture in the context of its production and consumption. Why should we talk about postmodern culture in our society? Does the Korean cultural industry produce postmodern culture and, if so, how is postmodern culture articulated in the context of the specific social conditions? Eagleton (1997: 5) recently raised this question at a conference on postmodernism in China:

> What do you do, in short, if postmodernity arrives on your doorstep before you have fully experienced the delights and disasters of modernity itself? How do you cope with the time warping consequent on having your current history elided between autocratic traditionalism on the one hand and the ambiguous promises of postmodernism on the other? How do you deal with the paradox that your own 'modernity' means joining a club which is now at the point of leaving modernity scornfully behind it?

Though Eagleton does not have any solutions to the questions, he poses that it might be plausible to take advantage of the 'gains of Enlightenment' by avoiding the 'evils of that creed'. Without raising and answering these questions, the introduction of the category of postmodern culture can yield neither theoretical solutions when exploring the possibilities of social transformation nor practical leverage in bringing a politics of culture. The purpose of this study is to interpret

the meaning of the postmodern discourse produced by Korean television advertising in the context of our specific social formation. In particular, this study
attempts to categorize postmodern advertisements, and to provide a thorough
description of their representations and images of reality.

In the first part of the study, we deal with the theoretical issues concerning
the emergence of postmodern advertisements. The second part analyses the
material condition of postmodern advertisements in Korean society, focusing on
changes in the advertising industry and consumer market.

The analysis was performed in two stages. In the first stage 104 postmodern
advertisements were selected from 761 broadcast during prime time between
March 1991 and February 1992. The research team[1] developed seven categories
of modes of representation such as the intermingling of the real and the fictional
and selected sixty-one advertisements after repeated watching of recorded video
clips (Table 1).

In the second stage of the study, we separately interviewed three high-
ranking production staff members at advertising agencies, who provide detailed
information about the production process. The interviews enabled us to examine
the planning process for some selected advertisements as well as the development of new editing technologies and creative techniques – including the styles
of setting, modelling and colouring. The production staff generally agreed with
our selection of the specific postmodern advertisements chosen by our research
team, with two exceptions.

In the third part of the investigation we attempted a discursive analysis of
postmodern advertisements by classifying the ways in which reality is represented. This last part will incorporate a thorough description of the meaning of
postmodern culture in television advertisements within the broader context of
contemporary Korean culture.

Table 1 Modes of representation of postmodern advertisements

Mode of representation	Total
Intermingling of the real and the fictional	12
Deconstruction of traditional narrative	10
Deconstruction of the concepts of time and space	7
Convergence of artistic and multiple genre	11
Feminist perspective	2
Modification of traditional camera movement	3
Collapse of harmonious colour combinations	3
Combination of several of the above modes	13
Total	61

Postmodern advertising as cultural discourse

Following the definition of J. B. Thompson (1990), the depth hermeneutics of postmodern advertisements consists of social analysis, discursive analysis and critical interpretation. Depth hermeneutics traces the ways in which postmodern cultural forms produce particular aesthetic systems through the interactions between the producer and the text, and between the text and the viewer. This study is therefore concerned with the factors involved in the production process and the experiences of postmodern culture and practices of viewers, rather than with the epistemological evaluation of postmodern discourse.

This section will clarify some theoretical assumptions so that the social, economic and technological conditions of advertising in general as well as postmodern advertisements in particular can be elaborated.

First, if we understand postmodernism as 'the cultural logic of late capitalism' (Jameson, 1991), advertising is one of the primary fields that generates postmodern culture and practices. Advertising, it may be argued, is a cultural sphere, primarily producing commodity aesthetics through which use value and exchange value contradict each other.

As a cultural mechanism of commodity aesthetics, advertising produces the appearance of use value (Haug, 1986: 16–17) which is manifest in the consumption of a commodity rather than the use of goods. Aesthetic innovation in advertising design, images and narratives puts the commodity in the consumer's everyday life. What advertisements in a consumer society promise is the appearance of use value (Leiss et al., 1986; Williamson, 1978; Wernick, 1992). Postmodern advertisements are new forms of discourse that engender distinct appearances.

Second, postmodern advertisements are closely related to the visual media. Differing from the language of the print media, the visual language of television, film and video produces a sequence of images and provides the viewer with an aesthetic populism. The visual media suitably delivers the language of postmodern sensibility that is characterized as a depthless collage of images, the absence of historical consciousness, an abundance of euphoria, a deconstruction of meaning-centred narrative and a fabrication of fantasy through pastiche (Baudrillard, 1983; Hebdige, 1988; Jameson, 1991). The aesthetic populism of postmodern culture fits into the 'crisis in the political economy of sign value', since 'advertisers not only confronted disaffected, alienated viewers armed to foil advertisements with their remote control zippers, they also faced the problem of differentiating their commodity-signs from the clutter of formulaic advertising' (Goldman and Papson, 1994: 24). Postmodern advertisements no longer hide the codes of the commodity aesthetic, but turn hyperreal codes into their signs.

Third, in addition to the relationship of advertising to commodity aesthetics and the visual media, the multinational cultural industry is the other crucial element in understanding postmodern advertisements. Nine Korean advertising agencies (Oricom, Korad, Kumkang, etc.) operated joint enterprises, and twelve agencies had contracts and technical tie-up with twenty-six multinational agencies in 1989.[2] With technical cooperation, foreign agencies transfer the know-how for advertising production and marketing strategies, and train production staffs in the Korean agencies (see Table 2).

In the process of acquiring production and managerial skills, Korean advertising agencies have adopted advertising strategies as well as the ways in which consumer cultural practices are represented and realized. Western sensibilities, including postmodern aesthetics, have emerged in Korean television advertisements. What such processes of transferring and acquiring implies is that the grand notion of 'copying' cultural practices, whether wittingly or unwittingly, has taken place in newly industrialized countries like Korea.

Fourth, the reinforcing relationship of television and new technologies creates favourable situations for postmodern advertisements that indispensably employ computer graphics and video editing technologies. New technologies make possible the introduction of innovations in visualization, colour combination and free-floating camera movement that facilitate the visual expression of postmodern sensibility.

Table 2 Billings of transnational advertising agencies tied with Korean advertising agencies (unit: one million won)

Agency	1990	1991	1996
Cheil-Bozel	84	147	63,612
McCann-Erickson	56	140	40,881
D Y & R	66	80	17,044
D D K	–	98	22,030
J W T	32	47	26,265
Total	238	512	169,832

Source: *Advertising Information* (1992) and *Trends in Advertising Industry* (1997)

Social analysis of postmodern advertisements

This section will examine the social and material conditions of postmodern advertisements, focusing on the changes in advertising production as well as in the consumer sectors.

There have been two contrasting positions concerning postmodern discourse among Korean scholars and artists. On the one hand, some claimed that the notions of the decentred subject, the decentralization of power and de-authorization may have an important bearing on the disintegration of authoritarian bureaucratic systems, the centralized power structure and the unequal distribution of social and cultural resources. As Hall (1992) and Grossberg (1993) clearly show in their discussion of globalization, when postmodern ideas are transferred to new social contexts, such a view dismisses the possibility of differential appropriation. For instance, some consumers at local level can appropriate the notion of postmodern discourse as a form of escapism from a disturbing and oppressive political terrain.

On the other hand, some groups of intellectuals who are concerned with the political contradictions resulting from the enforced division between South and North Korea and the monopoly capitalistic nature of Korean social formation argue that postmodern discourse is the economic and political expression and strategy of neocolonial domination. These contrasting positions, however, provide few analyses of concrete relations between cultural practices and their social consequences.

The question is, then, to elaborate the new politics of postmodern advertisements in different Korean contexts which are experiencing different historical trajectories towards modernity. In this respect, this study suggests three aspects of the background in which postmodern advertisements have emerged in Korea.

First of all, postmodern advertisements are consumed by a very well-defined group of consumers and for that reason have different political and cultural effects. Postmodern culture is the product of Western (post)industrialized societies that have been moving towards post-Fordist arrangements of production, and thus guarantee leisure time and buying power for cultural commodities. Owing to the tremendous growth in productivity and influx of surplus value by the multinational corporations into Western capitalist nations, working hours in the labour sector have rapidly decreased to thirty-five or forty hours per week (Table 3). While labour has decreased in value, entertainment and leisure have become more important. But the work hours, working conditions and distribution of wealth and social welfare in Korean society are decidedly different from Western industrialized societies.

As shown in Table 3, Korean workers have to work the longest hours of these eight nations: 54.2 hours, compared to 41.3 hours in Japan, 38.6 hours in France and Finland, and 48.2 hours in Singapore. Korean industry also recorded the highest number of industrial accidents: 83,000 industrial workers on average per year were killed or injured between 1984 and 1987 (*Yearbook of Labor Economy*, 1988).

With regard to the distribution of wealth, capital gains from sky-rocketing land prices provided a small number of landowners with a surplus of 17,000 billion won (about 24 billion US dollars) in 1988. The total GNP of South Korea amounted to 12,300 billion won in the same year. This has been termed a 'bubble

Table 3 A comparison of work hours among eight nations

Nation	(Hour/week)			
	1985	1986	1987	Average of 85–87
Korea	53.8	54.7	54.0	54.2
Japan	41.5	41.1	41.3	41.3
West Germany	40.5	40.4	40.1	40.4
France	38.6	38.6	38.7	38.6
Finland	32.3	33.4	32.2	32.6
Israel	38.6	38.8	38.3	38.6
Singapore	47.0	48.5	49.2	48.2
Peru	44.8	48.5	47.4	46.9

Source: *ILO Yearbook* (1988)

economy'. The total price of privately owned land is 10.6 times the GNP, in comparison to 0.6 times in the US, two times in the UK and seven times in Japan (Lee, 1989). These figures suggest that the number of families living in their own homes has been decreasing since the beginning of the 1980s.

Due to the unequal exploitation of surplus value from the increase in land prices and the policy of low wages for workers, the distribution of wealth has been deteriorating over time. Among the ten brackets of family income, the families in the top 10 per cent have 42.3 per cent of the income, and the four brackets at the bottom earn only 19.7 per cent of total income.

It may be meaningless to simply cite statistical data. Some explanation of these figures is necessary with respect to the structural relationship between labour and capital as well as the alteration of the labour process; for example, there is an increasing tendency to control labour via monopoly capital. Exploring this relationship is, of course, beyond the scope of our study. However, in order to deal with postmodern culture as a concrete reality, we should take into account the material and economic conditions that shape our everyday life.

The above discussion does not necessarily lead us to claim that these qualitatively different material and economic conditions mean that the postmodern discourse which originates in Western society is not applicable to Korean society. To judge whether an external culture form is applicable to a society, one has to predispose an appropriate form of culture to a receiving society. To push this position further it would be a cultural absolutism and essentialism. This is why we need to look at the articulation of the production, distribution and reception processes of postmodern discourses in their specific material and economic contexts.

Second, besides the above-mentioned material and economic conditions of postmodern culture, the emergence of the youth market must be considered. It is well-known that college students and upper-class youth have been the main target consumers of the advertising market since the mid-1980s. These young consumer groups are avid readers of foreign fashion magazines like *Vogue, Mode and Non-no,* and buyers of music video and video movies through which they develop a distinctive structure of feeling apart from other groups and generations in their society.

These postmodern advertisements typically feature such youth-oriented commodities as fashion clothing, cosmetics, CD players, soft drinks, confectionery and department store merchandise (Table 4). Their appeal is primarily to the youth market.

It should be mentioned that the so-called '*Apgu-jung*' culture (the new upper- and middle-class yuppie culture) is most readily encountered in the newly developed downtown, which is located south of the *Han* River and surrounded by luxurious shopping malls, upper-class restaurants and lavish apartment complexes. Those who consume and practice *Apgu-jung* culture come mainly from the ruling bourgeois class. They enjoy extravagant materialistic life-styles, foreign travel and participating in expensive sports like skiing and scuba diving, etc. The presence of this *Apgu-jung* culture is integral to postmodern discourse in Korea which advertising agencies appropriate in order to promote consumer culture.

The third background condition for postmodern advertisements in Korea is the use of technological innovation by means of which advertising producers are able to create fast-moving images and special visual effects. Our interviews with several production staff members reveal that advertising production enterprises usually have imported advanced technologies for computer editing and computer graphics (for example, ADO, Print Box) from Japan and the US. They supply the domestic advertising agencies with editing techniques and edited film clips containing special effects. Postmodern advertisements cannot be produced without these computer graphics and computer editing technologies.

Table 4 Types of goods and frequency of postmodern advertisements

| | March 1991 | | June 1991 | | December 1991 | | February 1992 | |
	Total	Post	Total	Post	Total	Post	Total	Post
Machinery	8	–	18	5	14	2	78	6
Confectionery	8	–	14	–	11	–	26	1
Soft drinks and alcohol	4	–	8	–	5	–	20	1
Food	12	–	16	–	5	–	50	2
Cosmetics	14	3	14	2	18	1	41	3
Department store	5	–	7	1	23	2	21	2
Shoes and clothes	47	7	48	6	48	5	74	12
Medicines	9	–	20	–	13	–	62	–
Total	107	10	145	14	137	10	372	27

Given these three background conditions of postmodern advertisements on Korean television, the question is not whether or not postmodern cultural forms are appropriate. Rather, it is crucial to elaborate the politics of postmodern culture in the concrete context of Korean society, which has 'different' contradictions to Western societies.

The second implication is that postmodern advertisements accompany the emergence of consumer groups who can afford and enjoy a postmodern sensibility (for example, *Apgu-jung* youth culture and their structure of feeling). Advertising agencies as culture industries play a mediating role, diffusing postmodern cultural taste to the general consumer through the mass media. One production staff member whom we interviewed outlined the mediating role between agencies and consumer, using an analogy: 'when a couple of young lovers walk arm in arm, the boy (consumers who have a certain type of taste) usually walks a step ahead of the girl. The ad agencies are like the girl who is a step behind, but holding hands with the boy.'

We now turn to a discursive analysis of postmodern television advertisements, paying attention to their specific modes of representation.

Features of representation in postmodern advertisements

Postmodern advertisements have a number of distinctive representational features: anti-form, irrational appeal, destruction of linear narratives, image-centred ways of seeing, and 'feminist'[3] perspectives. These discrete modes of representation in postmodern advertisements consist of the combination of several features. Hence, these categories are not mutually exclusive.

Regarding the feature of anti-form, the postmodern text permits more open signification than in modernist advertisements by intermingling reality and fictional reality and putting a visual frame within a frame; for example, a television on television.

When we look at the appeal of these advertisements, postmodern advertisements present little information about the utility of the goods, focusing instead on symbolic relationships in the context of consumption. This is why advertisements for medicines and food rarely take the form of postmodern advertisements.

Postmodern advertisements subvert traditional narrative structure by presenting fragmented sequences of images, affection and mood, and thus they make it hard for the viewer to reconstruct a story-line. In order to deconstruct conventional narrative structure, some advertisements simply juxtapose fragmented images that attract the viewer's attention and do not allow for the reading of any meaningful story-line.

While modern advertisements represent symbolic worlds of reality by integrating the linguistic and the non-linguistic (music, visuals and sound effects) in a consistent way, postmodern advertisements depend largely on non-linguistic codes and make use of overlapping and fragmented images.

Finally, feminist perspectives are often salient in postmodern advertisements. Whereas modern advertisements feature male-dominant ways of seeing, preserving the corresponding line of vision between camera and viewer, post-modern advertisements subvert traditional patriachical vision. Thus, post-modern advertisements portray female-centred action and emotion that deconstructs female stereotypes.

A description of postmodern advertisements

In this section we analyse the meaning of postmodern advertisements in the context of Korean society, their vision of the world, the ways in which social relations between man and woman are portrayed, and the way in which relations between (wo)men and things are constructed. Postmodern advertisements typically present distinctive social relations as well as a postmodern vision of the world. While in modernist advertisements a woman and a man often fall in love with each other and resolve their conflicts according to a conventional narrative structure, in postmodern advertisements, more often than not the couple either separate or divorce as a result of female initiative.

There is no world in this postmodern media space that promises a safe, stable or peaceful life. As this feature is epitomized in Levi's advertisement, 'Everybody leaves, everything leaves me, but *Levi's* stay with me' (quoted in Grossberg, 1988). People do not occupy spaces like the home, a restaurant, a club or a park. Instead they are situated in a borderless, dark, abysmal hyperspace as well as in disintegrated and disrupted spaces, such as that left after the Holocaust. In this world, time does not flow in a linear fashion from the past to the present and into the future. Thus the viewers can barely identify relations of 'before and after'.

Analysing the television advertising of Reebok sports shoes, Goldman (1992) points out that the Reebok advertisement's pastiche is a metaphor for individuality, as its 'metacommunicate indifference to instant style or the look' (p. 215). Differing from the modern convention of advertisements that portray goods with signs of individuality, Reebok dissociates its signs from the social; that is, from social status, class, or acceptance or desirability. The blankness and lack of engagement in the Reebok advertisement is itself turned into a signifier. Goldman refers to this as 'contradictions of a political economy of sign values'.

The postmodern world rejects any happy, harmonious and integrated vision of the world or of being in the world, and demolishes any shared structure of feeling. This is what Grossberg (1988) calls a discursive movement or strategy that represents 'authentic inauthenticity', 'realistic irony' and 'empowering nihilism'.

What has been described so far is the world and the vision of the world which is characteristic of Western postmodern advertisements. To interpret the meaning of postmodern advertisements, it is useful to compare the cultural frames of postmodern advertisements with those of modernist advertisements, whose creative strategies are 'personalization' and 'life-style' (Leiss *et al.*, 1986).

According to Leiss *et al.*, the cultural frame of narcissism combines goods with emotion and the psychology of users. Consumers are able to assume certain types of personality and style or to formulate their self-identities by consuming commodities. For example, a (fe)male model in narcissistic advertisements becomes an 'imaginary other' of the consumer/viewer.

The totemic cultural frame constructs an identity for the consumer group who shares a totem or emblem such as Coca-Cola red and enjoys a certain type of life-style (Table 5). The strategy of creating a life-style clearly demonstrates how consumers become members of a consumer community through symbolic totems. In both cultural frames of advertisements, as Leiss *et al.* argue, advertising plays a mediating role, connecting consumers and goods or offering promises for changes in consumers' social relations.

In contrast to modernist advertisements, postmodern advertisements present only vague relations between consumers and goods. As Goldman (1992) argues, more often than not the relations disappear and new relations of consumer and images emerge. The experience of seeing images does not permit any direct or indirect experience of the thing as referent. Rather, it means the reception of simulacra in which reality is not represented as a mechanical expression of originality, but as a hyperreality, constructed through the deprivation of authenticity and purity (Baudrillard, 1983; Grossberg, 1988). The distinction between the real and the represented disappears, and everybody lives in the world of simulacrum where goods provide consumers with no fixed identity but with the appearance of difference through a collage of fragmentary images.

Table 5 Historical changes in the cultural frames of modern and postmodern advertisements

Medium	Television	Video/cable	Multi-media
Marketing strategy	Active	Division	Division
Ads' strategy	Personalization	Life-style	Postmodern
Period	1950–60	1970–80	1980 to present
Elements of ads	Goods/typical model	Goods/activities (person and situation)	Collage of images
Analogy and emotion	Glamour/romance/ self-transformation	Leisure/health/ friendship	Fantasy/hallucination/ desire
Cultural frame of commodity	Narcissism	Totemism	Neo-utopia

Source: Two categories of narcissism and totemism are Leiss *et al.*'s (1986); the 'neo-utopia' is mine

The postmodern perception of reality includes nihilistic and cynical visions of the world that are also realized in the social contradictions between the corporate structures of capital and labour, neo-Fordist labour control, and anti-nuclear, feminist and the black movement, even though these overdetermined relations are difficult to identify.

We will now turn to the world of postmodern advertisements on Korean television; it is not surprising that these do not have the same nihilistic and cynical vision of the world. Unlike modernist advertisements, postmodern advertisements on Korean television depend entirely on new modes of expression rather than on a new vision of the world. Instead of embracing a nihilistic and cynical vision, Korean postmodern advertisements show a technological utopia where social contradictions will be resolved by the computer, bio-technology, the information super-highway, etc. Why aren't these Korean advertisements embedded in a nihilistic and cynical worldview and the absence of historical consciousness, even though visual and linguistic modes of representation clearly adopt the hyperreal conception of space and time?

On the one hand, the different social and economic conditions of Korea can explain the absence of the postmodern vision of a bleak world. As mentioned above, the complex economic and political terrains characterized by an unequal distribution of wealth, centralized bureaucratic state power and the oppression of social movements make it unpopular among consumers. The argument that the postmodern vision of the world can provide a promising and empowering consumer culture for Korean society is ahistorical, as well as a political illusion against the harsh realities of Korean society. Since social contradictions are transparently conceived, the nihilistic and cynical vision of the world is hardly acceptable to the Korean populace.

On the other hand, it is important to mention that the very competitive market of advertising forces producers to differentiate their advertisements from others. To accommodate the clients' demands that 'our goods must be something different or cool', producers of advertisements must exploit the large reservoir of free-floating signifiers in the Western postmodern mediascape. One producer we interviewed told us that 'a number of the owners of fashion companies have been trained as designers. So they are fairly familiar with postmodern cultural tastes and they want to give their goods a "postmodern look"'.[4]

The analysis of television advertisements shows that in parallel with the surge of postmodern advertisements, so-called 'human-touch' advertisements have been rapidly increasing, presenting traditional community- and family-oriented human relations. A series known as the 'Dawoo Family', Samsung's washing-machine and Choco Pie (chocolate pie) strongly demonstrate the worlds of traditional as well as communal values, norms and rituals. These goods have been successful in the Korean market. This is why both postmodern and 'human-touch' advertisements have become popular on Korean television advertising and why postmodern advertisements purposefully adopt the appearance of the hyperreal, rather than appropriate the postmodern vision of the world as a whole. I would like to call such a modality of cultural terrain in Korea a 'post-modern consumerism without postmodernity'. This refers to the cultural tendency whereby cultural products and practices (here postmodern advertise-ments) mainly focus on 'copying' the new and adopting the appearance of post-modernism, while not taking seriously postmodernism as an effort to overcome the contradictions of the modern.

Postmodern consumer culture without postmodernity

If postmodern advertisements in the US force a relentless hyperreal encoding by collapsing distinctions between the real and the simulated in the world of rep-resentation, how can we interpret the copying of hyperreal encoding in a differ-ent context? Put in a different way, how can we interpret the phenomena of imitating and assimilating the style of advertisements from the reservoir of post-modern signifiers while not taking into account the values, ideas and ways of thinking implicit in such advertisements? By asking this question, I am not deploring the absence of a postmodern worldview in Korean advertisements. The question is: Why don't Korean advertisements adopt the worldview and what are the implications of its absence?

There may be two ways of looking at this phenomenon. First, it may be an effect of structural dependence, in which postmodern consumer cultural forms are replicated and replace local products with mass-produced goods that usually originate in the West. The narratives of postmodern advertisements serve as the catalyst to introduce these advertisements and to teach the 'grammar' of inter-national advertising. As production staffs attested in our interviews, there is neither a time lag nor a distance lag when they make the same style of adver-tisements, because production teams usually check video clips of American and Japanese advertisements that are sent to them monthly by their foreign offices. Since 1993, they have been able to watch MTV's advertisements in real time on satellite television. In this sense, it is 'not yet post-imperialism' (Schiller, 1991) and 'the media are still American' (Tunstall, 1977).

From the problematic of global culture or globalization, some postmodern-ists (Featherstone, 1990) and postcolonialists may interpret this assimilation of postmodern advertisements as a newly emergent hybrid culture. In Bhabha's (1994) term, hybridization occurs in a 'Third Space' or 'in-between' space, not in and through original narratives. It is in this border space that intersubjective negotiation and translation and the hybrid constitution of culture become poss-ible. Following this theory of hybridity, the Korean advertising agencies as pro-ducers of popular culture have their own cultural competence and sensibility through which they can tune into the attitudes of their local consumers. Because the target of postmodern advertisements is the newly emerging youth, they adopt postmodern tastes and styles, inserting and translating their roots into local forms such as technopia or computopia.

There is no doubt that the intentions of the Western producers and the meaning of Western signifiers are not guaranteed; rather, they are always reinterpreted and reimagined.[5] However, for an imitated postmodern style to be an emerging hybrid culture as many postcolonialists claim, it should not be a mere adoption of styles, but the postmodern signifiers/signified appropriated by Koreans should challenge or discursively destabilize the regime of American commodified culture. As shown in the earlier discussion above, it is hard to find any creative appropriation or the constitution of new subject positions.[6] If postmodern advertisements in the West illustrate the crisis of signification, as Goldman (1992) argues, copying the appearance of the outside crisis at best results in a diversity of surfaces, rather than the transformation of a contradiction.

A newly emerging upper- and middle-class youth incorporates the free-floating postmodern signifiers as a display and class distinction, exhibiting a sophisticated and cosmopolitan look. The display of difference under the regime of commodity cannot be the expression of resistance.

It is important, however, to mention one interesting case of a new feminine subjectivity resulting from some postmodern advertisements in the Korean context. Not unexpectedly, there are some postmodern advertisements that subvert the traditional representation of the male–female relationship. Many fashion advertisements (for both foreign and Korean brands) include scenes of love and conflict: a woman aggressively attacks her partner; a woman demonstrates her anger and anxiety to others (either to men or to other women). These scenes are filmed with either close-up or extreme close-up shots, through which bodies and gestures of female characters are decentred.[7] But these advertisements are few and far between.

One question remains unanswered: Why is the vision of feminism adopted? and why aren't visions of cynicism or nihilism adopted as well?

It may be more appropriate not to choose one of these interpretations as a single correct theory: it is better to look at the articulation of different forces and processes within a field of interconnections among mediascape, financescape and technoscape.[8] In the production process of postmodern advertisements the centre–periphery relationship works not as a single determinant but as a framing force, which not only socializes Korean producers into particular cultural patterns (in this case postmodern styles and modes of encoding) but also offers and makes the American postmodern life-style a significant part of Korean youth's value structure.

We cannot ignore the fact, however, that copying and imitating was not the result of imperialistic imposition by the centre but a voluntary accommodation to the other culture by local producers of advertising. To local cultural producers, the Western postmodern advertisements are primarily rich sources of codes and symbols.

Notes

1   This study could not have been completed without the help of doctoral
    students Chang-yoon Chu and Soojung Kim.
2   As for the domination of multinational advertising agencies in the world
    market, see Kim (1995).
3   By feminist perspective I do not mean that postmodernism features a femin-
    ist perspective. I labelled some postmodern advertisements that represent
    non-traditional male and female relationships as feminist. There are certainly
    many modern advertisements which include other non-traditional gender
    relations.
4   He added that postmodern advertisements should not be broadcast on national
    television because the consumers of those goods are limited to small sectors
    of the youth market. It is not a well-planned market strategy to broadcast post-
    modern advertisements for goods whose consumers come from particular
    demographic and material backgrounds.
5   There are many anthropological studies which illustrate indigenization and
    creolization of Western commodity and its culture in different societies
    (Miller, 1987; Miller, 1994; Wilk, 1994).
6   In this context, it is very interesting that many postmodernists and post-
    colonialists have tried to find some positive appropriation, postmodern diver-
    sification, and hybridization in the cultural formation in the border space
    within the centre, rather than the periphery.
7   See Williamson (1978) , Wernick (1992), Goldman (1992), who explain that
    these discontinuous arrays of close-up and fractured images demand or allow
    the viewers to construct and fill in meaningful relations for themselves.
8   Appadurai's (1990) five descriptive categories should be put into a theoretical
    system of articulation rather than being considered as autonomous fields of
    forces.

References

Appadurai, A. (ed.)(1986) *The Social Life of Things: Commodities in Cultural Perspective*,
    Cambridge: Cambridge University Press.
Appadurai, A. (1990) 'Disjuncture and difference in the global cultural economy',
    Theory, Culture and Society, 7 (2–3): 295–311.
Baudrillard, J. (1983) *Simulations*, New York: Semiotext(e).
Berger, J. (1977) *Ways of Seeing*, London: Penguin Books.
Bhabha, H.K. (1994) *The Location of Culture*, London: Routledge.
Eagleton, T. (1997) 'The contradictions of postmodernism', *New Literary History*, 28:
    1–6.
Featherstone, M. (1990) *Consumer Culture and Postmodernism*, London: Sage.
Goffmann, E. (1979) *Gender Advertisement*, New York: Harper & Row.
Goldman, R. (1992) *Reading Ads Socially*, London and New York: Routledge.

Goldman, R. and Papson, S. (1994) 'Advertising in the age of hypersignification', *Theory, Culture and Society*, 11: 23–53.

Grossberg, L. (1988) 'Postmodernism and affect: all dressed up with no place to go', *Communication*, 10: 211–293.

—— (1993) 'Cultural studies and/in new worlds', *Critical Studies in Mass Communication*, 10(1): 1–22.

Hall, S. (1992) 'Cultural studies and its theoretical legacies', in L. Grossberg, C. Nelson and P. Treichler (eds) *Cultural Studies*, New York: Routledege.

Haug, W. F. (1986) *Critique of Commodity Aesthetics: Appearance, Sexuality and Advertising in Capitalist Society*, Cambridge: Polity Press.

Hebdige, D. (1988) *Hiding the Light: On Images and Things*, London: Routledge.

Jameson, F. (1991) *Postmodernism, or the Cultural Logic of Late Capitalism*, London: Verso.

Kim, K. K. (1995) 'Spreading the net: the consolidation process of large transnational advertising agencies in the 1980s and early 1990s', *International Journal of Advertising*, 14: 195–217.

Lee, J. S. (1989) 'Reduction of labor tax and an equal imposition of taxes', unpublished paper presented at the Peace and Democratic Party's Seminar on Government Economic Policy.

Leiss, W., Kline, S. and Jhally, S.(1986) *Social Communication in Advertising: Persons, Products and Images of Well-being*, Toronto: Methuen.

Miller, D. (1987) *Material Culture and Mass Consumption*, Oxford: Blackwell.

—— (1994) 'Creolizing for survival in the city', *Cultural Critique*, 27: 153–88.

Schiller, H. (1991) 'Not yet the post-imperialist era', *Critical Studies in Mass Communication*, 8: 13–28.

Thompson, J. B. (1990) *Ideology and Modern Culture: Critical Social Theory in the Ear of Mass Communication*, Cambridge: Polity Press.

Tunstall, J. (1977) *The Media are American*, London: Constable.

Wernick, A. (1992) *Promotional Culture. Advertising, Ideology and Symbolic Expression*, London: Sage.

Wilk, R. (1994) 'Consumer goods as dialogue about development: colonial time and television time in Belize', in J. Friedman (ed.) *Consumption and Identity*, Chur, Switzerland: Harwood Academic Publishers.

Williamson, J. (1978) *Decoding Advertisements*, London: Marion Boyars.

David Hesmondhalgh

INDIE: THE INSTITUTIONAL POLITICS AND AESTHETICS OF A POPULAR MUSIC GENRE

Abstract

This article is concerned with the complex relations between institutional politics and aesthetics in oppositional forms of popular culture. Indie is a contemporary genre which has its roots in punk's institutional and aesthetic challenge to the popular music industry but which, in the 1990s, has become part of the 'mainstream' of British pop. Case studies of two important 'independents', Creation and One Little Indian, are presented, and the aesthetic and institutional politics of these record companies are analysed in order to explore two related questions. First, what forces lead 'alternative' independent record companies towards practices of professionalization and of partnership/collaboration with major corporations? Second, what are the institutional and political-aesthetic consequences of such professionalization and partnership? In response to the first question, the article argues that pressures towards professionalization and partnership should be understood not only as an abandonment of previously held idealistic positions (a 'sell-out') and that deals with major record companies are not necessarily, in themselves, a source of aesthetic compromise. On the second question, it argues that collaboration with major record companies entails a relinquishing of autonomy for alternative independent record companies; but perspectives which ascribe negative aesthetic consequences directly to such problematic institutional arrangements may well be flawed.

Keywords

aesthetics; institutions; music industry; independent record companies

Indie is a popular music genre which, in the 1990s, has considerably outgrown its original audience among students and (lower) middle-class youth. It was at first a British phenomenon, and is often subsumed under the category 'alternative rock' in the United States and elsewhere. The mid-1980s' coining and adoption of the term, an abbreviation of 'independent' (as in independent record company) was highly significant: no music genre had ever before taken its name from the form of industrial organization behind it. For indie proclaimed itself to be superior to other genres not only because it was more relevant or authentic to the youth who produced and consumed it (which was what rock had claimed) but also because it was based on new relationships between creativity and commerce. The discourses of fans, musicians and journalists during the countercultural heyday of rock and soul in the 1960s and 1970s saw 'independents', small record companies with no ties to vertically integrated corporations, as preferable to the large corporations because they were less bureaucratic and supposedly more in touch with the rapid turnover of styles and sounds characteristic of popular music at its best. Such companies were often, in fact, even more exploitative of their musicians than were the major corporations (Shaw, 1978), but punk activists took the idea of independence and politicized it more rigorously (see Laing, 1985; Hesmondhalgh, 1997). Post-punk companies, often started by musicians or by record shop owners, saw independents as a means of reconciling the commercial nature of pop with the goal of artistic autonomy for musicians. Creative autonomy from commercial restraint is a theme which has often been used to mystify artistic production by making the isolated genius the hero of cultural myth. Indie, however, emerged from a hardheaded network of post-punk companies which made significant challenges to the commercial organization of cultural production favoured by the major record companies (Hesmondhalgh, 1997).

Given the long-standing, if muted, concern in cultural studies and the political economy of communication with efforts to transform the nature of cultural production, the lack of attention paid to this network of alternative production is remarkable. Its penetration went far beyond that of the 'small media' institutions often surveyed as examples of alternatives in academic work on the cultural industries (e.g. Herman and McChesney, 1997: 189–205). Such alternative media activism is usually concerned with the provision of small-scale alternatives 'outside' commercial popular culture, as it were. My concern here, though, is primarily with the historical trajectory of indie as a case study of what happens to oppositional moments 'within' popular culture. I focus on two important British independent companies, Creation and One Little Indian, to explore two related questions. First, *what forces lie behind the move of such alternative independents towards professionalization, and towards partnership/collaboration with institutions which these companies had previously defined themselves strongly and explicitly against?* In the case of One Little Indian, such collaboration took the form of partnership with an entrepreneur who had no background in the punk ethics and aesthetics of the company and, later, with the Dutch-based multinational corporation, PolyGram. In the case of Creation, it took the form of a particularly controversial sale of a stake in the company to Sony. I want to suggest that the motives involved in such professionalization and partnership are more complex than is implied in two discourses which have been prevalent in the indie sector as a means of explaining these processes: 'sell-out', which assumes that independents abandon previously held political and aesthetic commitments for financial gain; and 'burn-out', which is slightly more generous to independents and which assumes that institutional alterity can only be maintained for a short period before human and financial resources run dry.[1] The two companies make for an interesting comparison, because both came to be part of a boom in the popularity of indie in the 1990s via partnership with entrepreneurial and corporate capital, but they began from political and aesthetic positions which were markedly different from each other. One Little Indian provides the opportunity to examine the legacy of the most politically active role of punk, inspired by anarchism, rather than by the socialist politics prevalent in other companies such as Rough Trade. Creation Records, by contrast, throughout most of its history, showed little or no interest in political engagement, until its well-publicized links in 1996–97 with Tony Blair's Labour Party – and such links with a formal political party would have been scorned by the anarchists at One Little Indian. Creation was, instead, a company built very much around a set of aesthetic concerns: in particular, a reverence for a certain 'classic' pop/rock canon; and this fact is significant for my account, as will become apparent below.

The second question is: *in terms of institutional and aesthetic politics, what losses and gains are involved in the move towards such professionalization and corporate partnership/collaboration?* This type of question is at the heart of much debate about attempts to achieve difference in contemporary popular culture. Again, I am interested in complicating a discourse common within some sections of indie culture itself (especially its more politicized wing) which sees aesthetics as an almost inevitable outcome of certain institutional and political positions, whereby maintaining an institutional separation from corporations, or a place on the margins, is felt to guarantee aesthetic diversity and stimulation. As we shall see, this position was held by some former associates of One Little Indian. In fact, I want to suggest that the very basis of this second question is somewhat flawed, in that it assumes that institutional positions have traceable aesthetic outcomes. But I also want to criticize an aesthetic position which is characteristic of a much less politicized type of indie discourse (though, of course, aesthetic positions are always, if indirectly, political positions) and which is to be found at work at Creation Records. I would describe this aesthetic position as *classicist* and as *aestheticist*. Before discussing each of the companies in turn in the main body of this article, I outline the way in which indie, as a genre, grew out of punk and post-punk and how it developed in the 1990s.

The post-punk battle against the music industry and the coming of indie

The successes of the post-punk independents in the 1980s can be summarized in four categories (see also Hesmondhalgh, 1997).

1   They set up an alternative network of distribution which enabled not only the musicians signed to their labels, but also a string of other companies and musicians across the country, to reach a much wider public than would have otherwise been possible. This significantly counteracted the processes of concentration and oligopolization which had been characteristic of the recording industry, and of the cultural industries in general, for much of the century. Many people, who may not otherwise have had the opportunity to do so, were able to undertake paid creative work. The arrival of relatively cheap technology, in the form of reduced studio costs and less expensive musical instruments, can only be partly credited for this. A significant factor was that those who were drawn to punk argued for the active appropriation of these opportunities.

2   This institutional intervention was achieved through a more reflexive under-standing of the dynamics of the record industry than had existed up to that point. The commitment to independent production and distribution tran-scended romantic notions of musical creativity. Rather than naively contrast-ing the spontaneous art of independents with a corrupting and predatory commercial sector, some of the post-punk companies recognized that in a popular-cultural medium, independent ownership of production *and* distri-bution was the most effective route towards democratization of the industry. These post-punk independents proclaimed that at the heart of the politics of cultural production was the issue of how music came to its audiences, whereas rock discourse had tended to mystify and/or ignore this process (see Bloomfield, 1991).

3   Independent networks of production and distribution were extended beyond Britain and into Europe and the United States. Again, this was based on an awareness of the new conditions facing the music industry, as well as a pragmatic desire to expand audiences through exports. Although the post-punk project eventually burnt out, these international networks still exist today.

4   An aesthetic based on mobilization and access was developed. This encour-aged the unskilled and untrained to take the means of musical production into their own hands. By extension, there was also an emphasis on political activism in certain quarters. Not only was Rock Against Racism able to base its campaigns around punk's anti-nationalism, but socialists and anarchists were able to build post-punk institutions with a political edge. The sexual politics of punk were complex and contradictory, but women took new roles

in music and the commercial organization of recording, and expressed new
and suppressed themes and sounds.

But by 1986, post-punk's status as the most prestigious branch of alternative
music in Britain was under threat. At the same time, the term 'indie' was becoming widely used to describe a new phase in the cultural politics of alternative
pop/rock in Britain. Rather than the mélange of experimental influences covered
by the umbrella term 'post-punk', 'indie' described a narrower set of sounds and
looks. The 'whiteness' of the genre was the subject of much music press comment
in the mid-1980s.[2] While many musicians, fans and journalists had increasingly
turned to pop and black musical traditions, such as electro and hip hop, as fresh
sources of inspiration in the early 1980s, indie was constructing a canon of white,
underground rock references. The mainstream pop charts were dominated by
funk figures and rhythms, but indie records turned to 'jangly' guitars, an emphasis on clever and/or sensitive lyrics inherited from the singer/songwriter tradition in rock and pop, and minimal focus on rhythm track.[3] Dance rhythms
were, on the whole, resisted (and the exceptions tended to be the most popular
bands in the independent sector, such as New Order and Depeche Mode). In
terms of presentation, indie often prided itself on its care over design (23 Envel-
ope's work for the label 4AD and the work of Peter Saville for Factory being the
most prominent examples) but set itself against the concentration on 'image' in
the pop mainstream: important indie bands, such as the Smiths, refused to put
their pictures on record sleeves. There was a resistance to using promotional
videos. And the stage presentation of bands involved dressing down, a minimum
display of musical prowess, and a deliberate muting of charisma. All this represented an opposition to what Simon Reynolds called 'health and efficiency': the
perceived stress in dominant forms of culture on the body, and on aspirations to
professional success (Reynolds, 1988). As with so many oppositional genres in
popular music, then, indie was contradictory: its counter-hegemonic aims could
only be maintained, it seems, by erecting exclusionary barriers around the
culture.

Indie faced problems of popularity which had been gradually emerging
during the post-punk era of alternative pop/rock. There was a widening gulf
between, on the one hand, a stabilizing pop mainstream oriented towards video
promotion, and synergies with visual mass media,[4] and on the other, a post-punk
independent sector which set itself determinedly against these commercial
methods. This gap was manifested in the fact that the records in the independent
charts were beginning to make less and less impression on the pop charts. As the
New Musical Express (*NME*), one of the music press bastions of the independent
ethos in the UK, put it at the time: '[In the last twelve months] the indie alternative, taken as a whole, has seemed as far removed from the centre of the pop
action as at any time in the last decade' (Kelly, 1987).

Media outlets for indie were struggling too: although many local radio stations still had their own specialist indie show, it was becoming more and more difficult for post-punk independents to gain exposure for their sounds. BBC Radio One no longer provided much coverage of sounds from independent companies and, where it did, audiences were falling.[5] And, in 1987, the circulation of the *NME* itself had fallen below 100,000 for the first time in its thirty-year history (*BPI Statistical Handbook 1993*: 46).

Although the post-punk distribution network, the Cartel, was increasingly able to provide impressive support for the star names which sustained the indie scene in the late 1980s, the retreat of indie as a genre into a market niche meant that the independent networks were hit badly by the economic recession of 1988–92. Few star bands emerged to inherit the mantle of the Smiths, New Order and the like. There was a widespread sense that the punk legacy had run its course. More and more people who had been previously drawn to independent rock/pop were turning to dance music and/or the harder sounds of American bands such as Husker Du and the Pixies. There was a revival of general and music media interest in the sector when, in 1989, a number of British bands fused features of dance music with rock (in a subgenre which was briefly known as 'baggy', and which was associated with indie bands which had discovered post-house club culture, such as The Happy Mondays and The Stone Roses). But the early 1990s' bankruptcies of two key post-punk institutions, Factory Records and Rough Trade, seemed only to confirm notions of a 'crisis' in the indie world (see Maconie, 1992).

Yet by 1995, a version of indie had come to occupy the centre ground of British pop music in the shape of bands such as Blur, Oasis and Pulp, all of which had aesthetic roots in the post-punk rock tradition. This neo-indie triumph, labelled 'Britpop' in the music and news media in 1995–96, also had its *institutional* foundations in post-punk: many of the key bands were on, or had been on, labels that were fostered by the 1980s independent networks. In the meantime, however, much had changed. Post-punk independence had maintained its distance from major capital by forming alternative networks of distribution, marketing and manufacture, internationally as well as nationally. The 'Britpop' explosion emerged from companies which had survived the bankruptcies of the early 1990s to form much closer ties with the corporations.[6] One Little Indian and Creation were, in different ways, examples of such companies.

One Little Indian and the professionalization of the anarchists

For the post-punk vanguard (much of it based around Rough Trade), punk had provided an opportunity to experiment with the form of the pop song. For others, though, it was the authentic music of working-class youth; its fast, furious noise was felt to encode the anger of the dispossessed and disempowered. A

series of groups claimed the mantle of 'true' punk from the Sex Pistols and The
Clash, the core punk bands who signed to major companies. Some of these acts
descended into outright racism and fascism in the form of the Oi! movement,
propagated by *Sounds* journalist Garry Bushell (who later became the television
columnist of the authoritarian-populist *Sun* newspaper). Other descendants of
what Jon Savage (1991: 583) calls the 'social realist cadre' of punk, such as Sham
69 (on the semi-independent Chrysalis Records) reached the pop charts with a
football terrace aesthetic of working-class unity, expressed in soccer-style
chanted choruses. But a small group of anarchist bands, centred on the activities
of a group and label called Crass, achieved considerable success with a series of
strongly political records and events in the late 1970s and early 1980s, and did
so via independent production and distribution.

Crass was formed in 1978, and was centred around a collective based at a
rented farmhouse in Epping, to the north-east of London. The band's first record
was released on the Walthamstow shop label Small Wonder, but it formed its
own Crass Label in 1979. Between 1978 and 1983 (when it disbanded), Crass
was an almost permanent presence in the UK independent charts. Its music was
basic and, compared with the experimentalism of many post-punk acts, aesthet-
ically unadventurous. Marching drums and distorted guitar carried the rhythm.
Listeners' attention was directed to the angry lyrics, which were often about
sexual oppression and the danger of ecological disaster. The music, then, served
as something of a vehicle for the politics. Unlike earlier forms of directly political music, however (such as the folk/protest movement of the early 1960s in the
US), Crass chose to work across a range of techniques. Cover art, designed by
G., of the Crass collective, was particularly striking. The 1979 album *Stations of
the Crass* features a booklet detailing the crimes of organized religion (and, in this
respect, the band was working in a long tradition of anarchist anti-clericalism).
Crass extended its activities beyond recording and playing live gigs to carrying
out situationist-style actions. At the time of the Royal wedding between Prince
Charles and Lady Diana Spencer in 1981, for instance, Crass arranged with a
teenage romance magazine called *Loving* a deal whereby readers of the magazine
could send off for a special single to commemorate the event. Crass, which called
itself 'Creative Recording And Special Services' for the purposes of the action,
sent out anarchist material with the singles it dispatched to the (mainly) teenage
girls. The single itself was a parody of romantic conceptions of love. Crass then
contacted tabloid newspapers to draw attention to the outrage that an anarchist
band had pulled such a cruel trick on young readers – especially as the material
sent related to the *Penis Envy* album out at the time.[7]

Crass was more explicitly and actively political than most of the Rough
Trade bands and staff; and, as the above story indicates, feminism was central to
its work.[8] Nevertheless, the band relied on an 'outside' cultural entrepreneur
to facilitate its early recordings: there was no pure, original moment where
anarcho-punk was 'untainted' by entrepreneurialism. John Lauder, a computer

engineer, had built his own recording studio, Southern, in the garage of his house in Wood Green, North London. His wife Sue attended Walthamstow College with members of Crass, and they arranged to record their first single there, with Lauder engineering. This was the beginning of a long relationship, though not one based directly on a political alliance. Lauder himself may have been sympathetic to anarchism, but his own beliefs were mainly religious: he was a practising scientologist. But a string of anarchist-inspired bands (including Dirt, the Omega Tribe and, most notably, Conflict) recorded at the studios and had their records issued on the Crass label, and on its offshoot, Corpus Christi.

Distribution of the early Crass records was through the key post-punk shop/record company Rough Trade (see Hesmondhalgh, 1997) but Crass had little connection with the Rough Trade set-up, which was on the other side of London. Rough Trade's politics were more socialist, and according to Tim Kelly, who was unusual in that he worked in both places, musicians and staff at Rough Trade tended to be more interested in popular music history than the Crass anarchists (interview, 23 August 1994). By 1981, on the basis of the Crass label's continued success and high sales (Crass's 1979 album *Stations of the Crass* sold 250,000 copies, according to the band's Penny Rimbaud), Lauder was able to set up independent distribution from Southern Studios. They quickly gained the contract to distribute another key anarchist label, Alternative Tentacles, which had been set up by Jello Biafra of the US West Coast anarcho-punk band, The Dead Kennedys, in association with British manager Bill Gilliam. An alternative, anarchist network was being formed.

Today, although Lauder no longer has a stake in the company, Southern Distribution, now called SRD, is one of the UK's leading independent distributors, with over a hundred labels contracted to it for distribution and export. But this is only one example of an institution formed from an explicitly political, amateur set of practices in the early 1980s around Crass. The best-known instance of this anarchist heritage is One Little Indian itself, which was a direct progeny of Crass, formed by members of the anarcho-punk band Flux of Pink Indians in 1985 (and preceded by another small label, Spiderleg). After Crass played its last gig in 1984 and started to wind down its label (and other) activities, many Crass acts ended up on One Little Indian, including Annie Anxiety, the Very Things and Kukl, an Icelandic band which was later to become The Sugarcubes, One Little Indian's most successful early act.

In the early days of One Little Indian, the principal staff were Derek Birkett, the bass player with Flux of Pink Indians, who financed the company with a loan from his father; Tim Kelly, then also of Flux of Pink Indians; Mark Edmondson, who had lived at the Crass commune for a while, and who worked at Southern distribution when it started up; and Lauren Bromley, who was in charge of international licensing, and who had worked at CBS Records. All, apart from Bromley, were amateurs who were learning their trade as they went along. Their story indicates some of the problems associated with professionalization and growth in cultural institutions founded on an amateur ethos (see also Hesmondhalgh, 1997).

The music industry is a high-pressure business, but there are few opportunities for a professional training, which might provide assistance in coping with this pressure. In both major and independent companies there is a stressful continuum between leisure time and work. Evenings are often spent attending live concerts in order to stay aware of new developments and to maintain contacts. In independent record companies there are additional burdens. The people working together are often friends, and relationships are put under great strain by new and unexpected roles. Another problem is that of negotiating between the constant threat of bankruptcy and a strong resistance to 'selling-out' to majors, or even to 'straight' companies (those supposedly motivated neither by love of music, nor by politics). As Mark Edmondson put it,

> You get so many hangers-on. The night before gigs, you'd get people ringing you up at home saying can you put us on the guest list for the Sugarcubes, can you do this? You'd get Australian *Vogue* ringing up saying can we have the lead singer on our front cover, blah, blah, blah. I thought, 'this is getting fucking out of hand'. . . . You'd get these real bloody sharks that you'd have to deal with from commercial companies, tour managers, the whole bloody caboodle. . . . They're just horrible people, you haven't got anything in common with them at all, they don't like the same music as you, they're not coming from the same area at all.
>
> (Interview, 10 December 1993)

Of course, some aspects of these remarks are complaints which could be made by any overworked, disgruntled former employee (though Edmondson remained on very good terms with Birkett). But some of the distinctive features of work in independent cultural production emerge here: the disillusion caused by the lost hope that it might be possible to work with people of similar tastes and, by extension, people of similar political inclinations; and the frustration that the breakdown of distinctions between public and private life, work and leisure could be so invasive and unpleasurable. Even those who choose to continue to work in the record industry often express similar sentiments informally.

Such pressures drive many independent record company musicians and staff out of the industry altogether, and such cultural factors should not be ignored in examining why so many independent companies fold. For many anarcho-punks, combining political beliefs directly opposed to the accumulation of wealth and status, with a job involving frequent contact with conspicuous wealth and consumption, proved too much, and they left the industry. But some of the anarchists stayed on, and ventured further into the professional world which some of their colleagues chose to evade.

One Little Indian was as musician-centred as the other post-punk independents. In a 1988 interview with Tim Kelly, a journalist asked if One Little Indian was ever 'skint'. Kelly replied:

> Yeah, sometimes. Especially when bands spend six days in a good studio doing one single. And we always do a good sleeve. It costs a lot of money. We've got to sell a lot of records to make it all back. But the better we make the record, we think, we've got a better chance than if we start cutting corners.
>
> (Quoted in Gittins, 1988: 42)

Whereas the early anarcho-punk scene had paid great attention to good packaging and to selling records cheaply to fans, this was supported by remarkable sales. But with the decline of the alternative scene, including the specialist independent shops, money was not so readily available. Birkett complained in another interview (Gibson, 1988), from the same PR drive, that the first Flux of Pink Indians single on Crass sold more than 30,000, but that releases on One Little Indian struggled to sell anything like this amount. At Rough Trade a successful distribution operation had subsidized the label until it managed to develop its own stars. One Little Indian had to turn elsewhere for financing. In 1988, Birkett sold 60 per cent of One Little Indian to a Battersea businessman, Brian Bonner, who ran a pressing plant and video distribution company called Mayking.[9] The intervention of Bonner did not escape the vigilant attention of some within the independent 'scene' for whom Bonner represented a very different ethos from the company's anarcho-punk origins. Former Crass members, still in contact with One Little Indian throughout this period, told me that they did not trust Bonner's involvement. Brenda Kelly was in contact with the company through her work as editor of *The Catalogue*, and later as producer of *Snub TV* (1989–90), one of the few television fora for independent rock and pop in the 1980s. As she puts it,

> When it was bought by Mayking, it moved into Mayking's premises in Battersea and things changed a bit. It got complicated because it had a more ambivalent independent status. He [Bonner] is more like an investment banker than an A&R idealist, or someone from that old school of independence.
>
> (Interview, 30 April 1996)

For indie idealists, then, Bonner represents a more 'traditional' entrepreneur – that is, one who is considered to be motivated as much by commerce as by music or politics. According to Jenny Lewis, editor of the indie trade magazine *The Independent Catalogue* from 1992 to 1994 (interview, 14 June 1994) the sale to Mayking by Birkett was seen by many on the independent 'scene' as a precedent for One Little Indian's move, in the 1990s, towards becoming an international player via its licensing deals with PolyGram.

In the late 1980s, One Little Indian's star act was the Sugarcubes. The group's success in 1987 was almost certainly a factor behind Bonner's interest in buying the company the following year; and the need to give them the push they 'deserved' was definitely behind the company's need to find more capital, according to Mark Edmondson (interview, 10 December 1993). That the musician-centredness of One Little Indian inspired some loyalty in its musicians is demonstrated by the fact that the Sugarcubes' lead singer, Bjork, chose to remain with the company for the launch of her solo career in 1993. By then, though, she and One Little Indian had the finance and distribution muscle of PolyGram behind them. The ambivalence about success experienced by many of the professionalized amateurs around the anarcho-punk scene is cleverly represented on the cover of Bjork's first One Little Indian album, *Debut*, which consists of a simple monochrome image of Bjork, hands held to her lips. That this is a parody of vulnerability is confirmed by her direct stare to camera, and the presence of a plastic tear under each eye. The title *Debut* adds to the tease: this is her first solo album, but Bjork is an experienced player: no *ingénue* debutante. The sleeve design is by Paul White of the Me Company. White was an early associate of Derek Birkett, and was responsible for the design of many early One Little Indian albums. White, Birkett and Bjork are part of a network of musicians, record company employees and attached specialists who share a past commitment to anarchist ideals, including small-scale amateur recording activity. A purist view, with which many of these insiders began, and to which some of those who 'dropped out' from record label activity subscribed, would hold that such professionalization represents a dilution of earlier, amateur ideals.[10] The core of punk's democratization efforts were decentralization and access based on sub-professional activity; entry into a more established, parallel industry involves compromise, through contact with the 'bloody sharks' referred to by Mark Edmondson. Such purism often sees the process of professionalization as a sell-out: the abandonment of idealism for financial reward.

In order, though, for Derek Birkett (now the main owner-manager) to achieve for his key acts the international success of which he felt they were capable, he felt obliged to turn to a variety of capital sources. Was this a 'sell-out' in the widely used phrase from indie discourse which I discussed above? The term 'sell-out' masks not only a potential range of motivations behind collaboration with other sources of capital, but also the achievements which such collaboration sometimes allows. It could be argued, for example, that One Little Indian and Southern – the legacies of Crass – permit a space in the music industry for those uncomfortable with the slick world of the corporations and with the more entrepreneurial independents, by forming a protective shield, whereby corporate finance and corporate culture are kept at 'arm's length' distance from musicians and staff who share tastes and political backgrounds. A purist position which sees professionalization as 'co-optation' implies a way of living which is difficult for many people to sustain: a constant existence on an impoverished margin. The choice to set up more permanent positions and careers, while despised by many enthusiasts, is often based on a genuinely idealistic commitment to fostering talent, and to providing an alternative.

This purist position often has a corollary view of aesthetic processes which sees them as closely tied to institutional ones; perhaps exaggeratedly so. Bjork's *Debut* was widely acclaimed for its innovative soundscape (created by producer Nellee Hooper) and for its celebration of a positive identity for women in the 1990s (e.g. Price, 1993). The ex-members of Crass were, however, critical of *Debut* for its softer, 'highly produced' sound, and attributed this to the increasing encroachment of PolyGram and Mayking into the work of One Little Indian. According to this view, institutional and aesthetic politics are closely related. The concern with a smoother, richer sound which can be detected in the solo work of Bjork and in other acts on the label was misguided. The lo-fi punk sound was not only more exciting, it allowed mass participation by putting an emphasis on de-skilling. I assess this position, and attempt to look in more depth at the motivations behind independent professionalization and growth at the end of this article.

Creation, internationalization and classic pop dreams

'I Know Someone Who Knows Someone Who Knows Alan McGee'
(The Pooh Sticks, 1987)

'At the present time I myself am quite simply without peers. Self Publicist? Yeah! You'd better believe it'
(Alan McGee, 1984)

Like all sectors of media production, the independent music world is replete with gossip and speculation about the main 'personalities' in the field. Many of those who are subjected to such attention are of course musicians, but just as significant – and often more durable – are the label owner-managers. The head of Creation Records, Alan McGee, is probably the best known of the British small record company bosses of the 1980s and 1990s.[11] His label, founded in 1983, is the flagship company of British indie pop/rock and has the most prestigious, and therefore potentially most valuable, back catalogue of all the post-punk labels.

But even if, as media coverage often suggests, Creation is a company in McGee's image,[12] the development of the label, and its enormous success since its takeover by Sony in 1992, reflect wider issues about the politics of independent rock culture. When McGee sold a controlling stake of his company to Sony in 1992, this was interpreted by many advocates of independence as a third symbol of the end of the punk era, after the bankruptcies of Rough Trade and Factory in 1991: a sign of the times, but also a 'sell-out', a reversal of its earlier policy. But I want to argue that the sale of Creation should be viewed not as an abandonment of a post-punk goal of providing an institutional alternative to corporate rock and pop, but as a logical culmination of the company's desire to develop a new generation of classic pop stars in an era of increasing internationalization in the recording industry. For, in spite of some stylistic changes at the label, the *classical* nature of the company's rock/pop aesthetics and its focus on such aesthetics rather than on institutional politics have been very striking. Acts on the label have generally been in the mould established by rock and roll in the late 1950s, and continued by British beat bands in the early 1960s: bands consisting of four or five young men playing guitars and drums. The company is named after a 1960s British cult psychedelic band. Many of Creation's records, particularly in the 1980s, showed the influence of 1960s pop/rock instrumentation, in particular the Hammond organ and the 'jangly' guitar sound first used by George Harrison but developed by the Byrds' Roger McGuinn (see MacDonald, 1995: 85). Constant reference points for musicians and company staff are a lineage of classic British bands, such as the Beatles, the Rolling Stones, the Kinks and the Jam.

Will Straw (1991: 377–8) has noted 'the enshrining of specific forms of connoisseurship as central to an involvement in alternative rock culture' from the mid-1980s on in the USA and Canada.[13] Straw suggests that the interest within post-punk culture in the history of 'rock-based forms of recorded music' points to a much stronger link between post-punk and older, rock institutions than is generally recognized. The basis of the continuity between rock and post-punk alternative culture was, for Straw, their shared origin in a 'largely white bohemia'. Straw suggests that alternative rock culture is sexually as well as ethnically insular: collecting and studying old rock bands is a rite of passage for young men entering the 'scene'. The continuity between rock and post-punk alternative music culture which Straw identifies is observable in the UK too, and he is certainly right to draw attention to masculinity as a crucial area for understanding alternative or independent rock. Creation exemplifies such links. It is true that there was a period during which the work of Creation suggested a complicated mix of rockist nostalgia and post-punk experimentalism and a set of competing discourses about sexuality. The deliberately 'formless' studio experiments of My Bloody Valentine are far removed from the traditional rock song (based around the orgasmic guitar solo), as Reynolds and Press (1995: 220) point out.[14] And Primal Scream's 1991 album *Screamadelica* was the most successful attempt to fuse dance rhythms with a rock sensibility during the dance boom of the late 1980s and early 1990s.[15]

In fact, though, *Screamadelica* serves as a homage to the country blues-inflected work of the Rolling Stones in the late 1960s and Creation's project was always to create new superstars in this mould. The promotion of new star careers would necessarily involve considerable recording budgets and marketing costs, and these could not be sustained by a label low on business acumen and high on ambition. So a commitment to a certain notion of rock/pop meaning was vital in determining institutional policy (and the same was true at other post-punk labels negotiating the contradictions of their own cultural politics).

Creation had been quite successful in producing a series of indie stars (The House of Love, Primal Scream) as part of the independent networks in the late 1980s. What were they to gain from ties with the majors? Dick Green has stressed the particular importance of being able to coordinate international promotion (*Music Week*, 1994). From 1984 to 1990, Creation was licensed through the system of international affiliates which Rough Trade had successfully set up during the 1980s, such as RTD (Rough Trade Germany) and RTBV (The Netherlands). According to Green, it was difficult to promote bands adequately under this piece-meal arrangement because release dates for records could not be made to coincide with promotional tours. The Sony deal, according to Green, allowed 'unification' in Europe and the rest of the world outside of the US, where Creation had a deal with SBK, part of EMI (*Music Week*, 1994: 7). National pop stardom was not enough. The logic of the music industry as a cultural system is towards inter-nationalization, because of the economies which accrue to very big, as opposed to moderate, sales: the costs of development, marketing and recording are high; marginal costs for reproducing each copy are very small. But such economics are not enough in themselves to explain what happened in indie in the late 1980s. Creation's goal was to produce international stars, not merely in order to make money, but because the classic pop dream involves going global, in the mould of the Beatles' conquest of the global pop market in the 1960s. In other words, the aesthetics at work in the company helped to determine institutional policy.

As Alan McGee recognized in interviews, the price paid for the financial and coordination support of Sony was that Creation would have to 'deliver' internationally successful product: 'What's in it for Sony is these bands' record sales worldwide. They see me as a guy who can come up with alternative product and maybe give them two or three superstars' (quoted in Cameron, 1994: 20). By 1996, Creation had its first superstars – a band from Manchester called Oasis. In May 1994 I drove with Creation Records staff to a pub in Chelmsford, Essex to see Oasis play a gig to promote the release of its first single. About 200 people attended, in the wake of some limited, but very positive, music-press coverage. In early 1996 the same band, Oasis, was selling out two nights at a 100,000 capacity outdoor venue in the English Midlands, and had sustained a six-week run in the American top five with its second album. This was an unprecedented achievement for a British indie band. It consolidated the reputation of Creation Records as a key label in British rock history. It also affirmed, for many in the independent sector, the view that close deals with majors are the only way to achieve mass popularity.

Oasis was marketed from the start of its deal with Sony as an authentic British rock act for the global, or at least the US, market. An important context for understanding the purchase of Creation by Sony and the consequent success of Oasis is the changing status of 'alternative rock' in the USA in the early 1990s. American post-punk was, in the mid-1980s, still largely confined to an underground network of college radio stations, independent record companies and specialist retail shops (Wright, 1986). But, from the mid-1980s, MTV was increasingly able to provide a massive-scale promotional forum for alternative rock to audiences beyond the core constituency of college radio listeners, and the major cities in the United States began to develop their own alternative rock stations (Goodwin, 1993; Straw, 1993). Leading alternative bands were signed by majors during the late 1980s,[16] and the style achieved spectacular cross-over success in 1991, when Nirvana reached the top of the American album charts with its album *Nevermind*. During the 'grunge' period initiated by the popularity of Nirvana and other bands, alternative rock was able to draw upon heavy metal and hard rock audiences who had previously resisted the style.

British independent labels, however, were on the whole unable to capitalize on the possibility of selling 'alternative' acts in the USA. This was for two reasons. First, any labels, such as Rough Trade, who chose to work with their American equivalents, faced almost insurmountable problems in the American market: the absence of manufacturing and distribution possibilities, and the fragmentation of a huge market into regional divisions, with few national media outlets to bind them together (Wright, 1986). This was why many independent British labels chose to work with a major in the one-off case of the US, while using independent affiliates for all other territories in the world. But, second, even where British independents formed alliances with American majors, forms of British rock/pop labellable as 'alternative' were very difficult to sell in the late 1980s. Indie was not only resistant to the dance base of mainstream pop music; it also purported to be thoroughly antagonistic to the imagery and sounds of traditional rock culture (Reynolds, 1988). Very few bands from independent British labels achieved success in the USA, even within the alternative niche. When British bands turned towards dance fusions in the light of the publicity blaze around Manchester dance–rock fusions in 1989, the gulf between the European taste for dance music culture and the American preference for harder rock styles meant that bands like the Happy Mondays, on Factory, who were expected to do well when they toured the US in 1990, failed.

Creation was strongly linked with the kind of alternative music that the Americans did not take to: their leading band, Primal Scream, had a dance sound at the time, and became associated with the androgynous, neo-psychedelic 'shoe-gazing' style through the signing and development of bands such as Slowdive and My Bloody Valentine.[17] Following the sale of its stock to Sony, however, Creation changed its strategy. In 1994, in a special *Music Week* advertising supplement, Alan McGee declared his intention of returning to rock roots: '"We're getting back to basics", says Alan McGee. . . . McGee's current watchword is "authenticity" which he claims is to the Nineties what "marketing" was to the Eighties' (*Music Week*, 1994: 3).

'Back to Basics' was a term which had been used frequently in 1993–94 by John Major, the Conservative Prime Minister, to signal a return to 'traditional' morality. So, to some extent, McGee and the Creation copywriter have their tongues in their cheeks. It is clear too that the authenticity which McGee invokes is a self-conscious one. Nevertheless, if we look at the records being issued at this time on Creation, and at the promotional and marketing tactics adopted by the company in order to sell them, a conservative traditionalism is apparent. Primal Scream made an album (*Give Out But Don't Give Up*, 1994) explicitly based on the values of certain subgenres of Anglo-American rock in the late 1960s and early 1970s. The album was recorded in Memphis, and featured a confederate flag on its cover. The iconography and the sounds referred listeners back to the hedonistic, unreconstructed version of masculinity in southern rock (the Allman Brothers) and the Rolling Stones' British country-boogie on albums such as *Exile on Main Street* (1972).[18] The album was greeted with some derision by the British music press for its nostalgic classicism. Oasis, however, was successfully marketed as sufficiently innovative in its reinvention of the rock tradition to be worthy of credibility.

In 1991, Simon Frith commented that the case of the Stone Roses, who had not achieved the attention in the United States that they had gained in the UK, suggested the limits of a British belief in a traditional rock career model, whereby local cult success leads on to the American market, and to international fame (1991: 268). Frith has pointed out elsewhere that the model of rock success, which sees a band building a fan base by playing live, before getting signed up by record companies, true of bands as varied as the Beatles and the Grateful Dead in the 1960s, no longer holds. This is the case with Oasis: the band played a gig at a venue in Glasgow, which they knew Alan McGee would be likely to attend. The aim was to get a recording contract and then to build up a following – among journalists as much as fans. Management, band and record company coordinate marketing very carefully in advance. The marketing campaign for Oasis, however, suggests that some aspects of such traditional rock strategies are still operable for British independents in the 1990s. Breaking the band in Britain relied on the carefully controlled cultivation of a very small number of key journalists, who were introduced to the band (and partied with them) as they rehearsed, and played their first gigs in late 1993.[19] A reputation was built up via playing carefully selected live dates, and the issue of artificially rare 'white label' promotional records. Reports of the band's wild behaviour on tour and the fights between the two brothers at the core of the band drew on images from the classic masculinist rock tradition. (See, for example, the coverage of Oasis being thrown off a ferry due to a spot of bother in Harris, 1994.) American coverage duplicated the angles encouraged in the British media, and looked back to the notorious exploits of British acts such as Led Zeppelin, the Who and Herman's Hermits on the road in the 1960s and 1970s. Dick Green commented: 'To sell records, America needs to be taken into account. . . . Oasis are our one big hope to change this whole situation [the poor sales of UK acts]. They're a very direct rock & roll band' (quoted in Sinclair, 1995: 24).

The vast status of achieving success in America reflects in part that country's history as the origin of contemporary rock-based popular music; and the association of popular culture itself with American-ness. Success in the USA is the ultimate index of making it (e.g. Shelley, 1995). European success, by comparison, is sneered at, even though the size of the European market for recorded music was, by 1988, greater than that of the US.[20] The observation that a band is 'Big in Germany' is often used as a put-down of an act's limited appeal. During 1994 and 1995, as a series of indie bands broke through to the high reaches of the British charts, the music press and national newspapers were full of speculation about the fate of the 'Britpop' wave of talent in the US.[21] Because of the success of Oasis (and of other bands, such as the Boo Radleys, in the UK), of all the post-punk independent labels of the 1980s, Creation achieved most commercial success in the 1990s (though cuts in staff during 1998 suggest that the label is by no means invincible). But they have achieved their success via partnership with corporate capital; and, in order to 'deliver' their superstars, through a return to rock ideologies of authenticity and masculinity which many other independents had previously sought to challenge.

This move at Creation cannot, however, be blamed simply on the intervention of Sony. Creation had always positioned itself in opposition to the more idealistic post-punk independents. A piece Alan McGee wrote for the Rough Trade magazine *The Catalogue* in 1984, for example, mocked the older generation of indies, and set out his view of rock aesthetics: 'Tune in, drop out or are you all simply too old? . . . Timeless Classic Records Is Our Vision. . . . Remember great rock 'n' roll has very little to do with honesty. Liberalism does not appear on our pedigree' (McGee, 1984: 17). This suggests an adherence to an entrepreneurial notion of independence, as opposed to the emphasis on democratization at the other independents. Given that the same conceptions of musical quality are prevalent within many branches of the major companies, the move towards a buy-out could easily be reconciled with the company's former beliefs. The promotional strategies behind Oasis as a 'back to basics' rock and roll band are consistent with many aspects of the company's approach to rock aesthetics in the years before the Sony takeover.

The debate which took place in the music press in 1992 over the nature and status of the independent charts (the lists of the biggest-selling independently distributed records) further reveals a division of perspectives within the sector. The discussion concerned the fundamental principle established by the post-punk independents – the crucial role of independent distribution. The independent charts had, since the beginning of the 1980s, provided an important promotional forum for the products of independent distribution companies. But when indie became established as a genre, a musical sound as well as, or perhaps instead of, a sign of a political stance towards the music business, many industry insiders began to argue that the independent charts should be based on musical style, rather than on the basis of whether the distributor had ties to a major corporation (the definition of 'independent'). These issues first came to the fore in 1985–86, when *Music Week* started to publish independent charts defined on the basis of sound, rather than economic status.[22] The independent labels reacted angrily, and the issue helped lead to the launch of a new trade association for independents, Umbrella, in January 1986. *Music Week* reverted to a chart based on independent distribution, but the matter became current again in the 1990s for two main reasons. First, the dance genre (mainly pop versions of it, especially those created by Pete Waterman's PWL label) was beginning to dominate the independent charts, so some labels dealing with indie rock/pop started to argue for a generic chart, in order that their music could be publicized more effectively, without the confusion caused by the mixing of styles in the distribution-based chart. Second, the rise of 'pseudo-independent' labels such as Hut (part of EMI/Virgin) and Dedicated (part of BMG) was felt by many to be taking advantage of the independent charts: they were funded and owned by major labels, but used independent distribution to reach that chart. This led to a feeling that independent distribution was no longer a reliable index of difference from, and opposition to, the majors, and that the criterion of distribution might just as well be abandoned. It was the old guard of the post-punk independents that argued for the importance of independent distribution. The younger, newer labels favoured genre-based charts.[23] Significantly, Alan McGee took their side against the views of label bosses like Daniel Miller of Mute in arguing for the introduction of genre charts.[24] This was typical of McGee's pragmatism. Reflecting on the history of Creation in 1994, McGee presented the defeats of the independent ethos as inevitable: 'There's only two things that happen with independent labels,' he commented, 'you either get bought out or die. And that's it. There is no middle ground' (quoted in Cameron, 1994: 20). It was this pragmatism which helped to put Creation at the centre of the 'Britpop' boom of 1995–96. By early 1996, Holsten Pils was running a marketing campaign based around indie quizzes; and BBC Radio One, which in the UK dominates pop taste even more than does MTV in other territories, featured a series of young, emerging rock bands as its daytime staple. A direct legacy of the post-punk and indie sound and look had become central to British pop music. The meaning of this aesthetic had changed radically by this point, however, and had lost much of its oppositional edge. Indie was a term now generally used to describe a set of sounds and an attitude, rather than an aesthetic and institutional position. Indie was able to accommodate women musicians who were able to explore gendered experience in a sometimes powerful (P. J. Harvey) and often witty way (Elastica, Sleeper), but much of the genre had become associated with a backlash against feminism, in the form of new men's magazines which celebrated an unreconstructed version of young masculinity, a hegemonic sexual politics which went almost unchallenged. The 'whiteness' of the genre became even more pronounced; there was scarcely a black musician to be seen in the pages of the music press, except where jungle and trip-hop made appearances. The rockist aesthetic challenged by post-punk had made a comeback. Creation's success with Oasis was very influential in this process. And the narrow nationalism of the term 'Britpop' hardly needs comment (though the Irish roots of the two brothers, Noel and Liam Gallagher, at the centre of Oasis, make the relationship of Creation's leading band to the phenomenon quite complex).[25]

Forces towards partnership

One Little Indian's story is one of a move away from a punk ethos and aesthetic towards an attempt to intervene in the pop market, to challenge the 'mainstream' on its own terms. Creation, however, began from a very different political and aesthetic position, which revolved around the excitement and unpretentiousness of a certain classic pop sound, a hip pop canon. Returning to the questions with which I began, how, then, can we assess the development of these two labels as an example of the trajectory of an oppositional moment within popular culture? First of all, what forces lay behind the move towards partnership with the major corporations on the part of the indie sector? The discourses of 'sell-out' and 'burn-out' mentioned earlier are too simplistic to capture the difficulty of these issues. There is more at stake in these decisions than the desire to make money, or to give up the struggle for an easier route, as both the case studies show. A more complex account of the motivations behind growth, and ambitions towards popular success for artists can be found in Georgina Born's analysis of the subjectivities of cultural producers (1993a: 236–8). Born stresses the very different psychic drives involved in the desire for mass popularity, and the desire for 'alterity' (working outside dominant systems). In an attempt to avoid the moralism of an avant-garde position often associated with Adorno, she writes about the ambivalence of 'the global strategy'. There is the utopian pleasure of overcoming boundaries and reconciling difference; but there is also the darker side of the need for 'omnipotence, of banishing difference' (1993a: 236). Born stresses that these issues relate not only to the strategies of cultural producers, but to the pleasures derived by consumers from 'culturally imagined communities'. Popularity, in this model, is not a 'sell-out' but derives from fundamental but contradictory human drives. Alterity too has its positive and negative aspects: the exploration of the 'exotic or complex, as opposed to the banal', but also the denigration of the ordinary, and the idealization of the different.

Thinking through these psychic divisions is a useful tool for prising open the difficulties faced by post-punk in reconciling conflicting aims towards being different but also being popular. It may be that these are cleavages which will face any popular-cultural movement which hopes to challenge hegemonic systems. Perhaps it is only possible to reconcile them temporarily, as the initial impulses which allow for coalitions around democratizing aims fragment with time. How cultural producers deal with these contradictions is enormously affected by wider economic and organizational factors. The companies were constantly forced into certain practices in order to give 'their' music the promotional push they felt it deserved. In other words, discursive, psychological and aesthetic factors were applied in circumstances delineated by the economic logics of the cultural industries. Particularly important were the need to deal with risk by creating star names who would 'guarantee' future sales; the need for promotion, distribution and marketing; and potential access to the much larger audiences afforded by internationalization.

It is understandable that musicians and record companies should want their music to *matter*, to be consumed and battled over on the largest stages. The motivations behind collaboration, behind the goal of wider pop success at a national and international level go beyond the base desire for financial comfort and the competitive desire to beat all rivals. The desire to stay on the margins, so apparent in 1980s indie, can sometimes reflect a contempt for popular culture. At the same time, to dismiss vernacular notions such as 'sell-out' as simplistic is overly haughty. Such ideas can serve positive political ends by providing a rallying cry for alterity and difference.

Institutional and aesthetic 'consequences'

What were the consequences of professionalization and of partnership with the majors? Is it possible to speak of 'losses' and 'gains' in terms of institutional and aesthetic politics? I argued, in discussing One Little Indian, that such companies can form a protective layer between, on the one hand, the entrepreneurial and corporate worlds and, on the other, musicians and other record company staff who want to be involved in the production of music, but who feel uncomfortable with the prevailing culture of the music business. And Born's discussion, referred to above, highlights the problems of taking the other route, of aspiring towards marginality, of seeking refuge in the comforts of obscurity.

I think it is easier to talk of 'consequences' of such processes of professionalization and partnership in terms of institutional politics than in terms of aesthetic outcomes. In coming to work with the major corporations, One Little Indian and Creation were reflecting the failure of the post-punk challenge to the structure of the music industry. In an era of pragmatic acceptance of collaboration with major capital, there is a need to (re)develop a case against the majors which does not rely on a simplistic romanticism. At the core of the post-punk independent ethos was an important argument about *autonomy*. Financial investment on the part of major corporations entails potential control. In general, major companies monitor their partners in the independent sector closely. Many independents with ties to bigger companies claim that they work autonomously; but it is worth referring to a distinction which Graham Murdock (1982: 122–3) borrows from the sociology of economics, between allocative and operational control. Allocative control consists of formulating overall policy and strategy; decisions on whether to expand, and at what rate; financing issues; and control over the distribution of profits. Operational control, however,

> works at a lower level and is confined to decisions about the effective use of resources already allocated and the implications of policies already decided upon at the allocative level. This does not mean that operational controllers have no creative elbow-room or effective choices to make. . . . Neverthe-less, their range of options is still limited by the goals of the organisations they work for and by the level of resources they have been allocated.
>
> (Murdock, 1982: 122–3)

Murdock is referring primarily to the tension between newspaper proprietors and the editors beneath them, but I think the distinction is useful for post-Fordist networks of small and large record companies too (see Hesmondhalgh, 1996). The small company in partnership with a larger firm is in this position, i.e. of having decisions about finances and overall strategy ultimately made for them depending on which level of partnership they undertake (see Hesmondhalgh, 1996: 474). There will inevitably be pressure to adapt to 'the goals of the major organisation they work for', as Murdock puts it. Such partnerships, it should be noted, are potentially of enormous financial benefit to major corporations. A senior executive at one major record company told me that his firm would be aiming at gaining 80 per cent of their revenues from distribution, and only 10 per cent from bands signed directly to the company.[26] Independent companies which sign partnership deals are not only prone to takeover bids at a later stage; they also feed the relentless drive for profit which is the legal requirement of any corporation. These arrangements have been called 'symbiotic' (e.g. Frith, 1988) but the greater power is with the majors.

Many of the Britpop bands which achieved success in the 1995–97 period were on labels with close ties to the majors. Unlike Creation and One Little Indian, many of these companies entered into close alliance with major com-panies from their very inception. They were often production companies set up in order to push one band in particular. Brett Anderson of leading indie act Suede told *Billboard* in 1993 that 'The independent music industry is the only place that allows bands to develop. We don't intend to betray it and run off to some multi-national corporation' (*Billboard*, 1993: 75). But Suede is signed to Nude Records, which is co-run by Suede's manager Saul Galpern, and which was tied, like Cre-ation, to Sony's Licensed Repertoire Division (since renamed). Ash, whose debut album reached the number one position in the British album charts in May 1996, is on the Infectious label, which was set up by a former RCA A&R (Artist and Repertoire) director as his own 'independent' label, with a financing deal from his former employers, BMG.

1990s indie, then, marked a new era of major/independent collaboration. Another sign of the decline of the punk ethos as it transmuted into indie was the erosion of the 'micro-independent' sector. While dozens of very small record companies continue to spring up across Britain, they have much less access to a wider public sphere than previously (although John Peel's BBC show continues to promote them, and their products can still be found in a shrinking network of shops and fanzines). Now bands working in the indie genre aim to sign to 'pseudo-independent' companies in order to get public attention in the indie sector, before crossing over into the pop mainstream. These labels and the various marketing specialists they use are concentrated in a scene based around Camden Town, North London:

> If it sometimes seems to you, gentle readers, that the entire music business – performance, rehearsal, marketing, promotion, partying and relaxation – is currently taking place exclusively within a couple of square miles north of Euston [a major train station in North London] . . . well, you're almost completely right, as it happens.
>
> (Parkes, 1995: 29)

The decentralizing impulse of punk/post-punk had gone from indie and it migrated, in complicated ways, to dance music culture (see Hesmondhalgh, 1998).

But what of the musical culture associated with these institutional changes? To what extent is it possible to draw links between such institutional changes and the aesthetic-political nature of the texts and performances produced? Can we speak of aesthetic 'consequences'? I suggested above, in closing my discussion of Creation, that the story of indie as a whole is one of a move towards conformism and conservatism. On the surface, I might appear to be indulging here in a fairly traditional form of radical left commentary on the dynamics of popular culture, one which mourns the decline of an oppositional impulse precisely at the point at which it reaches beyond its original niche audience. But, in my view, it is not the fact of cross-over itself which limits the potential of 1990s indie. Rather, the political-aesthetic problem is one of a prevailing nostalgic classicism at large in indie culture (and One Little Indian's Bjork represents an exception to that). Such pastiche in the 1980s was a quiet challenge to the notions of authenticity on which much mainstream rock rested because it suggested the value of a return to hidden parts of the canon more concerned with a fey, pop sensibility. Indie's celebration of obscurity and failure was intended as a gesture of contempt for those who revelled in a notion of success founded on competitive individualism. But by the 1990s, the use of older sounds had become emptied of political meaning and was increasingly accompanied by a rockist self-indulgence, a flamboyant display of arrogance and wealth more or less undistinguishable from that which punk had so despised twenty years earlier. This is not to deny that some bands, some records, some moments, went beyond such conservatism and conformism. Oasis was widely criticized for its imitation of other bands and other songs, but its records were made emotionally complex by a mixture of ebullient optimism and aching yearning. Pulp's Jarvis Cocker brought to the mass pop audience uncomfortable narratives of sexual dysfunction and class anger. Nevertheless, 1990s indie as a whole was marked by nostalgia, political conformity, aesthetic traditionalism, a notion of personal and professional success indistinguishable from the aspirational consumerism of much of the rest of British society and a lack of interest in changing the social relations of production. Whatever the limits and contradictions of late 1980s indie, it at least offered a critique.

Even if I am right in characterizing 1990s indie in this way, however, it is still difficult to describe these features as the political-aesthetic *consequences* of major/independent collaboration, as the *outcome* of a set of institutional politics. As we have seen above, Creation's distinctive aesthetic position preceded the Sony takeover by many years. It was aestheticist in that it placed much more emphasis on what was produced, than on the social relations behind the commodity. It was classicist in that it adhered to a traditional rock notion of what constituted quality and success. The company's concern with a particular model of global pop success as the goal of musical activity helped to form its institutional politics: a pragmatic acceptance of the need for partnership with major capital. In other words its aesthetic position helped to form its institutional politics, rather than the other way round. This reverses the way in which often-noted moves from a (contradictory) oppositional politics towards something more conformist and conservative are explained 'within' popular culture. It is too simplistic to see the conservatism of 1990s indie as deriving solely from its institutional base in networks of collaboration with the major companies. This does not mean, of course, that aesthetics are autonomous of social forces as a whole; but we do need to be cautious in assuming that oppositional or conformist institutional politics lead to correspondingly oppositional or conformist textual forms (cf. Born, 1993b: 280).

I also want to question another vernacular view which sees too close a link between institutional and aesthetic politics, a position represented in the attitude of Crass, reported above, to the solo work of Bjork. According to this perspective, any move towards stylistic pluralism might be seen as evidence of institutional co-optation and compromise. The logical outcome of such a view is the advocacy of an aesthetic position which only values simplicity, on the grounds that it encourages widespread participation through de-skilling. There are echoes here of the ethos of collective participation in folk revivalism. Though very different from Creation's position, this too represents a nostalgic aesthetic, which implicitly argues for a return to a fantasized version of pre-modern social relations of production. One Little Indian had the courage to go beyond its punk

roots to explore and create a richer soundscape. This involved professionalization, with its higher production costs and the use of corporate capital in order
to market its products internationally. The price of such moves, though, is the
abandonment of the autonomy sought by punk.

Indie, then, represents the end of the post-punk vision of transforming the
social relations of musical production via the medium of the small record
company. I have argued elsewhere (Hesmondhalgh, 1997: 271–2) that post-punk
independence foundered on punk's own ambivalence about popularity. It proved
impossible to reconcile being 'outside' the music industry with producing a new
mainstream, because the terms of that new attempt were dictated by the capitalist economics which make the majors dominant. Indie represents the pragmatic 1990s response to that dilemma: a tendency towards classical pop
aesthetics, and 'arm's length' institutional ties with the corporations. But to point
to the failure of indie (amidst its many pleasures) is not to argue for a return to
a punk vision of an alternative cultural praxis. Times have changed: a different
era calls for a different cultural politics, but hopefully one which will take into
account the lessons of earlier failures.

Notes

1   For an academic treatment of this discourse, see, for example, Stephen Lee,
     who argues that 'Wax Trax's move toward the major labels represented in the
     employees' minds the only possible alternative to them' (Lee, 1995: 24).
2   Reynolds (1986) for example, remarks that indie-pop had 'abandoned R&B
     roots for albino sources like The Velvet Underground, Television, Sixties psy-
     chedelia, rockabilly, folk'. There were debates in the music press during 1986
     over whether The Smiths' single 'Panic' (Rough Trade, 1986) with its refrain
     'Hang the DJ', was a racist attack on black music (see Rogan, 1992: 255–6).
3   In the radio documentary, 'Creation Rebels' (BBC Radio One, broadcast 19
     February 1995) one musician recounts how label boss Alan McGee would
     always turn down the bass to a minimum whenever he played any new tracks
     by the band.
4   On this stabilization, see Straw (1991, 1993), Frith (1988) and Goodwin
     (1993), all of whom place video in the context of wider industrial and cultural
     change.
5   For prognoses of exposure problems for the independent sector, see Cramp-
     ton (1985) and Diggit (1985).
6   The growth of such alliances between majors and independents in the 1970s
     and especially in the 1980s led various commentators to question traditional
     models of independent cultural production. On this phenomenon in the
     recording industry, see Vignolle (1980), Frith (1988), Negus (1992); and for
     a different viewpoint, Hesmondhalgh (1996), where I survey a wider litera-
     ture on such links.

7   Details from an interview with Penny Rimbaud, G. and Steve Ignorant (3 March 1994). The fieldwork interviews cited here were carried out between 1993 and 1996 as part of research funded by the Economic and Social Research Council (UK). This article was submitted to *Cultural Studies* in July 1997 and resubmitted with minor revisions in July 1998. My thanks to all interviewees, especially Mark Edmondson; to Jo Forshaw for her generous help with contacts; and to Jason Toynbee for helpful comments on this material at a crucial time.

8   McKay (1996: 73–101) has traced the hippie roots of Crass, and has analysed the feminist and situationist elements in their politics.

9   In 1997 Mayking went into receivership and Birkett bought back his 60 per cent stake from Bonner.

10   For an early example of this purism, see Crass's 'Punk is Dead', from *The Feeding of the Five Thousand* (Small Wonder, 1978), which attacked other punk bands for 'selling out'.

11   The other most notable British owner-managers of the 1980s and 1990s were: Daniel Miller at Mute; Ivo Watts-Russell at 4AD; Martin Mills at Beggars Banquet; Tony Wilson at Factory; Geoff Travis at Rough Trade; and Pete Waterman at PWL.

12   For example, *Melody Maker* (1994); and 'Creation Rebels', BBC Radio One, broadcast 19 February 1995.

13   'Alternative rock' is the term which has generally been used in the United States for what in Britain was known as indie or 'independent' rock or pop. Lately, the term indie has become more widely used in the US. As with all genre terms, boundaries are always in dispute and there is no court to act as final arbiter of what constitutes indie and alternative rock/pop and what does not.

14   The £250,000 recording budget of My Bloody Valentine's 1992 album *Loveless* is often blamed for McGee and partner Dick Green's decision to sell 49 per cent of Creation to Sony in that year (e.g. *Melody Maker*, 1994).

15   I mean 'successful' here in the sense of gaining prestige. The album won the Mercury Music Prize in 1992, and was album of the year in the *New Musical Express* in 1991.

16   Corbett (1994: 48–9) tells the story of the transition of REM from independent act to major label signing (in 1988) as an example of the increasing entanglement of alternative ('local mode') and major ('systemic mode') commodities. Other major signings at about this time were Sonic Youth (from SST to Geffen) and Husker Du (from SST to Warners).

17   Of the British post-punk independents, 4AD managed to achieve most success in the American market, and they did so by signing American bands (The Pixies, Belly and the Breeders) and then licensing them back to American divisions of the majors.

18   See Reynolds and Press (1995: 52–3) for an analysis of the misogyny underlying the Rolling Stones' work of this period. Such rockist misogyny placed the Stones outside the 1980s indie canon, which was strongly influenced by feminism.

19   Information about the Oasis marketing campaign is drawn from interviews with Jonny Hopkins of Creation, and my fieldwork in 1994.

20   According to IFPI figures cited by Negus (1993: 298), the income generated from sales of recorded music in the EC (31 per cent of global total) exceeded the equivalent figure in North America (30 per cent) for the first time in 1988.

21   For example, the front page headline in *Melody Maker* on 9 December 1995 read: 'Britpop in the USA. Blur, Oasis: Will They Make It In America?'

22   Tony Wilson, head of Factory, argued for a definition of independence as 'that very simple and accurate description – records which are distributed by independent distribution' (*Music Week*, 1986: 6). In doing so he was taking an idealistic position, opposed to that of Alan McGee.

23   See the debate organized by the *New Musical Express* between Martin Mills (Beggars Banquet), Andy Ross (Food), Keith Cullen (Setanta) and leading indie DJ Steve Lamacq (then of the *NME*): transcribed as Maconie (1992). Only Mills, representing the post-punk generation, favoured charts based on independent distribution.

24   'The idea of what indie was and what indie is now is completely redundant. The idea of 40-year-old guys sitting round in a restaurant in West Kensington dictating who is and who isn't in the indie chart, I find utterly ludicrous' (Alan McGee, quoted in *New Musical Express* (1992)).

25   For a brilliant analysis of the politics of 'Britpop' and Oasis's complicated position within it, see Savage (1997).

26   The other 10 per cent came from licensing deals. I was told I could quote these figures, but that I should not mention the executive's name.

References

Billboard (1993) 'Suede', 13 February: 75.

Bloomfield, Terry (1991) 'It's sooner than you think, or where are we in the history of rock music?', *New Left Review*, 190: 59–81.

Born, Georgina (1993a) 'Against negation, for a politics of cultural production', *Screen*, 34(3): 223–42.

—— (1993b) 'Afterword: music policy, aesthetic and social difference', in Tony Bennett, Simon Frith, Lawrence Grossberg, John Shepherd and Graeme Turner (eds) *Rock and Popular Music*, London and New York: Routledge.

BPI Statistical Handbook (1993) London: British Phonographic Institute.

Cameron, Keith (1994) 'Doing it for the quids', *New Musical Express*, 19 February: 20–2.

Corbett, John (1994) *Extended Play*, Durham, North Carolina: Duke University Press.

Crampton, Luke (1985) 'An independent view', *The Catalogue*, April: 14.

Diggit, Will U. (1985) 'Numb 1 for music' [sic], *The Catalogue*, July: 15.

Frith, Simon (1988) 'Video pop: picking up the pieces', in Simon Frith (ed.) *Facing the Music*, New York: Pantheon.

—— (1991) 'Anglo-America and its discontents', *Cultural Studies*, 5(3): 263–9.

Gibson, Robin (1988) 'On the warpath', *Sounds*, 3 December: 19.

Gittins, Ian (1988) 'Acts of aggression', *Melody Maker*, 3 December: 42–3.

Goodwin, Andrew (1993) *Dancing in the Distraction Factory*, London: Routledge.

Gray, Herman (1988) *Producing Jazz*, Philadelphia, PA: Temple University Press.

Harris, John (1994) 'The Bruise Brothers', *New Musical Express*, 23 April: 10,11,49.

Herman, Edward and McChesney, Robert (1997) *The Global Media*, London: Cassell.

Hesmondhalgh, David (1996) 'Flexibility, post-Fordism and the music industries', *Media, Culture and Society*, 15(3): 469–88.

—— (1997) 'Post-punk's attempt to democratise the music industry: the success and failure of rough trade', *Popular Music*, 16(3): 255–74.

—— (1998) 'The British dance music industry: a case study in independent cultural production', *British Journal of Sociology*, 49(2): 234–51.

Kelly, Danny (1987) 'From C86 to Catch 22', *New Musical Express*, 11 April: 29.

Laing, Dave (1985) *One Chord Wonders*, Buckingham: Open University Press.

Lee, Stephen (1995) 'Re-examining the concept of the 'independent' record company: the case of 'wax trax!' records', *Popular Music*, 14(1): 13–31.

MacDonald, Ian (1995) *Revolution in the Head*, London: Pimlico.

Maconie, Stuart (1992) 'State of indie pundits', *New Musical Express*, 25 July: 10–12.

McGee, Alan (1984) 'Label spotlight: Creation Records', *The Catalogue*, November–December: 17.

McKay, George (1996) *Senseless Acts of Beauty*, London: Verso.

Melody Maker (1994) 'The story of Creation', 15 January: 36–8.

Murdock, Graham (1982) 'Large corporations and the control of the communications industries', in Michael Gurevitch *et al.* (eds) *Culture, Society and the Media*, London: Methuen.

Music Week (1986) 'Indie Wilson lays down the lore', 15 November: 4, 6.

—— (1994) 'Creation 10: a souvenir supplement to celebrate ten years of Creation Records', 19 March.

Negus, Keith (1992) *Producing Pop*, London: Edward Arnold.

—— (1993) 'Global harmonies and local discords: transnational policies and practices in the European recording industry', *European Journal of Communication*, 8(3): 295–316.

New Musical Express (1992) 'Indie majors split on chart', 25 July: 3.

Parkes, Taylor (1995) 'It's a NW1-derful life', *Melody Maker*, 17 June: 29–32.

Price, Simon (1993) 'Ooh, la, la, la', *Melody Maker*, 15 May: 8–9.

Reynolds, Simon (1986) 'Younger than yesterday', *Melody Maker*, 28 June: 32–3.

—— (1988) 'Against health and efficiency', in Angela McRobbie (ed.) *Zoot Suits and Second Hand Dresses*, Basingstoke: Macmillan.

Reynolds, Simon and Press, Joy (1995) *The Sex Revolts*, London: Serpent's Tail.

Rogan, Johnny (1992) *Morrissey and Marr: The Severed Alliance*, London: Omnibus.

Savage, Jon (1991) *England's Dreaming*, London: Faber and Faber.

—— (1997) 'The Boys' Club', *The Guardian* (*Friday Review* section), 4 July: 2–4.

Shaw, Arnold (1978) *Honkers and Shouters*, New York: Collier.

Shelley, Jim (1995) 'Rock and a hard place', *The Guardian* (*Weekend* Section), 22 April: 24–31.

Sinclair, David (1995) 'The British aren't coming', *Rolling Stone*, 9 March: 23–4.

Straw, Will (1991) 'Systems of articulation, logics of change: communities and scenes in popular music', *Cultural Studies*, 5(3): 368–88.

—— (1993) 'Popular music and postmodernism in the 1980s', in Simon Frith, Andrew Goodwin and Lawrence Grossberg (eds) *Sound and Vision: The Music Video Reader*, London and New York: Routledge.

Vignolle, Jean-Paul (1980) 'Mixing genres and reaching the public: the production of popular music', *Social Science Information*, 19: 79–105.

Wright, Peter (1986) 'The American way', *The Catalogue*, July: 25.

Selective discography

Bjork, *Debut*, One Little Indian, 1993.

Crass, *The Feeding of the Five Thousand*, Small Wonder, 1978.

—— *Stations of the Crass*, Crass Records, 1979.

—— *Penis Envy*, Crass Records, 1981.

My Bloody Valentine, *Loveless*, Creation, 1991.

Nirvana, *Nevermind*, Geffen, 1991.

The Pooh Sticks, *Alan McGee*, Fierce EP, 1988.

Primal Scream, *Scremadelica*, Creation, 1991.

Primal Scream *Give Out But Don't Give Up*, Creation 1994.

Laurie Ouellette

TV VIEWING AS GOOD CITIZENSHIP? POLITICAL RATIONALITY, ENLIGHTENED DEMOCRACY AND PBS

Abstract

This article draws on theories of political rationality, governmentality and cultural policy as well as historical analysis to examine how a philosophy of 'enlightened democracy' informed the historical formation of PBS. I analyse its early campaign to turn TV viewers into active citizens and show how the citizen subjectivities constructed presupposed a set of knowledge–power relations defined and managed by 'opinion leaders'. Following a cultural studies approach I analyse policy and popular discourses to show how requirements of professionalism, reason, civility and detached objectivity served as a means of differentiating good citizens and as a form of social control.

Keywords

citizenship; cultural policy; public television; enlightened democracy; political rationality; public affairs

IN JUNE 1972, in the midst of social and political unrest brought on by US involvement in Vietnam, campus activism, the Black Power movement, a wave of labour strikes and the women's movement, the TV critic for the Washington DC *Evening Star* declared that 'these are wonderful days for citizens who own television sets' (Thorpe, 1972: n.p.). As was typical of television criticism of the period, the praise was directed at the newly operational Public Broadcasting Service. From 1969 to 1973, when the service was partly blunted by the Nixon administration, PBS promoted a public affairs philosophy focused on transforming television viewers into active citizens. While the three commercial networks, with revenues of four billion dollars a year, were found by one study to devote an average of 2 per cent of primetime to news and public affairs ('Hoked Up', 1972: 23), the public channel devoted nearly one-third of its primetime schedule to expert analysis of current affairs, policy debates, election coverage, live coverage of government procedures and electronic town halls intended to reinvigorate participatory democracy (PBS, 1972).

The Advocates, a flagship PBS programme credited with reaffirming 'TV's worthiness', appeared regularly.[1] Each week on the show, two professional advocates argued liberal and conservative views on pending or theoretical legislative initiatives before a moderator and a studio audience, culminating in a mail-in vote that was sent to Congress, the White House and the news media. While advocacy-oriented and community-based public affairs programmes were marginalized and frequently mired in controversy when they appeared on PBS, the cultivation of citizenship epitomized by *The Advocates* was positioned as educational and politically balanced, and drew bipartisan support from policymakers and critics. The inherent paradox, however, was that the expansion of democracy via public television was presumed to require the ongoing guidance of elites best suited to the art of decision-making and the management of consensus. Initiatives like *The Advocates* extended the visibility of these processes, but the citizen subjectivities they constructed were loyal to discursive requirements of professionalism, reason, civility and detached objectivity – so that becoming a 'good citizen' also meant acquiescing to the expertise, cultural capital and behavioural proscriptions of a higher authority.

The early PBS public affairs philosophy has not received adequate scrutiny within the critical literature on US public television, primarily because the goal of addressing television viewers as citizen subjects 'who require information to participate fully in the nation's political and cultural life' (Engelman, 1996: 36) is seen as a welcome alternative to the consumer sovereignty promoted by commercial television.[2] While conservatives have lobbied relentlessly to 'zero out' subsidies to public broadcasting under the banners of 'liberal elitism' and an expanded cultural marketplace, the typical left response has been to protest the corrupting influence of corporate underwriting but to defend the value of public television as a democratic counterpoint to the marketplace of ideas (Hoynes, 1994; Croteau *et al.*, 1996; Ledbetter, 1997). Nicholas Garnham sums up this argument well when he asserts that a public communications system is 'indispensable to the development of full citizenship in complex societies' (1992: 19). I also see public television as an endeavour worth struggling for, but I disagree that its inadequacies can be so readily attributed to political economic factors only. By idealizing the 'development of citizenship' against the taint of 'creeping commercialism', scholars and reformers have often glossed over the power dynamics of public service culture.

Drawing from research I have conducted at the National Public Broadcasting Archives, I want to address this gap by charting the historical formation of PBS, with a focus on the discursive construction of its early citizenship campaign. Situating this campaign within the genealogy of the 'media and democracy' debate as it informed US broadcasting reform and the cultural and political tensions of the 1960s, I argue that PBS put forward a model of 'enlightened democracy' that complemented commercial television's hegemonic orientation with a different, 'governmental' logic. In broader terms, I am taking up Tony Bennett's call (1992a, 1992b, 1995) for a cultural studies approach to policy that moves beyond rhetorics of anti-commercialism on the one hand and counterhegemonic resistance on the other to engage the 'political rationalities' of public cultural institutions and the allocation of their resources.

PBS and a crisis of government

US public television came of age during the presidency of Lyndon B. Johnson and was ushered through Congress in 1967 as an extension of his Great Society programmes. A multiplicity of factors created a moment ripe for federal intervention in television, including fears that cultural distinctions were collapsing at the hands of the expanding consumer economy, anxieties about the quality of the 'vast wasteland' and its effects on the nation's knowledge class, and the difficulties of targeting influential customers with a mass medium that was not yet oriented to niche marketing. However, a call for the reinvigoration of democracy that referenced problems of mass apathy and minority deviance was officially evoked to justify the need for the new service, and the progressive and participatory elements of this discourse meant that PBS was introduced under different terms from the paternal European public broadcasting systems critiqued by Raymond Williams (1966). Bennett's Foucauldian approach to cultural policy is useful for making sense of this public service-oriented explanation, and for seeing PBS as a cultural institution called upon to activate *and* reform the citizenry, educate *and* differentiate television viewers according to particular relations of knowledge and power.

As Bennett notes, Foucault traces the emergence of disciplinary 'technologies of power' such as the prison and the asylum to the rise of modern forms of government (Bennett, 1995: 89). Foucauldian political theorists are concerned with the way such technologies construct a rationality of government, or a 'system of thinking about the nature of the practice of government (who can govern; what governing is; what or who is governed)' that is capable of making the activity both 'thinkable and practicable' (Gordon, 1991: 3). The term 'governmentality' is used to characterize efforts to regulate and manage the conduct of others as well as the way we come to regulate ourselves in light of 'certain principles and goals' that make the concept of self-government operable in capitalist democracies (Burchell, 1996: 19). The point to consider in the context of PBS is that citizenship is a social construct: citizens are not born but made. Describing this process, an introductory college textbook from the 1970s explained that

> Each and every individual must be capable of governing himself or herself. . . . Some have called it 'the making of citizens,' or citizen training, or civic education. More recently, we have come to call it political socialization, which implies a long process of introducing each individual into the political culture, learning how to accept social authority, and learning what is legitimate and what is not. Still others describe the process in more conventional terms, such as 'learning good behavior,' 'learning the rules of the game,' 'learning the American way of life'.
>
> (Lowi, 1977: 45)

Extending the analysis of political rationality to 'cultural technologies', Bennett charts a new mode of social control that developed in the late 1800s, as high cultural institutions such as museums opened their doors to the mass public. While hegemony theory has been used to analyse the struggle over dominance and consent waged through mass culture, he argues that museums are best understood as governmental apparatuses that rationalized the capitalist state in different ways. Their 'look and learn' orientation was indicative of governmental civilizing and 'self-shaping' campaigns (Bennett, 1995: 98) often designed to counterpose the degenerative effects (hedonism, crowd mentality, the decline of standards) attributed to mass culture (Kasson, 1978; Rubin, 1992). Museums were called upon to 'form and shape the moral, mental and behavioral characteristics of the population' with aims in mind ranging from uplifting popular taste to preventing rioting, says Bennett (1995: 21). This was pursued less through a demonstration of discipline and punishment (as with the prison) than efforts to instil in the mass public the 'capacity for self-improvement culture was said to embody' and the habit of emulating the conduct of one's betters (1995: 24, 47, 98). The purpose was 'not to render the populace visible to power but to render power visible to the people and, at the same time, to represent to them that power as their own' (1995: 98). Because the museum promised progressive reforms and democratic education for all, its political rationality as a governmental apparatus for guiding and shaping populations and for differentiating among them was obscured, says Bennett. By incorporating the 'citizenry into a set of power–knowledge relations represented to it as emanating from itself', it served as an 'instrument for the self-display of bourgeois-democratic society' (1995: 89–91, 98).

PBS operated with its own institutional logic, but it is also best seen as a governmental, rather than hegemonic apparatus. Like nineteenth-century public museums, it appeared at a historical moment when democracy was perceived to be breaking down, partly due to commercial television. Cultural reformers had, significantly, been arguing for a more edifying and educational alternative since the commercialization of radio (Douglas, 1987; McChesney, 1994), often with uplifting and classifying aims in mind, but their demands were marginalized by the free market 'supply and demand' rationalizations that oriented American broadcasting (Streeter, 1989). By the 1960s, however, the 'TV problem' had reached crisis point. The decline of public service programming and the escapist shows that populated the 'vast wasteland' were explained by private broadcasters and many policy-makers and critics as the consequence of 'giving the people what they wanted'. This explanation conjured up the troubling image of an apathetic and hedonistic mass public that refused to act as responsible citizens, and through its cultural choices, prevented opinion leaders from doing likewise. When urban rioting and anti-war protesting erupted later in the decade, its visibility on the evening news showed that if commercial television framed the activities as political 'deviance' (Gitlin, 1980), its conventions were less suited to teaching and instilling 'proper' modes of citizenship. These different but overlapping dilemmas warranted the creation of a new cultural technology that was capable of rationalizing US political democracy, and it is within this historical context that we can most clearly observe the governmental logic that guided the formation of PBS.

Toby Miller usefully describes the contradictions PBS was established to help manage as the need of the liberal capitalist state to produce 'ideal' citizen subjects 'trained to meet the conflicting needs' of the consumer economy and the political order. When 'television forwards image and emotion as opposed to sound and rationality,' he argues, 'the next move is often for television to become the source of power and the warrant/technology for training publics into a citizenry loyal both to the state and to a particular model of dialogue' (1993: 136). Because the commercial networks were pivotal to the expanding consumer economy, and because their quests for popularity necessitated an engagement with popularity and dissent, PBS was assigned the 'corrective' role defined by Miller. Like the relationship between mass culture and high cultural institutions, commercial and public broadcasting operated with distinct but complementary logics, so that television viewers could be simultaneously hailed as consumers and as 'citizens who must be reformed, educated, informed' so that they might 'better perform their democratic rights and duties' (Ang, 1991: 21).

We can see this governmental role articulated within the policy discourses that surrounded public television in the late 1960s. The Maryland Congressman who introduced the 1967 Public Broadcasting Act proposed that 'for a government by the people, a successful democracy depends on enlightened and well-informed citizens . . . public television can contribute to this end' (House, 1967: 103). The Senate Commerce Committee's Report concurred that 'particularly in the area of public affairs . . . noncommercial broadcasting is uniquely fitted to offer in-depth coverage and analysis which will lead to a better and enlightened public' (quoted in Karayn, 1972: n.p.). In his State of the Union address announcing public television, Johnson proposed that it would 'make our nation a replica of the old Greek marketplace, where public affairs took place in view of all the citizens' (quoted in Miller, 1993: 136). These discourses spoke to a decline of informed citizenship attributed to the 'TV problem', while promises of expanded participation in democracy spoke to the events of 1968. Equating the 'demonstrations, disorders, retaliatory blows and other extreme measures' with the breakdown of America's 'neural system', one supporter envisioned public television as a way to restore an 'affirmative relationship between the government and the people' (Blakely, 1969: 55).

But if the public service failures of commercial television could be explained by the perils of 'cultural democracy', and political unrest equated with the subversion of affirmative citizenship, it followed that public television must be protected from the corrupting influence of the masses. PBS was to be *for* the people not *by* the people, because its political rationality was rooted in their failed performance as citizen subjects. This logic rationalized the top-down, bureaucratic control of PBS as well as the allocation of its cultural resources and the unpopular conventions of its public affairs programmes. As Johnson explained, public television required careful management because 'in weak or even irresponsible hands, it could generate controversy without understanding; it could mislead as well as teach; it could appeal to passions rather than reason' (quoted in Macy, 1974: 29; and Miller, 1993: 136). Coupled with the expectation that public television must not effectively compete for commercial television's customers, these requirements positioned PBS as a culturally marginalized alternative. This paradox limited the reach of the governmental aims assigned to the new channel – after all, the public could not be forced to watch its public affairs programmes. Yet as the small PBS viewership was heavily concentrated among professional-managerial elites, a pattern that – similar to Bennett's account of the museum – was evoked to represent the model of 'enlightened democracy' constructed by public television as emerging from the citizenry itself. To see how this occurred, it is useful to consider the media and democracy debate in the US with an eye towards broadcasting reform.

The 'media and democracy' debate

As Stanley Aronowitz argues, twentieth-century American democratic ideals are rooted in the contradictory ideas of Thomas Jefferson and John Dewey. According to Jefferson, democracy required a universal public education system designed to effectively train the franchised populace for proper citizenship. Dewey, on the other hand, believed that the roots of democracy were in the face-to-face interactions of the agrarian town hall. Both visions were thought to be seriously compromised by industrialization, urbanization and the growth of consumer culture and mass media (Aronowitz, 1993: 75–83) – shifts that, as John and Barbara Ehrenreich (1979) argue, coincided with the rise of a pro-fessional-managerial class (PMC) in the US. According to their account, the concentration of wealth in the late 1880s could accommodate and indeed required an expanded class of managers, technocrats and professionals to run corporations and state bureaucracies, produce and circulate legitimate know-ledge, mediate the conflicts between capital and labour and produce a 'rational, reproducible social order'. The PMC assisted with the rationalization of indus-trial capitalism and the promotion of a national consumer culture – but it also produced fierce objections to some of the 'degenerative' symptoms of these transformations (Ehrenreich and Ehrenreich, 1979: 9–14).

Out of the PMC, progressive reformers emerged seeking to soften the harsh-est blows of monopoly capitalism, counter the seductive appeal of mass amuse-ments and bring order to a nation that had outgrown its previous system of 'loose laws and regulations' (Ehrenreich and Ehrenreich, 1979; Jowett, 1982: 218). When the surplus accumulated by industrial capitalists (Carnegie, Rockefeller) became a 'force for the regulation and management of civil society' and the expan-sion of the public sector, the PMC carried out the management of these opera-tions, note the Ehrenreichs (1979: 15). PMC reformers believed that with the 'careful and logical application of scientific principles to the management of government they could bring about opportunity, progress, order and community' (Jowett, 1982: 212). Their aims were often contradictory, in that they hoped to uplift the immigrant working class through rational science and create a 'pro-gressive version of the old community ideal' of *gemeinschaft*, but they hinged on the ideals (rationality, objectivity) that legitimated the PMC's authority (Ehren-reich and Ehrenreich, 1979: 17; Jowett, 1982: 212). In this sense, the PMC was pivotal to the 'show and tell' mode of governing which Bennett describes (1995: 98). Its call for public service culture as an alternative to mass amusements, for example, can be seen as a move to fuse citizenship with self-shaping strategies. As John Kasson argues, the progressive demand for rational recreation was fuelled by hopes that under 'enlightened municipal auspices' and expert supervision, culture could be deployed as a more 'constructive force in social integration and moral development'. The impetus was not to democratize public access to cul-tural resources, but to train citizens loyal to a particular model of democracy. 'Safe and sane Fourth of July celebrations would rekindle a sense of common faith', public parks would instil 'habits of discipline and cooperation' in the unruly poor and community centres would 'supplant poolrooms and saloons as agents in the acculturation of recent immigrants' (Kasson, 1978: 101–2).

A related logic can be seen operating in the 'media and democracy' debate as articulated within social science and broadcast reform discourse. Here again, the rational thinking, expertise and cultural guidance of the PMC were con-sidered essential to the smooth operation of democracy. By the early 1920s,

Walter Lippmann was arguing that the banalities, fragmentations and distortions of modern life had subverted the basis of popular democracy (Aronowitz, 1993: 80). In his classic work *Public Opinion* (1922), Lippmann called for a bureaucracy of 'objective' experts who could restore reason to politics, thus relieving the mass public from the 'impossible' task of forming a competent opinion. Cultural reformers, on the other hand, pushed for public service alternatives to commercial radio that could transform the masses into better, more discriminating citizens – although many also believed that 'quality' programmes would be lost on the 'moronic mob' (McChesney, 1994: 95–6). Like the promise of democratic education for all noted by Bennett, the early critics of radio hinged their discontents on the claim that a potentially uplifting mass medium had fallen into the hands of capitalist barbarians ill suited to such a task (Douglas, 1987: 313). By the early 1930s, 'educational radio' had become the leading rationale for reform because, in the words of Joy Elmer Morgan of the National Committee on Education by Radio, the majority of listeners would find themselves 'entrapped in a paradise of mediocrities' without the 'guidance of an educated minority' (quoted in Rubin, 1992: 272). Morgan also saw educational radio as a solution to unemployment and a safeguard against the collapse of civilization (1934; Hoke, 1932). While major reform was blunted by corporate lobbying campaigns and a lack of popular support, professional educators did eventually secure limited space on the ether, whereas labour unions and other 'special interest' groups were denied direct access (McChesney, 1994). The 'enlightenment' priorities of PBS can be traced to this precedent.

The dismal ratings of the public service programming that was broadcast on commercial radio (and later television) were often cited by network executives as evidence that the masses preferred entertainment to public affairs (Sarnoff, 1955; see also Boddy, 1990). This rationale obscured the contradictions that eventually necessitated PBS as well as the class coding of 'serious' alternatives. The suggestion that commercial television was a 'cultural democracy' gave credence to reform arguments calling for the preservation of political democracy with educational channels – but it also cast doubt on their ability to instil better habits and 'choices' in the mass citizenry. Paul Lazarsfeld and his colleagues at the Bureau of Applied Social Research solved this dilemma by rationalizing the paradox of the enlightenment rationale. Since the 1940s, the researchers had reported with dismay that college-educated professionals were the core audience for public affairs programming. In the influential *Personal Influence* study, they explained this skew with the concept of the 'two-step flow', proposing that information trickles down from 'experts who can be trusted to know what is really going on' to the 'less active sections of the population' (Katz and Lazarsfeld, 1955: 276). Males with college degrees were said to be the nation's 'opinion leaders', while public affairs leadership among women was said to increase 'with each step up the status ladder'. While more than half the wage earners surveyed reported turning to their peers for guidance on political matters, only 6 per cent of business leaders and professionals reported seeking advice from wage earners. To explain this lopsided exchange, the researchers proposed 'vertical influence'. The assumption was that ideas flowed from 'primary influentials' to certain wage earners, who then became 'informed' opinion leaders in their communities. The prospect of working-class autonomy was negated with the assertion that 'primary opinion shapers' were the males of the 'higher strata' who read more newspapers and magazines and 'possessed education and social prestige' (Katz and Lazarsfeld, 1955: 273, 285–6). With this theory, the researchers were able to reaffirm the liberal pluralist logic that oriented US media research (Hall, 1982).

The concept of the two-step flow obscured the relationship between class, cultural capital and the consumption of socially legitimated public affairs, representing the males of the PMC as model citizens and natural leaders. It also figured in reform discourse, in that programming oriented to an educated habitus, in Bourdieu's formulation (1984), was considered a national priority. By the 1950s, television had been installed in living rooms, the cold war was escalating and the decline of citizenship was regarded as a pressing problem. While some critics scorned early experiments in televised debates and panel discussions, believing that the new medium posed an inherent threat to democracy because it catered to 'popularity and emotion' over 'intelligence and reason' (Cherne, 1952: 14), others saw a chance to cultivate 'first class educational citizenship' (Hunter, 1961: 19). But commercial television, like radio, developed as an advertising-sponsored entertainment medium designed to pitch consumer goods to the widest possible audience. Under the banner of public service, reformers soon mobilized to create an educational alternative. Private benefactors like the Ford Foundation invested millions in the ETV infrastructure with the purpose of combating political apathy and a perceived lack of a 'realistic and meaningful sense of values' in the public (Ford, 1980: 2). Appalled by the 'vast wasteland', FCC Chairman Newton Minow was also a vocal supporter. Noting that the Russians and Chinese were using television to 'educate as well as propagandize', he promoted ETV as a way to bring 'to a mass audience the knowledge needed to keep our society growing, the cultural heritage to keep our society rich, and the information needed by our citizens to keep our society free' (Minow, 1962: 9). Quoting Aristotle, the manager of a local ETV station expressed this goal in more apocalyptic terms, arguing that in a democracy it was 'particularly necessary for people to be educated and informed,' because if they were not 'their bad judgments would plunge the state into disaster' (Schwarzwalder, 1959: 9).

By the 1960s, the enlightenment rationale for broadcasting reform was joined by a focus on the unmet informational requirements of opinion leaders. TV critics, reformers, social scientists and policy-makers believed that the college-educated 'minority' was especially poorly served by commercial television's lowest common denominator approach, particularly in the area of public affairs. Many believed an expanded, nationalized ETV system was needed to get vital information to such people ('A Panel', 1966). The skewed allocation of resources inherent to this focus was rationalized by the trickle-down benefits of the two-step flow. Harold Lasswell called for 'civil enlightenment' at a level of discourse that presumed a 'common audience framework of knowledge to which it is possible to add information and interpretive detail' (Lasswell, 1962: 102). The audience of informed opinion leaders envisioned by Lasswell was confirmed by Wilbur Schramm's (1963) social scientific study of the ETV audience. Rather than uplifting the masses, ETV was found to attract already influential and educated people. ETV viewers were better informed and more apt to read 'better' newspapers and 'talk and think about the news more'. They were also more active in professional, political and PTA organizations. Schramm attributed these findings to the 'strong achievement norm' shared by ETV viewers, an explanation that represented the model citizenship of the PMC as emanating from its greater self-discipline, intelligence and leadership skills. Still, the results of a current events quiz administered with the study suggested that the underfunded, localized ETV stations were not fully informing the nation's opinion leaders. As Schramm reported, it was 'easy to be shocked that two-thirds of our WGBH viewers had forgotten who Robert Oppenheimer was, if they ever knew' (Schramm *et al.*, 1963: 67–70).

The cancellation of network public affairs programmes such as Edward R. Murrow's *See It Now* coupled with perceptions of declining news standards and programme mediocrity in commercial television sparked demands for federal intervention. This moment marked the beginning of what Daniel Hallin describes as the decline of 'high modernism' in commercial television's journalism (1994). As James Baughman argues, it also signalled a crack in liberal 'idealism about the possibilities of the American system of broadcasting', which once expected capitalist owners to serve a mass market *and* a higher mission, or 'to be good entrepreneurs and good citizens' (1985: 173). While critics confused quality with their own educated tastes, their argument hinged on the alternating claims that commercial television was failing to produce an informed citizenry, and that the mass public had chosen triviality and 'instant gratification' to the detriment of the nation's opinion leaders (see e.g. Robinson, 1960; 'Public Taste', 1961; Ratner, 1969). The expertise and cultural guidance of the intelligentsia were seen as pivotal to the correction of these dilemmas. At a summit to discuss the problem of mass culture, former Kennedy adviser Arthur Schlesinger argued that it was the duty of the government to 'rescue' television because 'soap opera and give-away' shows make more money for the stockholders than 'news and Shakespeare' (1961: 149). Conceding that 'if horse opera sells more autos than Ed Murrow then the advertiser has to go for horse opera', the editor of *Harper's* magazine called for a tax on private broadcasters to fund a public service-oriented National Broadcasting Authority. Run by a board of directors that 'might include the president of Harvard, the heads of the Carnegie and Rockefeller foundations, and the director of the Metropolitan Museum', it would produce in-depth news, top-quality music and theatre, documentaries, the arts and public affairs. Under the arrangement, which drew praise from governmental officials, civic leaders and the mass culture critic David Reisman, the viewer who was 'not interested' in better television could simply turn to a western on CBS or a song-and-dance number on ABC (Fischer, 1959).

The revelation of quiz show fraud in the late 1950s gave reform discourse additional credibility. While the scandal placed commercial television's profit motives in the spotlight, the 'TV problem' was defined as a matter of discipline and taste, producing a cultural template for enlightened democracy on PBS. A classic example was Walter Lippmann's declaration: 'there is something radically wrong with the fundamental national policy under which television operates.' Writing in his *New York Herald Tribune* column, Lippmann cast commercial tele-vision as a 'prostitute of merchandising', but his main complaint was that a 'superb scientific achievement' had been misused at the cost of 'effective news reporting, good art, and civilized entertainment'. Conceding that the best way to produce wealth was through private enterprise, he argued that the reverse was true for ideas, and proposed that the people at 'Harvard and Yale and Princeton and Columbia and Dartmouth' find a way to run a public service network that would show 'not what was popular but what was good'. Presuming the network would not be popular, he argued: 'it might well attract an audience that made up in influence what it lacked in numbers' (1959: 26).

In his memoir (1967), Fred Friendly, the former president of CBS News who resigned when his network broadcast a rerun of *I Love Lucy* over hearings on the Vietnam war, articulated the TV problem through a more politicized, but no less hierarchical framework. Friendly did not question television's relationship to the consumer economy but he did attribute commercials and ratings for the decline of 'first-rate' news and public affairs. Friendly became a consultant to the Ford Foundation, and with its president, former National Security Adviser McGeorge Bundy, he advocated a fully-fledged public service system to operate in opposi-tion to both principles. Under Friendly's guidance, Ford remained a benefactor in the transition from ETV to PBS and helped fund early programmes, including *The Advocates*. By this point, the rationale for producing a 'better public' via tele-vision was bound up with a call to reach out to unruly and disenfranchised citi-zens. The uprisings of the era, coupled with worries that 'earlier American achievements in community-building' had been overrun by the automobile (Heckscher, 1968: 127–8), positioned PBS as a way to restore participatory democracy. This discourse promised gains for marginalized citizens – but its political rationality was rooted in an effort to restore social control by chan-nelling dissent into legitimate behaviours and official channels.

In the minds of reformers, participation hinged on enlightenment and ongoing guidance – conditions that required PMC leadership. When the Report of the National Advisory Commission on Civil Disorders reported that the typical ghetto rioter was a high school dropout ('Breeding', 1968: 66), this became paramount. With Ford's support, influential business and cultural leaders formed the National Citizens for Public Television, taking solving the 'nation's racial ills' as a priority (National Citizens, 1968). This was not a call for the real-location of cultural resources. Within policy discourse it was explicitly linked to citizen training strategies. According to US Commissioner of Education Howard Howe, the goal was to provide the sort of education that would prevent America's 'market places from becoming riot places' (1967: 13). With 'patient counseling and advice', explained liberal Senator Hubert Humphrey, helpless and disenfranchised groups could be moved 'into the mainstream of American life' (1966: 49). In an influential report, the Carnegie Commission summed up this reform logic succinctly, calling on public television to be a 'civilized voice in a civilized community' (1967: 18).

As the Ehrenreichs note, the upsurge of middle-class activism in the late 1960s challenged the traditional leadership role of the PMC. PBS was also per-ceived as a way to return student and anti-war protesters to reason and official procedures for expressing and remedying grievances. This aim was governmental rather than hegemonic, in that its purpose was to instil a logic of good citizen-ship that suited the capitalist state. As one supporter stated, public television's purpose was not to promote any particular ideology, but to make sure that 'those who govern will respond to fair and reasonable arguments' and 'those who are governed will respect the authority of the government and limit their protests to ways that do not wreck society' (Blakely, 1969: 57). Transforming 'discon-tents into proposals', 'high-decibel talk into high level discourse' and 'problems and issues into orderly procedures', it would revitalize the decision-making process (Blakely, 1969: 175).

Opinion leaders and PBS

PBS began operating in 1969 as the most visible entity of the national public tele-vision bureaucracy. In a 1970 speech before the National Press Club, John W. Macy, President of the Corporation for Public Broadcasting (CPB), articulated the new service's public affairs priorities. These included: (1) providing an alternative to the 'sensationalist' and 'distorted' news that commercial television was locked into due to its pursuit of ratings; (2) returning the public to the idea that through rational debate reasonable men could work to solve public issues; and (3) providing the viewer citizen with an opportunity for making judgements and opinions known on these issues. The move to create an electronic public sphere where citizens could look, learn and actively participate in proscribed ways was bound up in the corporate rationalization of the 'TV problem', the visi-bility of protesting in the network news and the need to differentiate and social-ize opinion leaders. It was envisioned as a cultural corrective, not a cultural transformation. As Macy (1970: 286–8) explained, none of this should be interpreted as criticism of the commercial networks or stations. By and large, they are doing – and doing very well indeed – what they must do under a system which measures survival and success in terms of mass-audience ratings that respond more to the stimulus of entertainment and excitement than to information.

The representation of commercial television as the consequence of audience demands for emotion, triviality, distortion and conflict – and the positioning of PBS as a cultural technology to reform these desires – fostered an emphasis on subdued aesthetics and educated ways of thinking and behaving. This meant that the public interest value of PBS was defined against the perils of unenlightened participation and popular reception. Most of the public affairs formats developed emphasized reason over passion, professionalism over advocacy, tedium over drama, expert over personality, civility over rudeness and officialdom over human interest and dramatic events. The view that 'too zealous an intent to entertain can lead to the falsification of what should be presented as unadorned as possible' (Blakely, 1969: 115) led to an emphasis on 'cross-talk' programmes based on print-oriented prototypes like *Newspaper of the Air* and *Newsroom*. These Ford-funded local ETV programmes were developed to offer serious alternatives to the 'trivial and meaningless' stories presented by 'plastic, deep-voiced readers of another's copy'. Featuring lengthy news reports and commentary from print journalists, and little visual or human interest material, *Newsroom* was 'an oasis of news in a television desert' distinguished by the adjectives 'authoritative', 'serious' and 'professional'. While its purpose was to 'provide the kind of coverage not available elsewhere' for all television viewers, an audience study turned up a rating of less than 1 per cent in every city surveyed. According to researchers, the programme was 'too written' and demanding for the average person to follow (CPB, 1969; Ford, 1970).

When the National Public Affairs Center for Television (NPACT) was created to produce programmes for PBS, it also stressed cross-talk formats like *Washington Week in Review*, a national version of *Newsroom* which focused on the doings of the Washington Beltway. NPACT's *A Public Affair*, intended to counterpose commercial television's horse-race approach to electoral politics, was similarly 'long on interviews, filled with visiting experts, marked by discussions', observed the *Washington Post* (Laruent, 1972: n.p.). In a democracy the 'quality of information you consume' is at least as important as the 'quality of the automobile you buy', said correspondent Robert MacNeil of its distinction (quoted in 'Public Television', 1973: E653). That the viewership for NPACT programming was 'of course, small' was officially explained by displacing class differences on to differences in 'selectivity' and the motivation to seek out quality information and analysis. The gap between public and commercial television mirrored that between ordinary daily newspapers and the 'selective, focused journalism provided by the *Wall Street Journal*', explained NPACT President Jim Karayn. The gendered dimensions of the parallel were acknowledged when Karayn proposed that the loss of public affairs on PBS would mean a 'castrated system' (Karayn, 1972: n.p.).[3]

Within the public television bureaucracy, discussions of the audience drew from the logic of the two-step flow. The PMC was seen as the natural viewership on the basis of its governing abilities, exemplary citizenship and discriminating tastes. Before Nixon accused public television of liberal elitism, supporters were arguing that public television must develop constituencies that would provide strong financial, political, social, intellectual and moral support (Blakely, 1969: 123). There was, however, also an institutional imperative to bring 'others' into the audience, especially when the news media began reporting PBS's minuscule ratings and that most people perceived the service as one for the higher educated segment of the population. But the political rationality that gave rise to PBS meant that the impetus to gear programming to the habitus of the PMC could not be questioned. Thus, the promise of democratic enlightenment for all existed in perpetual tension with a move to differentiate television viewers according to knowledge–power relations. Articulating the latter purpose, an unpublished study of the public television audience commissioned by Ford argued that

> The commercial networks aim primarily for the blue-collar class, and are grateful for white-collar viewers. Blue-collar households prefer the sitcoms and action series that are the staple of commercial television. The skew toward the better educated is a strength, not a weakness . . . if the skews were toward middle and lower-income, public broadcasting would be competing directly with the three large networks, who are already adequately serving those groups. Public television has to be an effective way to reach opinion leaders.
>
> (Statistical Research, 1974: 15)

Governmentality and social control

Beyond the creation of an informed citizenry, Macy also presented expanded opportunities for citizen involvement in the democratic process as a public affairs priority. However, such gains were contingent on discursive requirements and behavioural rules considered essential to enlightened democracy but threatened by the 'vast wasteland'. PBS was called on to manage the contradictory requirements of the consumer culture and the state theorized by Miller — which meant reconstituting citizen subjects loyal to a particular form of dialogue (1993: 136). The impetus to return television viewers to rational debate drew from the discourse of the Enlightenment, which saw reasoned deliberation as the foundation of Western democracy. While reason has historically been associated with educated white men and the written word, traits said to be irrational (such as emotion) have been associated with popular culture, including television, and are thought to be the legacy of women and the lower classes. The importance of 'unfiltered' objectivity on PBS as a counterpoint to 1960s demands for 'group access' to television and the 'maze of complexities' (the Fairness Doctrine, the Equal Time Provision) they produced for commercial broadcasters (Blakely, 1969: 165) drew on the claim that only professional experts were equipped to distinguish reality from the distortions that troubled Lippmann. However, as Michael Schudson argues, objectivity is not just a claim about what kind of knowledge is reliable. It is 'also a moral philosophy, a declaration of what kind of thinking one should engage in' as well as a logic that insulates and rationalizes professional authority, which can then serve as a mode of social control (Schudson, 1978: 7–8).

The promotion of rational thinking on PBS was more than an effort to enlist viewers in the productive, non-violent resolution of conflicts. It was also a cultural template for proper citizenship that hinged on knowledge–power relations that excluded emotionally and bodily-invested political participation, such as women's consciousness-raising groups, boisterous union meetings and bar-room debates, consumer boycotts and mass protests. The requirement of civility worked in complementary ways. As Kasson argues, the 'established codes of behavior' ascribed to civility have historically functioned as a social classification system 'against a fully democratic order and in support of special interests, institutions of privilege, and structures of domination' (1990: 3). The idealization of public television as a Habermasian public sphere orienting critical defences does not problematize its rules of conduct – rules that were ascribed to PBS at the historical moment when commercial television was thought to have undermined political democracy. The differentiation of opinion leaders was also a way to make proper citizenship – cerebral discussions of state affairs, calm and guided deliberation, voting – visible. Participation in these processes hinged on decorum, in terms of who could appear on the programmes and how they addressed viewers at home. Drawing from the work of Peter Stallybrass and Allon White (1986), Bennett (1995: 27) traces similar proscriptions to the exclusion of codes of behaviour associated with fairs and other places of popular assembly:

> No swearing, no spitting, no brawling, no eating or drinking, no dirty footwear, no gambling: These rules which, with variations, characterized literary and debating societies, museums and coffee houses, also, as Stallybrass and White put it, 'formed part of an overall strategy of expulsion' which clears a space for polite, cosmopolitan discourses by the construction of popular culture as the 'low-Other,' the dirty and crude outside to the emergent public sphere.

For most television viewers, adopting the subject position of a good citizen as constructed by PBS meant accepting an aesthetic and political order governed by a higher authority. It required either access or acquiescence to communicative 'codes' (Aronowitz, 1993: 90) rooted in the education, cultural capital and social habitus of the PMC. This requirement functioned as a form of social control, promoting the idea that 'action without knowledge and understanding, sooner or later, is wrong action' (Blakely, 1969: 90–3). While hegemony theory has illuminated how the conflicts of the late 1960s were negotiated and partially recuperated by commercial television (Gitlin, 1980; Spigel and Curtin, 1997), which had an economic motive to 'win' popularity, PBS's response was governmental in the Foucauldian sense. This is especially evident in the simulated and live official government activities that were broadcast. Based on ETV prototypes that televised students role-playing state procedures, these initiatives functioned as a display of official power. These initiatives were less about holding politicians accountable to the mass citizenry than about affirming the rationality of the existing decision-making process.

Live coverage of Congressional activities like the Senate Foreign Relations Committee's hearings on the resumption of bombing in North Vietnam was perceived not as an expansion of democracy, but as citizen education. The purpose, said Macy, was to demonstrate that 'laws are not made in a vacuum' and that those 'responsible for making them must consider many factors before recording a vote' (1970: 286). The purpose of NPACT's 'gavel-to-gavel' coverage of the 1972 Republican convention was to counter the 'stage-managed circus atmosphere' of commercial news by 'focusing exclusively on official business'. While commercial television played up the protesting but framed it as youthful deviance (Gitlin, 1980), PBS could not recuperate dissent in a similar way. The mandate to produce a 'better' and more enlightened public could not justify dwelling on civil disobedience. Conceding that 'nobody pretends this will be the most exciting program' on TV, a PBS spokesperson explained that if 'Gerry Ford is giving a very dull speech and a riot is going on outside, we will stay with Gerry Ford' ('Farewell', 1972: 61).

PBS formats based on the electronic simulation of the New England town hall were rooted in the democratic ideals championed by Dewey. However, they were also perceived institutionally as mechanisms for instilling active citizenship in the interests of the capitalist state. The formats were promoted as a way to restore community cooperation lost massification of society, but there was also concern about the 'kind of training' that was necessary to prepare television viewers for such roles. The solution proposed by one consultant was to balance the invitation for all 'citizens to exercise intelligent decision making' with an emphasis on 'the leadership segment of society', to ensure the quality of the town halls and their outcomes (Kettering, 1969: 35). That the PMC would mediate the initiatives went without saying. Referencing a situation at WJCT-TV in Jacksonville, Mississippi, where the public affiliate managed a potentially antagonistic encounter by placing some citizens in an expensive club and others in a community hall in a poor district while the 'experts held forth in the studio', Macy naturalized the power dynamics of this arrangement with the promise – rooted in the historical reforms of the PMC – of smooth reconciliation. Confrontations, he explained, do not 'lead to action' (1970: 286).

National town halls broadcast on PBS spoke of a similar tension between participatory democracy and social control. Co-funded by the CPB, government agencies and corporations, these initiatives, which were extensively publicized and encompassed programming as well as telephone advice hotlines, community outreach, study guides and the appearance of 'countless authorities', addressed the problem of deviant and disenfranchised citizens – particularly the student counterculture and the urban poor. While progressive in some respects, they were also a move to reform behaviours deemed degenerative or amoral by coupling 'problem-solving' with self-shaping rehabilitation strategies. The discursive framing of the ventures suggests how they sought to make power visible. For example, *The Turned On Crisis* was billed as an effort to 'detect, educate and rehabilitate drug users' funded in part by the National Institute of Mental Health. *VD Blues,* hailed as 'one of the most significant events in the history of television as a medium for education, enlightenment, and raised consciousness' (Resnik, 1972: 33), exposed the medical consequences of the 1960s sexual revolution, prompting a rush of visits to clinics, according to PBS publicity.[4]

The Advocates: TV viewing as good citizenship?

Not all PBS public affairs programmes were wedded to a model of enlightened democracy. The nod towards cultural pluralism demanded by the tensions of the era created space for innovative but marginalized alternatives. *Black Journal,* one of the few PBS programmes to feature black critics and journalists, subverted the philosophy outlined by Macy by collapsing its regulated boundaries (high versus low, reason versus emotion, politics versus pleasure) and by presenting 'experts' as representatives of popular movements who were invested in their outcome. Envisioned as a way to 'bring television back to the people' rather than citizen training, it featured discussions among reporters, professors, celebrities and leaders of the Black Panthers and the All-African People's Revolutionary Party as well as music and cultural performances. It refused the decorum of most PBS public affairs programmes and challenged their definition of legitimate knowledge by setting up call-in opportunities for viewers at home and featuring a black clairvoyant named Lillian Cosby, who successfully predicted the Nixon resignation.[5] As one critic observed, the difficulty was that *Black Journal* appeared on PBS, because its aura was a barrier to attracting a large black following (Gray, 1972). Still, the programme's transgressions were duly noted by the guardians of enlightened democracy, defined not as ideological deviance but as a failure of conduct and control. According to the *New York Times*, the problem with *Black*

Journal was that it opted for 'fast pace' and 'bridges of song' over reason and objective reporting (Gould, 1970: n.p.).

Within PBS publicity, *Black Journal* was positioned as evidence of cultural pluralism as opposed to a model of citizenship. The flagship public affairs programme, and the clearest example of the philosophy of 'enlightened democracy', was *The Advocates,* which debuted in 1969 with the goal of recasting 'the passive TV viewer in an active role, working and voting to make democracy a reality'.[6] Created by a Harvard law professor and co-funded by Ford and the CPB, the weekly debate epitomized the move to return reason to America's living-rooms by 'combining the vivid communication of television with the cool analytical power of experts'. The advocates, who were also lawyers, made their cases by calling witnesses and advancing arguments in a 'logical, orderly fashion'. Their presentations and cross-examinations culminated in a studio audience vote and the judgement of a 'decision-maker', usually a public official involved in the issue. Later episodes extended the final decision to viewers at home, whose votes were tallied and sent to Congress and other governmental agencies. For this service to democracy, PBS drew bipartisan praise from scores of commentators and the *Congressional Record*. While described as the closest television had come to a contribution to participatory democracy, the mail-in vote was the only participation offered. Similar to other PBS public affairs offerings, the purpose was to differentiate opinion leaders and demonstrate the ins and outs of proper citizenship.

The Advocates took up controversial issues ranging from the withdrawal of troops in Vietnam to school desegregation to whether to impeach Richard Nixon. But its governmental aim was to display legitimate ways to express and resolve conflicts. The intention was not to 'wade through the muck and mire of the past, viewing with alarm and advising us all to understand the social, political and economic forces that contributed to the mess.' It was to empower citizens to 'do something' about problems. This invitation was guided and controlled by the model of democracy constructed by the programme. According to *The Advocates,* this meant that there were only two positions on any issue, that experts were best equipped to define the issues, that both sides were equally defensible within the rational debate format, that mass participation was limited to the ritual of voting and that consensus could be achieved within the existing institutions of self-government. The programme's long and medium shots, lengthy unedited sequences, harsh lighting and minimal use of visuals constructed an educational aesthetic, relaying the idea that democracy was both a lesson and a solemn affair above the social world of popular culture and its audience.

The emphasis on rational science conveyed a similar message in a different way. The fairness of the debate format was stressed above the significance of any given issue, and the professional orchestration of balance was emphasized over the rightness or wrongness of the positions offered. PBS insisted that the 'two committed halves equal one balanced whole', a message that was emblematized by the programme's logo, which featured arrows pointed in opposite directions coming together as a unified symbol. On the one hand, the focus on rational debate among amiable opponents was a way to please funders (such as Congress) concerned with balance. But, similar to the dissonance between addressing an 'undifferentiated public of political equals' and screening out behaviours associated with popular assemblies which Bennett observes of the museum (1995: 90), it also facilitated the 'self-display' of bourgeois democracy and screened out 'unenlightened' popular participation. *The Advocates* epitomized the call for PBS to balance 'understanding and skills' with the upsurge of angry citizens who were demanding a 'piece of the action', the 'right to have a say', a share of the 'power' (Blakely, 1969: 171).

It was assumed, in the representation of 'balance', that everyone who appeared on the programme possessed the training and pedigree to articulate a position. According to PBS, it was essential to have professional advocates, because 'commitment alone may lead to gross errors of judgment'. Class differences were obscured by defining preferred dispositions as essentially democratic. The most important qualification for being an advocate was the disposition to avoid 'the temptation of making a highly emotional but fallacious argument'. To prevent this, the advocate was to present 'not his personal opinion, but responsible arguments for each side of the case'. On the first season they took arbitrary positions, and liberals often ended up 'playing' conservatives. In later episodes it was assumed that the advocates would be committed but able to adhere to requirements of professionalism and decorum. The two who appeared most regularly were Howard Miller, a University of Chicago law school graduate who was said to balance his arguments with 'lessons in philosophy, history, and the morality of Western man', and Harvard Law School graduate William Rushner, a former Wall Street lawyer and publisher of the *National Review*. While they 'disagreed about the issues', the men described themselves as close friends who shared a commitment to a process of dealing with conflicts. It was the televised display of this *process,* not the content of the debates or their role in informing the public, that defined the programme's governmental logic. As Rushner explained,

> I think our common ground comes mostly in having the same kind of job to do and the same kind of attitude towards it. I've said to people who've asked whether I get along with Howard, that I do. The reason is, we have a great many more things in common, in terms of the problems we face, than we have separating us . . . remember we're both trained lawyers, and lawyers tend to think in much the same way. So even if we have different or diametrically opposed points of view on a topic, the way we will go about 'slicing up' the topic and analyzing it will be a lawyer's way. . . . For two men, speaking calmly and intelligently, to disagree profoundly about an issue may be polarization; but to have people yelling 'pig!' at each other,

or shouting 'burn, baby, burn!' is a different kind of polarization – it is non-communicative polarization. I don't think *The Advocates* contributes to it; I think quite the reverse.

('Advocates', 1971: n.p.)

Suggesting how the aim described by Rushner may have been perceived by the PBS audience, one viewer sent the following comment: 'This is the best one I have ever seen and it was so fair and dignified that at the end I liked the lawyers and witnesses for both sides equally well and could have voted either way.'

The individuals who 'put such a show together' included a roster of journalists, lawyers and political scientists that would have pleased Lippmann. The people who appeared as moderators, decision-makers and witnesses also formed a 'guest list that reads like Who's Who'. The primary moderator, Victor Palmieri, was the president of an investment company who had served as deputy executive director of Lyndon Johnson's National Advisory Commission on Urban Problems, commonly known as the Riot Commission. Nearly everyone who testified as a witness was college educated, often male and frequently a government official, politician, author, professor or other type of professional ('top men, well informed', said *Daily Variety*). The studio audience, which was not permitted to question or comment, was also almost exclusively white and middle class. If this was not the case, audience members were required to accept middle-class dress codes and rules of appropriate behaviour, such as 'behaving with reasonable calm' and avoiding heckling. On the few occasions when people outside of these categories were invited to play a role, they were positioned by the logic of the programme in ways that undermined their knowledge and credibility. For example, in an episode about the Princeton Plan, a proposal to allow students time off from school to volunteer for electoral campaigns, a construction worker was called to testify as a 'hard hat' with 'no particular purpose except he was against special favors to college kids'.

Working-class guests who appeared on *The Advocates* were also a source of fodder in the popular press. In an episode dealing with a welfare reform bill, a San Francisco fish worker was called to testify that he earned less from his job than mothers who received welfare, and took the opportunity to elaborate on his views beyond the proscribed line of questioning. Later in the programme, a welfare mother who was in the studio audience shouted out opinions and stormed out of the building in protest. Contrary to the enthusiastic press coverage *The Advocates* generally received, the TV critic for the *Boston Globe* reported that the welfare episode was 'not particularly illuminating'. He conceded it provided 'some laughs' when a 'belligerent witness told how he felt in earthy terms, including a swear word here and there' and a woman became unruly and 'shouted epithets that reached the microphone', but 'the cause of enlightenment wasn't served much until an assistant secretary of labor . . . showed up near the end and

explained the provisions and implications of the measure in voluminous detail'
(Shain, 1969: n.p.).

While the testimony of people with lived knowledge directly relevant to the
legislation was discredited as uncivilized and unenlightened, the Congressman
who served as the decision-maker was praised for his efforts in welfare reform,
which included 'simulating' the life-style of welfare recipients to see if changes
in the system were justified. Quoting a PBS publicity item, many TV critics who
reviewed the episode noted that the Democrat and his wife 'ate for a week on
foods available for the welfare-budget of 66 cents per day and found that with
ingenuity a healthful menu was possible'. Qualifying this finding with another
PBS quote, they explained that of course, 'Mrs. Bingham is a nutrition expert
with knowledge unknown to the majority of the welfare recipients'. The knowledge–power relations set up by *The Advocates* divorced politics from the experiences and emotions of subordinated classes – and in so doing cast democracy as
a high affair properly managed by professionals.

According to the Ehrenreichs, the middle-class radicalism of the late 1960s
signalled a crisis for the capitalist state at the point when students began questioning their privilege and authority and identifying with the adversary positions
of the black revolutionary movements and, eventually, the economic conditions
of the white working class. *The Advocates* spoke to this crisis in an attempt to
return campus activists to rational debate as the proper way to handle disputes,
and an effort to instil dispositions and behaviours suitable for opinion leaders.
PBS encouraged local stations to actively promote the programme on campuses,
seeking out 'student representatives' who could help build an audience by word
of mouth. Issues that were of interest to student protesters, such as Vietnam,
amnesty for draft dodgers and FBI surveillance of the New Left were debated,
and students were often called to testify on these episodes. The legalization of
countercultural activities like marijuana smoking was also debated, as was the
institutionalization of legitimate opportunities for political participation epitomized by the Princeton Plan. There were counterhegemonic gains, in that the outcomes of the debates sometimes challenged government policies, but the
knowledge–power relations embedded in the format of the programme recon-
stituted dissent as professional reform logic. For example, following the debate
on Vietnam culminating in a decision to withdraw US troops, PBS issued a press
release suggesting that the public opinion produced in a reasoned, orderly way
on *The Advocates* was credible – which implied that the unruly demands of the
anti-war movement were not.

A similar effacement of agency was evidenced in episodes addressing the
demands of the women's movement. *The Advocates* debated a number of issues
relevant to women, including the Equal Rights Amendment, work schedules to
accommodate parenting, no-fault divorce and access to birth control. These
episodes offered a higher profile for female experts, and one exceptional pre-
Roe *vs.* Wade debate over the legalization of abortion featured a female lawyer

defined as a 'women's liberation activist' as the advocate.[7] However, democracy was still contingent on the codes of thinking, behaving and governing required by *The Advocates*. This meant that modes of political expression associated with women, such as sharing personal, often painful and emotional experiences, had to be incorporated within the logic of rational debate, if included at all. It meant that the non-hierarchical models of decision-making idealized by the women's movement could not be implemented. And it meant that grassroots organizing was largely irrelevant. If change was the sole consequence of an expert debate followed by a vote and an official procedure, it followed that active struggles were not really necessary. Therefore, PBS could issue a press release crediting *The Advocates* with the passage of liberalized abortion legislation in several states without even mentioning the women's movement.

The Advocates made an effort to reach a broad, presumably male audience by using sports figures in promotional campaigns describing *The Advocates* as 'The PBS Fight of the Week'. But research showed its audience to be comprised mainly of PMC males, as *TV Guide* suggested when it called the programme 'The thinking man's fight of the week' (Gunther, 1973: 10). PBS proudly admitted the skew in publicity aimed at opinion leaders, noting that 'In a medium that has bred the sixty-second attention span, *The Advocates* requires thoughtful attention for an entire hour. And it's getting it.' This discourse placed the impetus for resisting commercial television's seductive appeals, and for becoming a good citizen, solely on the viewer. In broader terms, it obscured the tension between the demands of the consumer economy and the political order with the logic of individual responsibility. The binary between good and bad citizenship was echoed in the popular press, where reviewers constructed hierarchies between the responsible citizens who watched *The Advocates* and the hedonistic, apathetic masses who preferred 'the movies on ABC and the second half of Hee Haw' ('Television Review', 1970: n.p.). Viewer letters excerpted by PBS in the debate tallies forwarded to public officials and the news media often drew from the discourse of the 'TV problem' to construct similar binaries. The following comments, for example, suggest that *The Advocates* offered the symbolic material for middle-class viewers to assert their rational thinking, self-discipline and good taste:

> Friends – and you are my friends when you present such thought provoking programs, implying that some of us out here in the Vast Wasteland can and do think. Not many TV programs pay us this compliment.

> A truly splendid program. Of all the myriad and generally spiritually demeaning offerings on television only your broadcasts are consistently interesting and civilized. Keep up the good work.

This construction of good citizenship affirmed a hierarchical model of democracy congruent with the social scientific logic of the two-step flow.

According to *TV Guide*, *The Advocates* was hardly a success by 'mass' standards, but it attracted 'influential people' and had 'an impact where it counts' (Gunther, 1973: 7). While political participation did not extend beyond the ritual of voting, the 22,000 plus votes received each month were taken as public opinion that mattered. Neither the sociodemographic profile of the PBS audience nor the fact that pre-addressed postcard ballots were available only to public television's contributing viewer-members were seen as reason to qualify the results of the debates. What was emphasized was the bipartisan nature of the voting audience – a pattern that was then evoked to affirm PBS's ability to produce political balance and liberal pluralist consensus. The 'vote swings heavily from conservative to liberal and occasionally perches in the middle of the fence,' explained a PBS press release, and the majority of 'liberal positions on social issues' were balanced by some 'very conservative thinking on the subjects of law and order and the economy.' As the Ehrenreichs argue, such 'balance' is precisely what one would expect from the reformist faction of the PMC.

The Advocates rationalized a model of government that stabilized the capitalist political structure by affirming the necessity of dominant institutions and the leadership abilities of white male PMC elites. Television viewers who refused to take part in the programme were positioned as hedonistic and apathetic citizens unworthy of active participation in self-government. Viewers who didn't play by the rules were not good citizens but deviants, as epitomized by an incident where the 'pot cigarettes' sent in following the debate over marijuana were 'promptly turned over to the police because under existing federal and most state laws, the possession of marijuana is a crime'. In 1973, PBS was partially restructured by policies established by the Nixon administration intended to curb its perception of 'East coast liberal bias'. To the dismay of many TV critics and viewers, public affairs programmes were among the first casualties. While some were rescued by viewer contributions and corporate sponsorship, *The Advocates* was cancelled in 1974, when it failed to secure a benefactor and the local station support necessary for public subsidies. By this point, civil disobedience had subsided and Ford had moved on to other projects. Cable was also being developed to reach niche markets, alleviating the problem of differentiating 'news junkies' and opinion leaders with 'lowest common denominator' television programming. Ironically, before it was dropped, *The Advocates* pondered whether Congress should initiate impeachment hearings on Richard Nixon, resulting in a forty/sixty split in favour of the procedure. As with an earlier episode debating whether Spiro Agnew's tax evasion plea bargain should be accepted, the purpose was not to promote ideological reconciliation, but to affirm the rationality of democratic institutions during a moment of crisis. Summing up this logic, one viewer letter proclaimed, 'Your program was fantastic . . . once this corruption is eliminated our government will be the better for it and faith in the process will be restored.'[8]

The campaign to instil good citizenship is not as explicit on PBS today, but we can see traces in the subdued officialdom of *The News Hour*, the 'enlightened democracy' of *Washington Week in Review*, the periodic effort to educate the public with campaign specials and the audience of opinion leaders drawn to these pro-grammes, and to PBS as a whole. At a time when debates about the future of public television are dominated by a free market conservative discourse seeking to stamp out the enterprise, a cultural studies approach to policy can unpack the political rationality of PBS, with an eye towards equalizing the allocation of its cultural resources. Here, I have shown how the idealization of citizenship as an empowered subject position glosses over the distinct but complementary know-ledge–power relations constructed under the banner of democracy and 'public service'. In an era when the governmental aims ascribed to PBS are no longer as contingent on public television, it is harder to sustain the rationale for public media, and easier for conservatives to cast PBS as a dated service whose func-tions are now met by channels like CNN and C-SPAN. The reconstitution of public television will require new rationales that go beyond the focus on anti-commercialism and whether programmes have or have not 'provocatively chal-lenged' the status quo (Ledbetter, 1997: 217). As Bennett argues, the design of equitable cultural policy necessitates a change in the *relations* between cultural institutions and the public. 'The ultimate referent of mass society,' notes Aronowitz, 'is the historical moment when the masses make the (still) contested demand for the full privileges of citizenship, despite the fact that they are obliged to work at mundane tasks, are typically untrained for the specific functions of governance, and are ensconced in the routines of everyday life' (1993: 77). In light of my research, I am suggesting that demands for participation that subvert established binaries between mass and political culture, and for access that is not predicated on educated, masculine and Eurocentric ways of thinking and behav-ing, are necessary to move beyond a marketplace construction of 'cultural democracy' and a liberal ideal rooted in enlightenment and social control.

Notes

1   My analysis is based on research conducted at the National Public Broadcast-ing Archives, University of Maryland, College Park, MD (hereafter NPBA) as well as the Museum of Television and Radio, New York, NY (hereafter MTR). I have examined official sources (policy discourse, CPB and PBS records, social scientific audience research, publicity, programming philosophies, early PBS programmes) as well as popular sources (popular journalism, TV criticism, viewer letters, viewer-member programme guides). This article draws from my Ph.D. dissertation, 'A chance for better television: PBS and the politics of ideals, 1967–1973', University of Massachusetts-Amherst, September 1998. Thanks to Justin Lewis, Susan Douglas, Lisa Henderson, Carolyn Anderson and a *Cultural Studies* reviewer for helpful comments on earlier drafts.

2   Cultural studies in the US has been slow to take up the politics of public broad-casting, although Ien Ang's (1991) theoretical critique does include some dis-cussion.

3   In addition to references cited, my analysis here draws on programme sum-
     maries, institutional records, publicity and press reviews collected in the
     following NPBA files: PBS Public Information, NPACT Press Packet, 1972,
     Box 7; PBS Public Information, NPACT Publicity, Box 2; PBS Program Files,
     Washington Week in Review, Box 77.

4   See PBS Program Files, *Turned On Crisis,* Box 74; PBS Program Files, *VD Blues,*
     Box 76.

5   See PBS Program Files, *Black Journal*, Box 13; episodes are also available for
     viewing at MTR. Another early exception was *Black Perspectives on the News.*
     Both programmes were marginalized within the PBS schedule and by the press
     commentary that circulated around its public affairs line-up.

6   *The Advocates* debuted on PBS on 5 October 1969 and appeared weekly until
     23 May 1974. It returned on a bi-weekly basis for the 1978–79 season, and
     for a series of episodes prior to the 1980 election of Ronald Reagan. The series
     was co-produced by KCET-Los Angeles, with Tom Burrows as executive pro-
     ducer, and by WGBH Boston, with Greg Harney as executive producer, and
     the Ford Foundation, under Friendly's guidance, played an active role. My
     analysis is based on an examination of PBS press releases, detailed programme
     summaries and guest lists, publicity, and the materials sent to public officials
     and the media in the form of a weekly report entitled *The Nation Responds.* The
     report included excerpts from viewer letters which I examined as another
     layer of evidence. I also examined seventy-one reviews that appeared in maga-
     zines and local newspapers between 1969 and 1970. Most of these were col-
     lected by PBS in a report entitled *The Critics Respond to The Advocates.* My
     analysis is also based on episodes of *The Advocates* available for viewing at MTR.
     Because the archival materials were often not dated or titled, and to avoid a
     cumbersome number of references, I have not cited each document. If not
     attributed, quotations are drawn from materials collected in PBS Program
     Files, *The Advocates*, Box 1 and 2.

7   On the basis of PBS programme summaries I have examined, this episode
     appears to be the only time when a woman appeared as an advocate, and the
     only time an advocate was also described as an activist.

8   It is worth noting that a year later, PBS featured 'gavel-to-gavel' coverage of
     the Watergate hearings. According to research, the viewership for the PBS
     telecasts (as opposed to those who watched excerpts on commercial television
     or didn't watch at all) contained more college-educated professionals, more
     people who voted in the last election and more people who had made a public
     speech at some point in their lifetime. The appeal to 'go getters' was used to
     defend tax subsidies on the basis that politically active citizens need to be better
     informed (Wotring and Leroy, 1974; Leroy, 1975; Fletcher, 1977).

References

'A Panel Speaks on Public Affairs Programming' (1966) *NEAB Journal,* January–
     February: 54–66.

'Advocates Define Their Terms' (1971) *Image*, WNET-TV, New York, 2 May: n.p. NPBA, WNET Collection, Program Guides, Box 4.

Ang, Ien (1991) *Desperately Seeking the Audience*, New York: Routledge.

Aronowitz, Stanley (1993) 'Is a democracy possible? The decline of the public in the American debate', in Bruce Robbins (ed.) *The Phantom Public Sphere*, Minneapolis: University of Minnesota Press.

Baughman, James (1985) *Television's Guardians: The FCC and the Politics of Programming, 1958–1967*, Knoxville: University of Tennessee Press.

Bennett, Tony (1992a) 'Putting policy into cultural studies', in Lawrence Grossberg, Cary Nelson and Paula Triechler (eds) *Cultural Studies*, New York: Routledge.

—— (1992b) 'Useful culture', *Cultural Studies*, 6(3): 395–408.

—— (1995) *The Birth of the Museum*, London: Routledge.

Blakely, Robert (1969) *The People's Instrument: A Philosophy of Programming for Public Television*, Washington DC: Public Affairs Press.

Boddy, William (1990) *Fifties Television*, Urbana, IL: University of Chicago Press.

Bourdieu, Pierre (1984) *Distinction: A Social Critique of the Judgment of Taste*, trans. Richard Nice, Cambridge, MA: Harvard University Press.

'Breeding Ground for Riots' (1968) *Saturday Review*, 20 April: 66.

Burchell, Graham (1996) 'Liberal government and the techniques of the self', in Andrew Barry, Thomas Osborne and Nicholas Rose (eds) *Foucault and Political Reason: Liberalism, Neo-Liberalism and Rationalities of Government*, Chicago, IL: University of Chicago Press.

Carnegie Commission (1967) *Public Television: A Program for Action, The Report of the Carnegie Commission on Educational Television*, New York: Bantam.

Cherne, L. (1952) 'Biggest question on TV debates', *New York Times Magazine*, 2 March: 14.

Clark, Charles S. (1992) 'Public broadcasting', *Congressional Quarterly Researcher*, 18 September: 812.

Corporation for Public Broadcasting (CPB) (1969) *Newsroom: An Audience Evaluation for KQED-TV*, unpublished report, NPBA, reference shelf.

Croteau, David, Hoynes, William and Caragee, Kevin (1996) 'The political diversity of public television: polysemy, the public sphere and the conservative critique of PBS', *Journalism & Mass Communication Monographs, 157*. Columbia, SC: AEJMC.

Douglas, Susan (1987) *Inventing American Broadcasting 1899–1922*, Baltimore, MD: Johns Hopkins University Press.

Ehrenreich, John and Ehrenreich, Barbara (1979) 'The professional-managerial class', in Pat Walker (ed.) *Between Labor and Capital*, Boston, MA: South End Press.

Elmer Morgan, Joy (1934) 'A national culture-by-product or objective of national planning', *School and Society*, 28 July: 114.

Engelman, Ralph (1996) *Public Radio and Television in America*, Thousand Oaks, CA: Sage.

'Farewell to Razzmatazz' (1972) *Newsweek*, 21 August: 61.

Fischer, John (1959) 'TV and its critics', *Harper's,* July: 12–18.

Fletcher, James E. (1977) 'Commercial versus public television audiences: public activities and the Watergate hearings', *Communication Quarterly*, 25(4): 13–16.

Ford Foundation (1970) *Newsroom: A Report,* unpublished report, NPBA, reference shelf.

—— (1980) *Ford Foundation Activities in Noncommercial Broadcasting*, New York: Ford Foundation.

Foucault, Michel (1991) 'Governmentality', in Graham Burchell, Colin Gordon and Peter Miller (eds) *The Foucault Effect: Studies in Governmentality*, Chicago, IL: University of Chicago Press.

Friendly, Fred (1967) *Due to Circumstances Beyond Our Control*, New York: Vintage Books.

Garnham, Nicholas (1992) 'Citizens, consumers, and public culture', in Kim Christian Schroder and Michael Skovand (eds) *Media Cultures: Reappraising Transnational Media*, London: Routledge.

Gitlin, Todd (1980) *The Whole World Is Watching*, Berkeley: University of California Press.

Gordon, Colin (1991). 'Governmental rationality: an introduction', in Graham Burchell, Colin Gordon and Peter Miller (eds) *The Foucault Effect: Studies in Governmentality*, Chicago, IL: University of Chicago Press.

Gould, Jack (1970) 'A black critic for a black show?', *New York Times*, 11 October: n.p., NPBA, PBS Collection, Program Files, *Black Journal*, Box 13.

Gramsci, Antonio (1971) *Selections from the Prison Notebooks*, New York: International Publishers.

Gray, Karen (1972) 'Black journal: an overview', *Educational Broadcasting Review*, 6(4): 231–2.

Gunther, Max (1973) 'The thinking man's fight of the week', *TV Guide*, 14 April: 7–10.

Hall, Stuart (1982) 'The rediscovery of "ideology": the return of the repressed in media studies', in Michael Curevitch, Tony Bennett, James Curran and Janet Woollacott (eds) *Culture, Society and the Media*, London: Methuen.

Hallin, Daniel (1994) 'The passing of the "high modernism" of American journalism', in Casey Ripley, jun. (ed.) *The Media & The Public*, New York: H.W. Wilson Co.

Heckscher, August (1968) 'The quality of American culture', in President's Commission on National Goals, *Goals for Americans*, New York: Prentice Hall.

Hoke, Travis (1932) 'Radio goes educational', *Harper's*, September: 473.

'Hoked up Conspiracy' (1972) *The New Republic*, 22 July: 23.

House Committee on Interstate and Foreign Commerce (1967) *Public Television Act of 1967: Hearings on H.R. 6736,* Remarks of Representative Samuel N. Friedel, 90th Congress, 1st session, 11–21 July: 103.

Howe, Harold (1967) 'Tenth anniversary program of KTCA-TV', 17 September, unpublished transcript, NPBA, reference shelf.

Hoynes, William (1994) *Public Television for Sale: The Media, The Market and the Public Sphere*, Boulder, CO: Westview.

Humphrey, Hubert (1966) 'Remarks to the convention', *NAEB Journal*, January–February: 49.

Hunter, Armand L. (1961) 'The way to 1st-class educational citizenship', *NPBA Journal,* July–August: 19–23.

Jowett, Garth (1982) 'The emergence of the mass society: the standardization of American culture, 1830–1920', in Jack Salzman (ed.) *Prospects: The Annual of American Cultural Studies*, New York: Burt Franklin & Co. Inc.

Karayn, Jim (1972) 'In defense of public television', *Wall Street Journal,* 15 November: n.p., NPBA, PBS Collection, NPACT, Box 2.

Kasson, John (1978) *Amusing the Million: Coney Island at the Turn of the Century*, New York: Hill & Wang.

—— (1990) *Rudeness & Civility*, New York: Hill & Wang.

Katz, Elihu and Lazarsfeld, Paul (1955) *Personal Influence*, Glencoe, IL: The Free Press.

Kettering Conference on Public Television Programming (1969) 'Transcript of proceedings', 25–28 June, unpublished report, NPBA, CPB Collection, Box 34.

Laruent, Lawrence (1972) 'Vanoucur-MacNeil start a new kind of news', *The Washington Post*, 3 September: n.p., NPBA, PBS Collection, NPACT, Box 2.

Lasswell, Harold (1962) 'The future of public affairs programs', in Institute for Communication Research (ed.) (1962) *Educational Television: The Next Ten Years*, Stanford, CT: Institute for Communication Research.

Lazarsfeld, Paul (1946) *The People Look at Radio*, Chapel Hill: University of North Carolina Press.

Ledbetter, James (1997) *Made Possible By. . . . The Death of Public Broadcasting in the United States*, New York: Verso.

Leroy, David (1975) 'Looking back: the audience for impeachment', *Public Telecommunication Review*, 3(2): 23–25.

Lippmann, Walter (1922/1954) *Public Opinion*, New York: Macmillan.

—— (1959) 'The TV problem', *New York Herald Tribune*, 27 October: 26.

Lowi, Theodore J. (1977) *American Government: Incomplete Conquest*, Hinsdale, IL: Dryden Press.

McChesney, Robert (1994) *Telecommunications, Mass Media & Democracy: The Battle for Control of U.S. Broadcasting, 1928–1935*, New York: Oxford University Press.

Macy, John (1970) 'The critics of television: a positive answer', speech before the National Press Club, 15 January, rpt in *Vital Speeches of the Day*, 15 February: 286–8.

—— (1974) *To Irrigate a Wasteland*, Berkeley: University of California Press.

Miller, Toby (1993) *The Well-Tempered Self: Citizenship, Culture and the Postmodern Subject*, Baltimore, MD: Johns Hopkins University Press.

Minow, Newton (1962) 'Our common goal: a nationwide ETV system', *NAEB Journal*, January–February: 1–9.

National Citizens for Public Broadcasting (1968) *The State of Public Broadcasting: A Report to the American People*, New York: National Citizens for Public Broadcasting, NPBA, reference shelf.

Public Broadcasting Service (1972) *PBS on Record: The Public Broadcasting Service Programming October 1971–October 1972*, Washington DC: Public Broadcasting Service, NPBA, reference shelf.

'Public Taste Molds TV' (1961) *Broadcasting*, 18 September: 26.

'Public Television: In the Balance' (1973) *Congressional Record,* 5 February: E653.

Ratner, Victor (1969). 'The freedom of taste', *Television Magazine*, November: 54.

Resnik, Henry S. (1972) 'Putting VD on public TV', *Saturday Review of Education*, 14 October: 33–8.

Robinson, Hubbel (1960) 'You, the public, are to blame', *TV Guide*, 26 November: 14.

Rubin, Joan Shelley (1992) *The Making of Middlebrow Culture*, Chapel Hill: University of North Carolina Press.

Sarnoff, David (1955) 'The moral crisis of our age', *Vital Speeches of the Day*, 1 December: 118–19.

Schlesinger, Arthur (1961) 'Notes on a cultural policy', in Normin Jacobs (ed.) *Culture for the Millions?*, Princeton, NJ: D. Van Nostrand Company, Inc.

Schramm, Wilbur, Lyle, Jack and de Sola Pool, Ithiel (1963) *The People Look at Educational Television*, Stanford, CT: Stanford University Press.

Schudson, Michael (1978) *Discovering the News*, New York: Basic Books.

Schwarzwalder, John (1959) 'Educational television and the sense of urgency', mimeographed commencement address presented to the University of Minnesota, 16 July, NPBA, reference shelf.

Shain, Percy (1969) 'Hot TV debate on Advocates debut', *Boston Globe*, 13 October: n.p. NPBA, PBS Collection, Program Guides, *The Advocates*, Box 1.

Spigel, Lynn and Curtin, Michael (eds) (1997) *The Revolution Wasn't Televised: Sixties Television and Social Conflict*, New York: Routledge.

Statistical Research Inc (1974) 'Public broadcasting audience analysis', unpublished report, 31 May 1974, NPBA, reference shelf.

Stallybrass, Peter and White, Allon (1986) *The Politics and Poetics of Transgression*, London: Methuen.

Streeter, Thomas (1989) 'Beyond the free market: the corporate liberal character of U.S. commercial broadcasting', *Wide Angle*, 11(1): 4–17.

'Television Review' (1970) *Alhambra California Post*, 5 October: n.p., in 'The critics respond to *The Advocates*', unpublished report, NPBA, PBS Collection, Program Guides, *The Advocates*, Box 1.

Thorpe, Day (1972) 'A political bonanza for viewers', *Evening Star*, 2 June: n.p., NPBA, PBS Collection, Program Files, *The Advocates*, Box 2.

Williams, Raymond (1966) *Communications*, London: Chatto & Windus.

Wotring, C. Edward and LeRoy, David (1974) 'The decline of the Watergate audience', *Public Telecommunication Review*, 2(1): 28–33.

Jacinth Samuels

DANGEROUS LIAISONS: QUEER SUBJECTIVITY, LIBERALISM AND RACE

Abstract

The emergence of queer theory has posed an incipient and significant challenge to the essentialism which has typically characterized theories of sexuality. In an attempt to eschew the totalizing effects of the categories 'gay' and 'lesbian', queer theorists advocate a subjectivity which celebrates sexual difference without concern for achieved or ascribed characteristics. It is this remarkable capacity for inclusivity, attributed most immediately to the gender and race neutrality of 'queer', which is of particular interest here. More specifically, this article examines queer subjectivity's relation to a liberal humanist discourse whose purported universality requires the production of abstract, sovereign subjects without concern for their social location. The article in turn examines how the liberal premises which underlie queer subjectivity actually facilitate the reappropriation of 'queer' while undermining similar attempts to resignify racial epithets. Far from being a neutral subject position which ensures the liberty and autonomy of its inhabitants, the racial epithet here reinscribes the difference which the 'queer' subject and its liberal humanist prototype are perpetually trying to mask. I contend that it is this discrepancy in the capacity to mask difference – via a proximity to or distance from the liberal subject – which permits the reappropriation of 'queer' while racial epithets continue to remain taboo in the cultural mainstream.

Keywords

queer theory; sexuality; subjectivity; race; liberalism; identity

Introduction: Queering theory

PERHAPS NOWHERE ELSE has the incipient challenge of queer theory been more keenly evidenced than in its unrelenting assault against the hetero/homo binary which is both intrinsic to and naturalized within modern Western theory.[1] The term 'queer' thus

> offers a comprehensive way of characterizing all those whose sexuality places them in opposition to the current 'normalizing regime.' '[Q]ueer' has become convenient shorthand as various sexual minorities have claimed territory in the space once known simply, if misleadingly, as 'the gay community.' As stated by an editor of the defunct New York City queer magazine *Outweek*, 'When you're trying to describe the community, and you have to list gays, lesbians, bisexuals, drag queens, transsexuals (post-op and pre), it gets unwieldy. Queer says it all.'
>
> (Epstein, 1994: 195)

The need to 'say it all', that is, the desire to conceptualize and articulate a plurality of sexual subjectivities, within a space uncircumscribed by the limitations of its own boundaries, is the impetus behind the creation of the term 'queer theory' – itself a response to the perceived lacunae in both heterocentric and gay and lesbian theory, the latter symbolized by the discord invoked by the very expression 'gay and lesbian'.[2] In other words, queer theory attempts to 'unpack the monolithic identities 'lesbian' and 'gay', and subsequently demonstrate how these categories are in fact overdetermined by factors such as heterosexuality, race, gender and ethnicity (Hennessy, 1994: 87). Some queers may even go so far as to abjure *any* investment in 'gay' and 'lesbian' identities, dismissing the practice as the politically disadvantageous occupation of homogeneous markers which serves only to cosmetically reverse the polarity while doing little to unsettle heterosexual privilege (Morrison, 1992: 16–17).

It is ironic that the anti-essentialism and inclusivity that are intended to distinguish queer theory from its gay and lesbian antecedents should also constitute the bases of its strongest criticism. At issue is whether the race and gender neutrality which is ostensibly synonymous with a queer identity (Watney, 1994: 15) actually subsumes more experience than it represents.

> Despite the barrier-crossing queer intends, can it do so without also masking difference? My fear is that 'queer' might flatten the social, cultural, and material distinctions and liabilities confronting each type of queer and the different stakes for each. While, in theory, queer invites the possibility of building alliances based on our common identity on the fringes, it is equally possible that it performs the same elision it was intended to remedy.
>
> (Penn, 1995: 33)

Far from being gender neutral, critics argue that 'queer' erases lesbian specificity and harbours the same implicit masculine bias found in 'homosexual' or 'gay' – initially generic referents encompassing both male and female homosexuality which have gradually developed an almost exclusive association with the former (Jeffreys, 1994: 469).

Advocates of 'queer' counter that the phrase 'gay and lesbian' has itself merely supplanted the previously standardized 'gay' or 'homosexual'. 'Queer', by contrast, signifies a critical distance from the institutionalized and formulaic coupling that is 'lesbian and gay' (de Lauretis, 1991: iv). Their opponents, on the other hand, contend that such claims are rendered possible only by virtue of their ahistorical and apolitical foundations.

> [T]he notion that . . . 'lesbian and gay' is now . . . an 'established and often convenient, formula,' sometimes arrogantly dismissed as 'retro' by queer activists and theorists alike, diminishes the courage exhibited by those who daily risk . . . relationships and reputations by writing, teaching, taking courses in, and living gay and lesbian lives. In the academy . . . queer may be the latest in intellectual chic, but to indulge the presumption that 'lesbian and gay' has somehow become mainstreamed and assimilated is, at best, wishful thinking. At worst, it is a gross misrepresentation of the place occupied by most lesbians and gay men in the academy and the larger culture.
>
> (Penn, 1995: 33)

The difficulty is that much of the scepticism surrounding the inclusivity of 'queer' is couched in adhominem appeals to lost 'specificity' and/or 'experience', arguments that are themselves fraught with an instability which is rooted in a presumptive 'essence' whose existence must be both demonstrated and defined. Hence although many critics remain suspicious of the race and gender neutrality of queer, their arguments become self-vitiating when grounded in the very essentialism which queer theorists have accused them of advocating.

One alternative to this dilemma is to investigate the *premises* which underpin queer theory's claim to inclusivity. Heralded as a means by which to articulate the complexity of multiple oppressions, 'queer', and its ability to transcend difference, is contrasted to 'gay' which 'is widely understood to mean "white," "male," "materialistic," and "thirty-something"' (Watney, 1994: 15). My concern is therefore with queer theory's remarkable capacity for inclusivity and its relation to a liberal humanist discourse whose purported universality similarly requires the production of 'abstract, genderless, colorless sovereign subjects without regard to their "social positioning"' (Brown, 1995: 142).

Theorizing queer subjectivity as the simultaneous production *and* contestation of the political terms of liberalism[3] necessitates a genealogy of the queer subject, exposing those politicized imperatives which avow particular identity categories as causal when they are actually the products or *effects* of institutions, practices and discourses (Butler, 1990: x-xi). This approach is inspired by Wendy Brown (1995: 3) insofar as it too takes as its focus those emancipatory political projects which reproduce the very mechanisms of which they are an effect but nevertheless purport to oppose. My own investigation therefore centres on the structural similarities between 'queer' subjectivity and that of the liberal human-ist subject most appositely exemplified in John Rawls' influential text, *A Theory of Justice* (1971).

Rawls and the queer subject

Rawls attempts to redress the inequities that have historically plagued the judicial system by proposing a theory of justice whose principles are collectively deter-mined by occupants of the 'original position', a hypothetical environment wherein inhabitants are necessarily ignorant of their achieved and ascribed characteristics. These restrictions allow the original position to be constituted as an 'initial status quo' wherein any fundamental agreements or conclusions con-cerning the principles of justice are inevitably fair – a phenomenon which Rawls terms 'justice as fairness' (1971: 12).

Yet it is precisely these restrictions – those which Rawls deems essential to attaining rational agreement on first principles of justice – which form the basis for comparison between the Rawlsian and the queer subject. Entry to the original position is, for example, conditional upon the participant's willingness to deliber-ate from behind a 'veil of ignorance', the goal being to mask and thereby *neutral-ize* the impact of any factors which would prompt people to exploit circumstances to their own advantage. Hence the Rawlsian subject, now rendered ignorant of its sex, race, class, ethnicity, gender, etc., provides an apposite model for any subject which is at least partially defined by the absence of such characteristics. In this respect the queer subject, similarly 'veiled' in its own obscurity, may be likened to the former; both subjects, united in the quest for neutrality, sustain their existence through the absence or, at the very least, mitigation of presence.

It seems odd then that a subject position which is defined largely by what it excludes could be deemed inclusive, much less accessible, but Rawls deftly cir-cumvents this problem by emphasizing the original position's conceptual status. Any number of people may 'simulate the deliberations of this hypothetical situ-ation, simply by reasoning in accordance with the appropriate restrictions.' Exactly *when* one enters the original position or even *who* does so is irrelevant because the veil of ignorance ensures the uniformity of all available information (Rawls, 1971: 138–9).

The original position is therefore distinguished by the sheer fluidity of its spatiality, a quality which facilitates the seemingly effortless entrance/exit of its participants. Here, once again, we discover an area consistent with queer subjectivity for which the notion of 'space'[4] is also essential. Queer subjectivity occupies a 'new space in the domain of sexuality: a postgay, postlesbian space' (Morton, 1995: 369) which, like the original position, can be entered and/or exited at will. It is a space whose fluidity reflects an identity which refuses to name itself and which heralds the declaration that '[t]o be gay is to have a mere identity; to be queer is to enter and celebrate the ludic space of textual indeterminacy' (Morton, 1995: 373).

The ability to move freely into and out of a space/subject position, be it Rawlsian or 'queer', presumes the liberty of an autonomous subject – liberty and autonomy being constitutive elements of liberalism. Thus liberty, for Rawls (1971: 202), is premised upon agents who are free to act without restriction – a definition which affirms both the sovereignty of the liberal subject and the freedom to *do* what one *desires* where not prohibited by law (Brown, 1995: 154). Insofar as liberty is juxtaposed not to slavery but a will-less absence of choice (Brown, 1995: 154), the autonomous subject is characterized by 'the absence of immediate constraints on [his] entry into and movement within civil society' (Brown, 1995: 156). To the extent that liberalism deems race, class, gender, sexuality, etc. to be indicative of such 'constraints', their removal is a necessary condition for both the liberty of the Rawlsian and 'queer' subjects and the autonomous exercise of their respective will.

Rawls' theory of justice is clearly indicative of a neo-Kantian theoretical heritage which defines moral subjects on the basis of autonomy, rationality and an uncompromising distinction between reason and affectivity. Given Kant's conviction that moral legislation is contingent upon the freedom and equality of rational beings, the deliberations of those in the original position must, in turn, be the product of rational choice rather than bias, ascriptive or achieved characteristics (Rawls, 1971: 252). Subjects within this Kantian ideal are thus akin to 'geometricians in different rooms who, reasoning alone for themselves, all arrive at the same solution to a problem' (Benhabib, 1987: 91). Hence the Rawlsian subject, much like its Kantian predecessor, inhabits a unitary subject position which occludes subjectivity outside of itself.

> In his attempt to do justice to Kant's conception of noumenal agency, Rawls recapitulates a basic problem with the Kantian conception of the self, namely, that noumenal selves cannot be individuated. If all that belongs to them as embodied, affective, suffering creatures, their memory and history, their ties and relations to others, are to be subsumed under the phenomenal realm, then what we are left with is an empty mask that is everyone and no one.
>
> (Benhabib, 1987: 89)

Nor would it seem that the queer subject is any more suited to resolving this dilemma. On the one hand, 'queer' celebrates the diversity of those who experience heterosexist oppression without invoking an essentialized identity, but at the same time 'the most appealing aspect of a queer identity is the refusal to name what that identity means' (Slagle, 1995: 97–8). Perhaps this refusal is less the result of a principled aversion to essentialism than it is the discomforting knowledge of what such a disclosure would occasion. That is, once the veil of ignorance 'relieves' participants of all individuating characteristics, the parties are no longer *similarly* but rather *identically* situated (Sandel, 1982: 131), thus effectively erasing the basis for any claim to diversity. Moreover, with each subject being driven by precisely the same motivations and knowledge, the original position essentially consists of a single 'disembodied, pre-social or transcendent self reasoning to reflective equilibrium' (Frazer and Lacey, 1993: 46).

The interrogation of the Rawlsian subject necessarily casts doubt on assertions that the fluidity of queer subjectivity is a deliberate strategy designed to avoid both the strictures of definitional boundaries and their intrinsic essentialism (Morrison, 1992: 14). Rather than simply a means by which to ensure both poetic and political licence, the indeterminacy of 'queer' masks the same problem that the veil of ignorance is intended to obscure. Once the veil can no longer bear the weight of its own scrutiny, it is not *people*, but a solitary subject who is exposed by the accident of its drooping facade. The veil tumbles to reveal 'no real plurality of perspectives in the Rawlsian original position, but only a definitional identity' (Benhabib, 1987: 90). Hence,

> the judgements are those of the philosopher himself, the construction of the original position having served only to obscure, to neutralize, substantive assumptions which should have been spelled out and defended. Far from being the product of an abstract, transcendent process of reasoning, the theory of justice is revealed as chosen from a very specific social position, that of a white, middle-class, liberal American male.
>
> (Frazer and Lacey, 1993: 55)

These sentiments are echoed in the critique of a queer discourse which tacitly adapts male subjects as its implicit referent (Kader and Piontek, 1992: 9). The problem stems from those objectives, defined as either Rawlsian or 'queer', which are nevertheless similarly rooted in *liberal* idealism. The veil of ignorance is deemed unproblematic by Rawls because it is considered a necessary condition for the achievement of rationality and morality among subjects. Only rational, moral subjects – so designated, tautologically, by virtue of inhabiting the original position – are imbued with the unity of thought, or logic of identity, needed to achieve rational agreement on first principles of justice. Queer subjectivity, though not explicitly concerned with *rational* consensus, is none the less specifically designed to achieve the same inclusivity/universality and equality which are foundational to the liberal tradition. Hence the agent of 'equality' need not differ substantively from the agent of 'rationality', 'fairness' or 'justice': they are, in fact, the same. Moreover,

[t]o the extent that the attributes of liberal personhood and liberal justice are established by excluding certain beings and certain domains of activity from their purview, liberalism cannot fulfill its universalist vision but persistently reproduces the exclusions of humanist Man. The hollowness of liberalism's universalist promise, then, inheres . . . in its depoliticization of invidious social powers . . . [and] in its often cruel celebration of fictional sovereignty.

(Brown, 1995: 164)

A revelation of this magnitude is bound to have serious consequences for the inclusivity which is similarly integral to the production of queer subjectivity. Positioned rather precariously between the postmodern critique which spawned its creation, and the liberal strategies which it actively employs in an attempt to distinguish itself from its predecessors, the queer subject is subsequently constitutive not of a genuinely autonomous, anti-essentialist subject, but rather the unwitting *reproduction* of the very liberal humanist subject which it was originally intended to critique.

What's in a name?

If the queer subject is indeed a liberal subject, then to what extent have recent attempts to reappropriate 'queer' – through its positive resignification – been facilitated by the liberal premises which underlie queer subjectivity? My intent is to examine the role that liberalism plays in both the reappropriation of 'queer', however problematic, and the improbability of reappropriating other historically derisive epithets like 'nigger'. It is an undertaking requiring some familiarity with a past which must first be garnered through an etymology and history of 'queer'.

The word 'queer', derived from the German *quer*, meaning crooked or awry (Thorne, 1990: 413), did not acquire an overtly sexual connotation until the 1920s when it was commonly used to refer to male homosexuals (Beale, 1989: 359; Dunkling, 1990: 206; Simpson and Weiner, 1989: 1014). Although the terms

queer, fairy, and *faggot* were often used interchangeably . . . each term also had a more precise meaning among gay men. [For example], [b]y the 1910s and 1920s, the men who identified themselves as part of a distinct category of men primarily on the basis of their homosexual interest . . . usually called themselves *queer*. Essentially synonymous with 'homosexual,' *queer* presupposed the statistical normalcy – and normative character – of men's sexual interest in women; tellingly, queers referred to their counterparts as 'normal men' (or 'straight men') rather than as 'heterosexuals'.

(Chauncey, 1994: 15–16)

'Queer' thus enjoyed popular usage among homosexual men until it was gradually supplanted by 'gay', a process initiated during the 1930s[5] and virtually complete by the end of the following decade. 'Gay' generally reflected the sentiments
of younger men who criticized their elders for the continued use of a pejorative
term which emphasized their distinction from straight men who associated
'queerness' with gender deviance (Chauncey, 1994:19). Unlike earlier terms
which catalogued several *types* of homosexually active men, 'gay' amalgamated
them, 'deemphasiz[ing] their differences by emphasizing the *similarity* in character they had presumably demonstrated by their choice of male sexual partners'
(Chauncey, 1994: 20–1).

By the 1950s, 'queer', formerly used to distinguish a particular type of *male*
homosexual, now inferred both 'a homosexual of either sex' (Wentworth and
Flexner, 1975: 415), and an insulting slur that was taboo[6] in most standard use
(Wilson, 1993: 354). It is within the context of the term's historical degradation
that attempts to reappropriate 'queer' were first initiated by the activist group
'Queer Nation'. Established in 1990, and modelled after the political stratagems
of AIDS activists, Queer Nation was mandated to transform public sexual discourse (Berlant and Freeman, 1993: 198) by destabilizing both the boundaries
of public and private space and, consequently, the notion that sexuality need be
confined exclusively to the latter domain. Employing tactics which ranged from
the 'invasion' of straight bars and shopping malls, to staging 'kiss-ins' in designated public spaces, Queer Nation sought to demonstrate that the naturalization
of any site as 'heterosexual' was necessarily contingent upon the invisibility of
gays – hence the use of exhibitionism to render such spaces 'psychically unsafe
for unexamined heterosexuality' (Berlant and Freeman, 1993: 207–8).

Ironically, the name 'Queer Nation' was initially a joke, a 'temporary
moniker' which, once accustomed to, became a means for the unceremonious
redoubling of 'queer' back on to itself (Slagle, 1995: 94). Queer Nation's strategy of challenging hegemonic assumptions, through the feat of their reversal,
encouraged others to likewise invoke the 'Q-word' as an act of linguistic recla-
mation, essentially appropriating the term so as to negate its power to wound
(Epstein, 1994: 195), the goal being to repossess, invert and, ultimately, celebrate the hateful epithets thrown at gay people over the decades (Browning,
1993: 34).

What is then suggested by the attempt to reclaim 'queer' is a profound
appreciation for the relationship between language and subjectivity. As Judith
Butler notes (1993: 226),

> [t]he term 'queer' has operated as one linguistic practice whose purpose
> has been the shaming of the subject it names or, rather, the producing of a
> subject *through* that shaming interpellation. 'Queer' derives its force pre-
> cisely through the repeated invocation by which it has become linked to
> accusation, pathologization, insult. This is an invocation by which a social

bond among homophobic communities is formed through time. The interpellation echoes past interpellations, and binds the speakers, as if they
spoke in unison across time. In this sense, it is always an imaginary chorus
that taunts 'queer!'

Insofar as the epithet 'queer' produces a pathologized subject, its user is spon-
taneously produced as a symbol of 'the normative', a gatekeeper intended to
quell any incursion into the discursive boundaries of sexual legitimacy. The irony
here, of course, is that '[m]uch of the straight world has always needed the queers
it has sought to repudiate through the performative force of the term' (Butler,
1993: 223); one such example is provided by the gay community in early twentieth-century New York.[7]

> The process by which the normal world defined itself in opposition to the
> queer world was manifest in countless social interactions, for in its polic-
> ing of the gay subculture the dominant culture sought above all to police
> its own boundaries. . . . In defining the queer's transgressions against
> gender and sexual conventions, 'normal' men defined the boundaries of
> acceptable behaviour for anyone who would be normal; in attacking the
> queer they enforced those boundaries by reminding everyone of the penal-
> ties for violating them.
>
> (Chauncey, 1994:25–6)

It is as a result of these historical boundaries that 'queer' is defined in opposition
to the 'normal', rather than the 'heterosexual', thereby identifying normaliza-
tion, rather than simple intolerance, as the site of violence. The innovation of
'queer' as a strategic appellation thus inheres in its simultaneous critique of the
normal and its phobic manifestation: queer-bashing (Warner, 1991: 16).

But attempts to reclaim 'queer' have hardly been met with blanket enthusi-
asm. Indeed, for some, the very question of the term's emancipatory potential
warrants critical reflection rather than unbridled optimism, their reservations
exposing the ineluctable weaknesses of a strategy which is itself deemed problematic at best.

> 'What harm does "queer" do? A great deal. It tells both ourselves and
> heterosexuals that we are so fundamentally different from them that they
> couldn't possibly understand who we are and what we're about. It rein-
> forces the already all-pervasive notion that gay people lead lives that are
> totally unlike those led by straight people. That can only harm us.' For
> [some], the Queer Nation slogan 'we're here, we're queer, get used to it'
> provokes the response, 'they never will'.
>
> (Penn, 1995: 31)

For others, this response confirms not the futility of reappropriating 'queer' but rather a fundamental misunderstanding of what this project entails.

> ['Queer'] represents a very contested site . . . partly because it started out as a pejorative term and has been consciously reclaimed as an honorific term; partly because it's an experiment . . . with finding a non-gender-specific name for a variety of sexual experiences and practices. Part of what interests me a lot about it is that in reclaiming the term, I don't think that what's being done is to disavow a lot of the negative stereotypes associated with it, but rather to reinhabit them in different ways.
>
> (Chinn et al., 1992: 80–1)

The ability to 'reinhabit' and therefore renounce negative stereotypes, via 'queer' subjectivity, mirrors the Rawlsian subject's ability to transcend the 'constraints' of race, class, gender, etc. by virtue of inhabiting the original position. What is presumed, in both cases, is a liberal subject whose sovereignty is implicit in its own volition – a phenomenon manifested in the queer subject as the capacity to choose not only *whether* to 'reinhabit' a term but also *how* to do so. To reinhabit 'queer', on a semiotic level, is therefore to sever the fixed/determined relationship between the signifier and the signified – the denotative term and its negative connotation. The ruptured association is then supplanted with a subject whose textual indeterminacy facilitates its slide along a chain of signifiers, thus freeing it to explore a variety of eccentric possibilities or simply to pursue the pleasure of the text (Morton, 1993: 135).

Given the linguistic, and hence political reappropriation of 'queer', one might reasonably anticipate the same result for a word like 'nigger'[8] which shares a similar history of brutality and shame. To the contrary, however, attempts to resignify 'nigger' are undermined to the very extent that they are modelled on the reappropriation of 'queer'. The remainder of this article examines how the same liberal premises – specifically equality, liberty and autonomy – which facilitate the reappropriation of 'queer' necessarily inhibit any attempt to do so with 'nigger'.

The American use of the word 'nigger', derived from *niger* (the Latin word for black), dates back to 1700 where it appears (as *niger*) in the diary of Samuel Sewall (Mencken, 1962: 628–9; Morris and Morris, 1817: 409). Other accounts trace the word's origin to the sixteenth-century northern English pronunciation, *neger*,[9] or its Irish dialect, *naygur* (Major, 1994: 319; Mencken, 1962: 629). Although the term's origin may be a matter for debate, the consensus regarding its historical connotation is unequivocal: 'nigger' is an insulting, contemptuous and racist slur, particularly when invoked by whites towards blacks as a linguistic relic of bondage (Dunkling, 1990: 184–5; Litwack, 1979: 252; Simpson and Weiner, 1989: 402; Thorne, 1990: 360). As with the production of a shamed subject through the interpellation of 'queer', 'nigger' produces a pathologized subject through the performative force of its invocation. The epithet, 'nigger', signifies abjection, blackness and evil among a host of other characteristics which collectively attest to its subject's inferiority. Through its abject alterity, the 'nigger' provides the discursive foundation on which claims to racial supremacy, and its corollary rewards, are both made and legitimated.[10]

But, as one commander of an antebellum black regiment found, the term's designation as a racial epithet hardly precluded its use among blacks themselves: 'White was the tint of nobility; black the symbol of degradation. If one coloured man wanted to insult another, he called him a nigger. To call him "a charcoal nigger" was the blackest insult of all, making him the furthest remove from the nobility of whiteness' (Litwack, 1979: 254). However, the use of the epithet would prove more than an ephemeral tendency among post-emancipatory blacks. In 1939, Lucius Harper (managing editor of the Chicago *Defender*) observed that '[nigger] is a common expression among the ordinary Negroes and is used frequently in conversation between them. It carries no odium or sting when used by themselves, but they object keenly to whites using it because it conveys the spirit of hate, discrimination and prejudice' (Mencken, 1962: 626). Thus, in contrast to its one-dimensional use by whites, when employed by blacks the term 'nigger' had a variety of connotations ranging from an indictment of slavish personalities to an expression of endearment which conveyed undertones of warmth and goodwill while serving as an ironic reminder of a shared past (Dunkling, 1990: 184; Litwack, 1979: 254; Major, 1994: 320).

The somewhat modest attempts to resignify 'nigger' in the past have recently been rejuvenated by the popularity of 'Hip Hop'.[11] For some members of Hip Hop culture, the term 'nigger' is no longer exclusively associated with derision, as evidenced by its general substitution for words like 'friend', 'brother', 'man', 'person', 'girl' or 'woman' (Major, 1994: 320). Rather, the word 'nigger', now pronounced and spelled 'nigga', suggests a broad spectrum of possible interpretations wherein the phrase 'She my main nigga' becomes an acceptable reference to a close friend (Smitherman, 1994: 167).

As with the attempt to reappropriate 'queer', efforts to do so with 'nigger' or its Hip Hop variant, 'nigga', have met with staunch criticism.

> [T]he frequent use of *nigga* in Rap Music . . . and throughout Black Culture generally, where the word takes on meanings other than the historical negative, has created a linguistic dilemma in the crossover world and in the African American community. Widespread controversy rages about the use of *nigga* among Blacks – especially the pervasive public use of the term – and about whether or not whites can have license to use the N-word with the many different meanings that Blacks give to it.
>
> (Smitherman, 1994: 168)

It would seem that the dilemma lies in denying whites licence to a term which arguably describes them too, the rationale being that '[e]ven white people can be

niggers [because] "nigger" does not imply race'. In reference to the US government, for example, Rap artist Queen Latifah was quoted in *Newsweek* as saying:
'Those niggers don't know what the fuck they doing' (Major, 1994: 320). In fact,
the inclusion of whites under the banner 'nigger' may usher in the incipient term
'wigga' or 'wigger'.

> [L]iterally, a white *nigga*, in the Hip Hop sense, [the 'wigger' is] a European
> American who strongly identifies with African American Culture – e.g.,
> baggy jeans . . . into Spike Lee films . . . and Rapper Ice-T. [W]iggers 'don't
> just appreciate black Culture, they have absorbed it. They consider Black
> Culture their culture. . . . Wiggers have turned stereotypes upside down.
> They've taken a racial epithet, reworked it and come up with a word that
> is not an insult, just a description'.
>
> (Smitherman, 1994:168)

Thus, it appears that with the advent of 'wigger', the resignification of 'nigger'
comes full circle. Once a term of opprobrium, 'nigger' has now ostensibly
become a race-neutral subject position, fully accessible to all who choose to
occupy it. Whether the epithet is 'reworked' or, in the case of 'queer', 'reinhab-
ited', its reappropriation is accomplished via the autonomy of a willed subject –
a liberal subject which is free to occupy the subject position of its choosing
without regard for the exigencies of race, class, sexuality or gender.

However, upon closer examination, the logic of liberalism appears to be
more abortive than supportive of this resignification. For instance, the claim that
'nigga' is now devoid of all racial connotation remains unsubstantiated since the
term is squarely situated within a Hip Hop lexicon which is itself a definitively
black cultural form. Nor can 'wigger' be successfully invoked as an example of
the inclusivity and, hence, neutrality of 'nigger' because it explicitly signifies the
whiteness of the subject to which it refers. In fact, the very invocation of 'wigger'
ironically racializes as *white* particular occupants of a subject position which is
purported to be race neutral. Moreover, since the term 'wigga' apparently has
no lexical complement – that is, a term (most logically 'bigga') which denotes a
black 'nigga' – one may surmise that such a term would be obviated by its own
redundancy: 'nigga' always already signifies blackness.

Given the racialization of 'nigger', attempts to reclaim the epithet cannot rest
on the liberal premise of equality – a condition of sameness – since the term is
exemplary not of equality, but its conceptual opposite: difference (Brown, 1995:
153). Far from being a neutral subject position which ensures the liberty and
autonomy of its inhabitants, 'nigger' merely reinscribes the difference which the
queer subject and its liberal humanist prototype are perpetually trying to mask.
And it is this discrepancy in their capacity to mask difference – via their relative
proximity to, or distance from, the liberal subject – which permits the reappropriation of 'queer' while 'nigger' remains taboo in the cultural mainstream.

Perhaps nowhere was the extent of the term's taboo status more evident than during the 1995 murder trial of O. J. Simpson. Repeatedly billed by the media as 'the trial of the century', the defence case hinged largely on their capacity to destroy the credibility of a key prosecution witness, Detective Mark Fuhrman. During a particularly memorable exchange, F. Lee Bailey – the senior member of Simpson's 'dream team' of attorneys – asked Fuhrman if he had, within the past decade, ever referred to an African-American person as a 'nigger'. In the face of Fuhrman's categorical denial, the defence produced a series of audiotapes on which the detective could be heard using the word a total of forty-one times. Fuhrman was subsequently impeached and his credibility as a seasoned police veteran was quickly supplanted by the image of a racist white cop who was out to frame a black defendant.

When highlights of the Bailey/Fuhrman exchange were rebroadcast a year later on the television programme *Hard Copy*,[12] the use of the word 'nigger' was noticeably absent. The censorship of the term, performed in a manner much like the deletion of a common expletive, raises some compelling questions. How do we explain the decision to censor the term in light of the type of programme on which the segment was aired – a tabloid television show whose primary journalistic objectives are titillation and shock value? Who did the censors presume would be offended by the word's utterance? Was it those who are so named by the epithet or was it the white, middle-class, liberal North American audience who at once vilified Fuhrman and yet metaphorically sat co-accused, the horror of Fuhrman's racism raising all too unsettling questions about the possibility of their own?

The 1996 perjury trial which ensued as a result of Fuhrman's testimony provides a slightly different example of what is essentially the same phenomenon. One week after his trial, Fuhrman appeared on the ABC news magazine *Prime-Time Live*[13] where not once – during an interview which revolved around his use of the word 'nigger' – did he or his interviewer, Diane Sawyer, ever say the word. In fact, the only thing more peculiar than the half hour spent discussing a word which is never spoken are the lengths to which Sawyer and Fuhrman go to avoid doing so:

SAWYER: You could not forget having, forty-one times, said a word that is so charged it is designed to wound and exert superiority over and do harm to people . . .

FUHRMAN: Well I did. When I heard my words on those tapes, I probably felt worse than anybody could feel. Not because I forgot about 'em. Because I did 'em.

SAWYER: And to all of the listeners tonight, in this country who are black, a final word about what you think that word does mean, and when it should be used.

FUHRMAN: It shouldn't be used. And I'm sorry to be the one to bring it to the forefront in such a grossly insensitive way.

By directing Fuhrman's comments to the programme's *black* audience, Sawyer infers a tacit knowledge of the epithet's association with this particular group of people. The initially unidentified *persons*, deemed most vulnerable to injury, are now named through the force of their isolation from the remainder of Sawyer's, presumably unafflicted, audience. Thus declarations as to the race neutrality and inclusivity of 'nigger' would appear to ring hollow here insofar as the epithet's 'victims' are constituted via their *exclusion* from a larger mainstream in which both Sawyer and Fuhrman assume implicit membership.

Interestingly enough, both Fuhrman's use of the word 'nigger', and the media circus which was its aftermath, did much to overshadow the significance of another trial which took place earlier the same year. In 1996, Bernard Goetz – dubbed 'the subway vigilante' – became the defendant in a fifty-million-dollar civil suit stemming from the 1984 shooting of four black teenagers. Presumably in an attempt to establish racism (rather than self-defence) as the motive for the shootings, the prosecution noted that Goetz had used racial slurs towards blacks and 'hispanics' three years prior to the incident. While Goetz, unlike Fuhrman, did not deny using the slurs, his defence was that he was on angel dust at the time and had since expressed regret over their utterance.[14]

What is evident in each of these, albeit sensational, examples is a complete disavowal of the word 'nigger'. Whether it is censored or excused as the anomalous product of a dissociative state, those who invoke the term are also loath to own it, and herein lies another obstacle to its reappropriation. How is it possible to reclaim a term that cannot be spoken, the severity of whose proscription necessitates its very euphemism? And yet how do we reconcile this proscription – that which dare not speak its name – with a common knowledge of the term's daily invocation, whether whispered, spoken, screamed or yelled?

Conclusion

Surely these difficulties are not unique to the resignification of any one epithet but are also characteristic of others which fail to affirm liberal humanism's sovereign subject. Thus while the reappropriation of 'queer' has garnered institutional sanction – as evidenced by the rapidly emerging field of queer theory/studies – we are unlikely to witness a corresponding proliferation of 'dyke' or 'faggot' studies. Although the term 'dyke' has been reclaimed for many lesbians, perhaps much more so than the use of 'fag' among gay men, both terms nevertheless signify gender in much the same way that 'nigger' or other racial epithets signify race. In so doing they contravene liberalism's principled commitment to equality and the view that such differences constitute morally irrelevant categories.

It is then perhaps most fitting that the refusal to be labelled 'morally irrelevant' – or banished to a depoliticized periphery whose amorphous and homogeneous citizens are crowded under the banner of 'diversity' – has inspired the marginalized to re-evaluate their shamed and collective history of exclusion. With the realization that categories are historically produced comes an understanding that their marginalized or deviant status is integral to the legitimation of the 'normal'. In defiance of the terms of the dominant discourse, 'dykes', 'faggots', 'coloured girls' and 'natives' have become the reappropriated identity categories of the marginalized, just as their (public) use had begun to fade beneath the veneer of political correctness (Brown, 1995: 53).

The irony is, of course, that such categories are hardly irrelevant, morally or otherwise. In fact, as liberalism's claim to a universal identity grows more emphatic, so does the need for this declaration to be mandated or *imposed* (Goldberg, 1993: 6). As Marx argues in *On the Jewish Question*, the dissolution of difference is formal rather than substantive in that the state only exists insofar as such differences are presupposed in civil society. Thus the state is not only cognizant of its politicization, but 'manifests its universality only in opposition to [difference]' (1978: 33). Hence the importance of examining these constructed differences through a genealogy which interrogates both the naturalized, abstract character of the liberal humanist subject and its aversion to theorizing marginalized identities as the *effects* of power. Within this context, liberalism's uncompromising denial of self, the ineluctable price of political membership, guarantees only equal blindness from – as opposed to equal recognition before – a state which simultaneously depoliticizes and presupposes individuality (Brown, 1995: 56–7).

The more amenable to diversity liberalism professes to be, the less tolerant of difference it becomes (Goldberg, 1993: 6). Such is the nature of the persistent dilemma whose resolution constitutes an illusionary choice between either the denial or tolerance of difference, options both equally problematic and identical in outcome.

> The liberal would assume away the difference in otherness, maintaining thereby the dominance of a presumed sameness, the universally imposed similarity in identity. The paradox is perpetuated: The commitment to tolerance turns only on modernity's 'natural inclination' to *in*tolerance; acceptance of otherness presupposes as it at once necessitates 'delegitimation of the other'.
>
> (Goldberg, 1993: 7)

In this we see the paradox that haunts not only queer subjectivity, but any other politicized identity which similarly invokes liberalism as its underlying premise. 'Queer' may designate a flexible space which accommodates various and fluctuating positions (Alexander, 1993: 3), but the ambiguity of 'queer', much like that of the original position, creates a space wherein diversity may be tolerated only through its denial. The danger is therefore in seeking a form of political recognition which merely resubordinates the subject on which such claims are founded.

The interrogation of queer subjectivity should not be interpreted as a call for its categorical dismissal. To the contrary, it is not simply a question of whether or not ostensibly subversive political strategies truly are subversive, but rather '*what kind* of politicization, produced out of and inserted into *what kind* of political context, might perform such subversion'[15] (Brown, 1995:55). Recognizing the significance of both specificity and context is a necessary precaution against the unreflective and unexamined adaptation of liberalism's political promise. And to the extent that queer theory fails to take such precautions, we may only speculate as to the implications of this refusal not only for the future of queer studies but for its capacity to forge political alliances with other marginalized subjectivities.

Acknowledgement

I would like to thank Lealle Ruhl, Mariana Valverde and Janice Hill for their help in bringing this article to fruition.

Notes

1   For an in-depth discussion, see Judith Butler (1991) and Diana Fuss (1991).

2   Teresa de Lauretis contends that the differences between 'gays' and 'lesbians' are elided more often than implied by the phrase 'lesbian and gay'. Queer theory therefore endeavours to eschew the ideological liabilities which are assumed via the uncritical adaptation of either term (1991: v–vi).

3   Wendy Brown notes that '[l]iberalism is a nonsystematic and porous doctrine subject to historical change and local variation. However, insofar as liberalism takes its definitional shape from an ensemble of relatively abstract ontological and political claims, it is also possible to speak of liberalism in a generic fashion, unnuanced by time or cultural inflection' (1995: 142).

4   My use of the term 'space' throughout this article refers not simply to the area engaged metaphorically by an intentionally nebulous subject, but also encompasses the theoretical arena in which such a subject position can even be imagined. The intent is to emphasize rather than obscure the theoretical premises which ground concretely an otherwise seemingly abstract subject.

5   The demise of 'queer' at this time was undoubtedly exacerbated by media hysteria which linked homicidal 'sex deviates' to threats against the nation's women and children (Chauncey, 1994: 19).

6   Indeed, one dictionary entry for the term came complete with the following caveat: 'So strong is the effect of this [i.e. derogatory] meaning that you must be careful to use context to make clear and unambiguous any other sense of this word you might use' (Wilson, 1993: 354).

7   Although New York was 'regarded [by homosexuals] as the "gay capital" of the

nation for nearly a century', activities here were most likely *prototypical* rather than *typical* of other urban centres (Chauncey, 1994: 28).

8   The use of the term 'negro' was also a controversial issue among blacks, particularly during the 1950s and 1960s. For more on the debate surrounding the propriety of terminology, see Bennett, jun. (1970) and Smith (1992).

9   This was itself an attempt to pronounce 'negro', the Spanish word for black (Major, 1994: 319).

10   For an analysis of this binary within the context of colonialism, imperialism and slavery, see Bhabha (1990); Brantlinger (1986); Fanon (1963, 1967) and JanMohamed (1986).

11   'Hip Hop' refers to black 'urban youth culture, associated with rap music, break dancing [and] graffiti; [it is] probably derived from the [1970s] partying style of DJs playing hype ("hip") music at a dance ("hop")' (Smitherman, 1994: 134).

12   This episode aired on 7 March 1996.

13   This episode aired on 8 October 1996.

14   *Prime News*. CNN. 8 April 1996.

15   Comedian Chris Rock's use of the term 'nigger' during a standup routine may indeed elicit genuine laughter from his predominantly black audience, just as lesbian and bisexual women may frequent establishments which they themselves have dubbed 'dyke bars', but each example represents a psychically safe space where the emotional history of the epithet is mitigated or, at the very least, shared. The contingency of either space becomes glaringly apparent the moment one steps outside of the sociocultural and geographical boundaries which constitute its constructed borders. The argument is therefore not that the invocation of 'queer' or 'nigger' can never truly signify an instance of subversive activity but that such instances must be acknowledged as contextually specific rather than offered as irrefutable evidence of each term's universal and legitimate reappropriation.

References

Alexander, Doty (1993) *Making Things Perfectly Queer*, Minneapolis: University of Minnesota Press.

Beale, Paul (ed.) (1989) *A Concise Dictionary of Slang and Unconventional English*, Berlin: Langenscheidt.

Benhabib, Seyla (1987) 'The generalized and the concrete other', in Seyla Benhabib and Drucilla Cornell (eds) *Feminism as Critique*, Minneapolis: University of Minnesota Press.

Bennett, Lerone, jun. (1979) 'What's in a name?', in Peter Rose (ed.) *Americans From Africa*, New York: Atherton Press.

Berlant, Lauren and Freeman, Elizabeth (1993) 'Queer nationality', in Michael Warner (ed.) *Fear Of A Queer Planet*, Minneapolis: University of Minnesota Press.

Bhabha, Homi K. (1990) 'Interrogating identity: the postcolonial prerogative', in David Theo Goldberg (ed.) *Anatomy Of Racism*, Minneapolis: University of Minnesota Press.

Brantlinger, Patrick (1986) 'Victorians and Africans: the genealogy of the myth of the dark continent', in Henry Louis Gates, jun. (ed.) *'Race,' Writing, and Difference*, Chicago, IL: The University of Chicago Press.

Brown, Wendy (1995) *States of Injury*, Princeton, NJ: Princeton University Press.

Browning, Frank (1993) *The Culture of Desire*, New York: Crown Publishers.

Butler, Judith (1990) *Gender Trouble*, New York: Routledge.

—— (1991) 'Imitation and gender insubordination', in Diana Fuss (ed.) *Inside/Out*, New York: Routledge.

—— (1993) *Bodies That Matter*, New York: Routledge.

Chauncey, George (1994) *Gay New York*, New York: Basic Books.

Chinn, Sarah *et al*. (1992) 'A talk with Eve Kosofsky Sedgwick', *Pretext*, 13(3–4): 79–95.

De Lauretis, Teresa (1991) 'Queer theory: lesbian and gay sexualities; an introduction', *Differences*, 3(2): iii–xviii.

Dunkling, Leslie (1990) *A Dictionary of Epithets and Terms of Address*, London: Routledge.

Epstein, Steven (1994) 'A queer encounter: sociology and the study of sexuality', *Sociological Theory*, 12(2): 188–202.

Fanon, Frantz (1963) *The Wretched of the Earth*, trans. Constance Farrington, New York: Grove Weidenfeld.

—— (1967) *Black Skin, White Masks*, trans. Charles Lam, New York: Grove Weidenfeld.

Frazer, Elizabeth and Lacey, Nicola (1993) *The Politics of Community*, Toronto: University of Toronto Press.

Fuss, Diana (1991) 'Inside/out', in her (ed.) *Inside/Out*, New York: Routledge.

Goldberg, David Theo (1993) *Racist Culture*. Oxford: Blackwell.

Hennessy, Rosemary (1994) 'Queer theory, left politics', *Rethinking Marxism*, 7 (3): 85–111.

JanMohamed, Abdul R. (1986) 'The economy of Manichean allegory: the function of racial difference in colonialist literature', in Henry Louis Gates, jun. (ed.) *'Race,' Writing, and Difference*, Chicago, IL: The University of Chicago Press.

Jeffreys, Sheila (1994) 'The queer disappearance of lesbians: sexuality in the academy', *Women's Studies International Forum*, 17(5): 459–72.

Kader, Cheryl and Piontek, Thomas (1992) 'Introduction', *Discourse*, 15(1): 5–10.

Litwack, Leon F. (1979) *Been In The Storm So Long*, New York: Vintage Books.

Major, Clarence (1994) *Juba to Jive*, New York: Penguin Books.

Marx, Karl (1978) 'On the Jewish Question', in Robert C. Tucker (ed.) *The Marx-Engels Reader* (2nd edn), New York: Norton.

Mencken, H. L. (1962) *The American Language*, New York: Alfred A. Knopf.

Morris, William and Morris, Mary (1817) *Morris Dictionary of Word and Phrase Origins* (2nd edn), New York: Harper & Row.

Morrison, Margaret (1992) 'Laughing with queers in my eyes: proposing "queer rhetoric(s)" and introducing a queer issue', *Pretext*, 13(3–4): 11–36.

Morton, Donald (1993) 'The politics of queer theory in the (post)modern moment', *Genders*, 17 (Fall): 121–50.

—— (1995) 'Birth of the cyberqueer', *PMLA*, 110(3): 369–81.

Penn, Donna (1995) 'Queer: theorizing politics and history', *Radical History Review*, 62 (Spring): 24–42.

Rawls, John (1971) *A Theory of Justice*, Cambridge: Belknap Press.

Sandel, Michael (1982) *Liberalism and the Limits of Justice*, Cambridge: Cambridge University Press.

Simpson, J. A. and Weiner, E.S.C. (eds) (1989) *The Oxford English Dictionary* (2nd edn), Oxford: Clarendon Press.

Slagle, R. Anthony (1995) 'In defense of queer nation: from identity politics to a politics of difference', *Western Journal of Communication*, 59 (Spring): 85–102.

Smith, Tom W. (1992) 'Changing racial labels: from "colored" to "negro" to "black" to "African American"', *Public Opinion Quarterly*, 56(4): 496–514.

Smitherman, Geneva (1994) *Black Talk*, Boston, MA: Houghton Mifflin.

Thorne, Tony (1990) *Dictionary of Contemporary Slang*, London: Bloomsbury.

Warner, Michael (1991) 'Introduction: fear of a queer planet', *Social Text*, 29: 3–17.

Watney, Simon (1994) 'Queer epistemology: activism, "outing," and the politics of sexual identities', *Critical Quarterly*, 36(1): 13–27.

Wentworth, Harold and Flexner, Stuart Berg (eds) (1975) *Dictionary of American Slang* (2nd supplemented edn), New York: Thomas Y. Crowell.

Wilson, Kenneth G. (1993) *The Columbia Guide to Standard American English*, New York: Columbia University Press.

Paul Mason Fotsch

CONTESTING URBAN FREEWAY STORIES: RACIAL POLITICS AND THE O. J. CHASE

Abstract

This article first considers how the O. J. Simpson freeway chase, the popular film *Speed* and television programmes such as *Cops* help construct the space of the automobile and freeway as a shelter from racially marked urban dangers, supporting deeply racialized politics in the United States. This politics is exemplified by the success of large capital interests in aligning themselves with the white working and middle class to form what Thomas and Mary Edsall call a top-down coalition or what might be seen in Gramscian terms as a hegemonic bloc.

Significant to enabling this coalition was the postwar subsidization of the suburban white life-style, including the construction of interstate freeways. The other side of white suburban security was the entrenchment of poor people of colour in central cities, and the second section of this article describes the role freeway construction played in this entrenchment. Freeway and suburban segregation also creates the distancing which allows the distorted narratives of the inner city described in the first section to become widely accepted.

The third part of the article returns to the O. J. Simpson chase, this time to consider both the possibilities and limits the freeway can create for public expressions. While the freeways may make older forms of face-to-face contact more difficult and increase the segregation of communication between different socioeconomic groups, its highly monitored nature also enables expressions which trouble the dominant view of the city. Still, the ability of these momentary voices of dissonance to inspire a strong challenge to this dominant view and its corresponding politics is questionable.

CULTURAL STUDIES 13(1) 1999, 110–137

Keywords

Los Angeles; segregation; crime shows; mass media; public sphere; cars

O N 17 JUNE 1994 MILLIONS of people watched a white Ford Bronco containing O. J. Simpson drive at 35 to 45 miles per hour along the Los Angeles freeways followed by ten patrol cars: this event contains rich possibilities for the examination of American culture, but I wish to focus on it solely as a moment in the cultural history of a US urban transportation form. The automobile/freeway form has impacted greatly on daily life, and this event, rather than being wholly bizarre as many news reports described it, in many ways embodies the freeways' evolving impact. Most importantly, the O. J. event displayed the social isolatability of the freeway and the auto, the distancing it allows between driver and surrounding environment. On the one hand, as a 'victim', O. J. was protected by the ability of Al Cowlings to drive continuously without interference from crossing traffic or unfriendly pedestrians. Although pedestrians did come on the freeway, the police shielded the Bronco in a way they could not once it left the freeway and entered surface streets. On the other hand, as an 'accused killer', O. J. was encircled, contained and isolated from surrounding neighbourhoods. In being viewed by millions, this isolating feature of the freeway reinscribed itself into popular discourses found elsewhere in US society. These discourses legitimate social and racial hierarchies that divide contemporary metropolitan regions of the US.

The freeway is part of dominant narratives which view African-American and Latino residents of the central city as largely responsible for the conditions of poverty and violence amidst which they live. In the first part of this article I explore how the freeway takes on these narratives by being embedded in contemporary media technologies such as the television, radio and car phone, an embeddedness exemplified by the O. J. Simpson chase. In the second two sections, I propose two counternarratives to the dominant freeway narrative outlined in the first section. In the second part, the auto freeway transportation system is read historically by showing how the construction of this system actually helped to create the ghettos which – as part of media-constructed narratives sketched in the first section – it now helps to legitimate. In the third part, I return to the O. J. event and briefly discuss perhaps the most unusual aspect of the event: the extraordinary number of people who gathered on the freeway to wave and cheer. Unlike with the isolating aspects of the event discussed in the first section, there were not as many ready narratives to understand the freeway's sudden role as a public meeting place. I suggest the freeway is part of a contemporary, highly mediated, public forum which might further help to sustain the social divisions discussed in the first two sections of the article.

The freeway as urban shield

The narrative of isolation surrounding the urban freeway begins with its connection to the suburban goal of escaping urban populations. Historically, the movement to exclusive suburbs has come from a desire to escape not just the crowding and industrial pollution of the central city but also the type of people who were increasingly moving into the city. At the turn of the century, advocates of the suburbs linked both the poor living conditions and the radicalism that led to strikes and anarchist bombings to the culture of new immigrants (Marsh, 1990: 69–71). Today, suburbs are both racially and economically diverse and include, for example, African-Americans who live in Oceanside north of San Diego, Chinese immigrants in Monterey Park just west of downtown LA, and Mexican Americans who are a significant part of several cities in Orange county. But more importantly, between and within suburbs and cities, tremendous racial and economic segregation continues to exist.[1] William Sharpe and Leonard Wallock argue that a reason for this segregation remains 'the wish to escape racial and class intermingling' (1994: 9).

The escape from these populations to the suburbs was first enabled by rail transportation, but going by rail required contact with residents of the city which suburbanization intended to avoid. The auto allowed suburban residents to avoid contact with urban residents but suburbanites who went to the central city for work, shopping or entertainment still frequently had to drive through inner city neighbourhoods. The freeway allowed even further distancing from the residents of these neighbourhoods by allowing drivers to go through them on the way downtown without having to stop or see anyone.[2] Thus, the freeway both enables the suburb to be at a distance from the space of urban populations and embodies this distancing in its design.

The O. J. chase made clear that not only can the freeway shield the driver from urban populations, it can also help shield 'dangerous drivers' from others. During the chase the freeway was closed off both in front and behind the Ford Bronco, and there was a noticeable increase in tension when the Bronco left the freeway for the 'surface streets'. In contrast, on public transportation, if one person makes trouble, all the passengers have to deal with it, whether this 'troublemaker' is simply playing a radio loudly or hassling the bus driver. A dramatic example took place in December 1993 when Colin Ferguson shot twenty-three people, killing five on the Long Island Railroad (Faison, 1993). This example shows how 'the violence of the city' cannot be contained on public transit. In contrast, on the freeway an automobile can easily be isolated and prevented from impacting on surrounding drivers.

Of course, the freeway is not always a completely protected space, as became evident several years ago when people began to fear being shot on the LA freeway. More recently, in the autumn of 1996, the rear windows of over 200 cars were shattered by unknown projectiles. The perpetrators were later identified as 'gang members' on probation (Allen, 1996). Although this type of accident is very rare compared to accidents with other drivers, it has done much more to create a fear of driving LA's freeways (Pringle, 1996). Here, the purpose of the freeway as a shield has deteriorated; holes have literally been shot through the shield. Yet the fact that these incidents received such widespread publicity precisely indicates how people expect the freeway to be a space free of dangers characteristic of the city.[3]

The O. J. event also demonstrates how the feeling of safety and isolation linked to the freeway is extended by the media technology which surrounds it. First, helicopter television is in part a creation of the freeway, since the demand for traffic monitoring requires helicopters. The helicopter is one element of a complex technological monitoring system which includes video cameras and radar that can capture traffic violators and mechanical counters which aid in tracking delays. Yet the helicopter's role in monitoring traffic has been extended to the monitoring of criminals or potential criminals, as was seen not only in the O. J. Simpson chase but also in the coverage of the LA uprising.[4] Since the O. J. chase it has become routine to compare televised freeway chases to the event. In fact, the helicopter televised chase has become a genre in itself. For example, on 29 May 1997 the lead story on all three San Diego local television news programmes was the televised pursuit of a suspected bank robber that took place on the Southern California freeways; in the story much attention was paid to the methods the police used to pursue and stop the driver with tire spikes while keeping the other freeway drivers shielded from danger. The televised chase is also a frequent element of the television programme *Cops*, where they have filmed episodes based entirely from the helicopter. Furthermore, a video of 'Best Chases' has been advertised for sale during *Cops*, and programmes such as *Choppers on Patrol* and *World's Scariest Police Chases* have been broadcast on Fox and the Discovery Channel.

These programmes, like the O. J. chase, make clear the ideal manner in which the helicopter can isolate and follow the chase of a dangerous driver. This is done in a way that could not take place on a commuter rail system. For example, the isolation of the dangerous passenger within the LIRR train as the shooting took place was not possible from the distant safety of the helicopter. The helicopter provides both an enhanced vision of what takes place, by providing a perspective of what is immediately surrounding the driver on all sides, and it also creates an additional distancing that television already provides; not only does one not have to fear for oneself, one does not have to fear for the person who is providing the information. The distancing role of the media can be traced back to the newspaper: Walter Benjamin saw the newspapers' goal precisely to distance the reader from the shock of directly experiencing what takes place in the world. 'If it were the intention of the press to have the reader assimilate the information it supplies as part of his own experience, it would not achieve its purpose. But its intention is just the opposite, and it is achieved: to isolate what happens from the realm in which it could affect the experience of the reader' (Benjamin, 1969: 158). Another illustration of this can be found in the traffic broadcast. Here the broadcaster announces accidents on the freeway not so that one may share in concern for those who have been injured, but so that the driver may avoid the accident and take another route.

This parallel distancing of the media and the freeway is described by Margaret Morse in an essay entitled 'The ontology of everyday distraction'. She argues that the television, freeway and shopping mall together create a distancing effect that allow the 'postmodern development of what (Walter) Benjamin called the "*phantasmagoria of the interior*," a mixture of levels of consciousness and objects of attention' (Morse, 1990: 201). In contrast to the largely distractive character of this distancing experience which Morse describes, I am suggesting that the distancing has an important narrative content concerning the dangerous character of the city which the freeway, television and mall[5] are distancing one from. To the extent that O. J. was seen as a black man with a gun,[6] he symbolized a danger of the inner city which needed to be isolated and contained.

Like the O. J. chase, the film *Speed* demonstrates how the freeway and its surrounding communication technologies isolate and contain danger while at the same time aiding its construction into a television format. In the film, the bus which is carrying a bomb that will explode if it goes below 55 mph is directed on to the freeway where it can maintain a high speed and be isolated from other traffic. The helicopter initially plays a crucial role in directing the bus off and back on to the freeway where it can avoid traffic. But as, predictably, the bus begins to be monitored by the many television helicopters, communication from the helicopter is no longer an asset. Instead, the helicopter broadcasts appear to heighten the crisis by preventing the police from making any rescue attempt. On the one hand, this shows that helicopter coverage of the freeway is not always an asset in providing safety. At the same time, it reaffirms the continuous impact which helicopter TV has on the experience of the freeway.

The technology of car phones also has an impact on the space of the freeway. In the O. J. chase it was used to maintain contact with Al Cowlings, the driver of the Bronco, reaffirming the distant monitoring of the television. The car phone plays a similar role in the film *Speed*. When the hero, played by Keanu Reeves, realizes the bus has a bomb on it, he must hijack a car to chase after it.[7] This car happens to have a car phone in it and the hero asks the driver to call 911. Here, the ability to call for help from one's car on the freeway demonstrates an additional sense of safety created by the car phone. Car and cellular phones are marketed on their ability to help drivers in distress. They provide a particular feeling of safety for those who own them, but owners can also and are encouraged to help others by calling 911 at no charge. This creates the image that one can help someone else or, equally important, report any activity which looks suspicious, while remaining within the protection of one's own car; thus the car phone adds to the surveying potential of the freeway.

The danger to be contained in the film *Speed* is marked as urban primarily through passengers on the bus; the film makes clear that the one time the freeway cannot shield someone from urban danger is when one is taking mass transit in the form of an express bus. While the freeway isolates the bus from the surrounding neighbourhoods and side-streets, those on the bus must deal with the poor and disenfranchised who are part of urban neighbourhoods and are most likely to ride the bus. This is particularly true in Los Angeles where those who can afford it usually drive a car. In the film, bus riders must confront first a man with a gun – presumably a Latino without papers to prove his residency – but more centrally, the threat of being blown up by a man who is not even on the bus.[8] In short, while the freeway signals a sense of safety and distance in the film, mass transit signals danger. But even more important for my argument, because the bus is marked as something the urban poor ride, as with the O. J. chase, the film places the freeway within a narrative which views the inner city as dangerous and requiring isolation.

The freeways' place amidst urban danger is also made dramatically clear in the film *Falling Down*. The film begins with the protagonist, Bill Ferguson, abandoning his car while stuck in a freeway traffic jam and climbing a hill which isolates the freeway from a neighbourhood referred to in the movie merely as 'gangland'. One police officer in the film calls the neighbourhood a 'shit hole'. The neighbourhood is filled with abandoned lots and graffiti-covered walls, and after an altercation with two Chicano gang members, Bill becomes a target of a drive-by shooting. The film follows Bill's violent rampage across LA as he walks 'home' to see his ex-wife and daughter in Venice Beach. The rampage is apparently provoked by the loss of his job and his inability to see his daughter, but it is his frustration with the freeway traffic jam that is the immediate trigger. Again, as with the freeway shootings and window smashings, the freeway is failing to perform its function of isolation. On it, Bill is caught within the disturbing and foreign elements of the city, from the poor immigrants listening to a Spanish language radio station, to the wealthy businessmen screaming into their car phones. But it is the city off the freeway – the Korean merchant who 'can't speak English' and the gang members who demand he respect their territory – that escalates his behaviour into violence. It is this image of the 'inner city' which the freeway and auto usually shield from the driver's view.

The narratives about the inner city found in the O. J. chase and the films *Speed* and *Falling Down* are made even more clear if we consider how they fit within an enormous genre of film and television chase scenes. As already noted, the O. J. chase especially signalled the 'live action' and 'real life dramatizations' of shows such as *Cops*, *Real Stories of the Highway Patrol*, *Rescue 911*, *Real TV* and *America's Most Wanted*. These shows directly portray the parallel between the distancing safety of the camera and that of the automobile. In *Cops*, as one cruises along in the cop car the feeling of safety is fortified by the rifle in the front seat and the knowledge that the driver is well armed. Moreover, when the police car moves off the freeway and into the danger of inner city neighbourhoods, it reaffirms the contrast between the safety of the freeway and the danger of the 'surface streets'. In other words, it asserts the dichotomy between the freeways as distant, safe places and surface streets as chaotic, dangerous places since the surface streets are where the criminals are to be found and chased down. *Real Stories of the Highway Patrol* declares the safety of the freeway in a more direct way by showing how dangerous elements can be easily and safely sequestered to the side of the road where they will pose no danger to passing traffic.

What these shows do in conjunction with affirming the safety and distance created by the auto and freeway system is to legitimate the need for this distancing. Their message is that the urban neighbourhoods which the police in *Cops* cruise through are filled with irresponsible law-breaking people; thus they confirm a desire to distance oneself from these neighbourhoods and the danger they contain. This message is conveyed first through the fact that the majority of both victims and suspects on shows like *Cops* and *America's Most Wanted* are poor and black or Latino. Crime is something identified with these groups. But more importantly, members of these groups are largely represented as responsible for their condition. *Cops* sets up a simplistic dichotomy between 'good guys' and 'bad guys', not just in the theme song of the show – 'Bad Boys' by Inner Circle – but in frequent statements made by the officer narrators who refer to the 'bad guys'. This portrayal constructs the criminals or suspects in the show as inherently 'bad' or inferior people. The idea that poor urban residents as a whole are immoral and irresponsible comes through most when the officers in *Cops* are called to the scenes of 'domestic disturbances' or reports of child neglect which are often drug related. The police peruse the run-down homes of the poor finding evidence of drug abuse, very little food in the refrigerator and generally unhealthy living conditions. In sum, the social hierarchy which is mapped out in the poverty of the inner city and the wealth of the suburbs is portrayed as a natural consequence of the lack of morals and responsibility among these inner city residents.

The stereotypes portrayed in shows like *Cops* confirm the constructions of race which replaced genetics with culture as an explanation for inferior social status. Steinberg (1989) traces the popularization of this cultural inferiority theory to Nathan Glazer and Daniel Patrick Moynihan's 1970 book *Beyond the Melting Pot*. Glazer and Moynihan argue that 'American society provides ample opportunity for class mobility, and it is black cultural institutions – "home and family and community" – that are problematic' (Steinberg, 1989: 119). Similarly, shows like *Cops* construct a subtle racism which says not that all blacks and Latinos are unlawful and lazy (after all, some of them are cops, proving that mobility is possible), but a significant proportion of them who live in the city lack the values of hard work necessary to succeed. It is not uncommon to hear an officer comment, with obvious disdain in his voice, about the suspects being on government aid. This supports the popular belief that people on welfare are irresponsible and lacking proper American values.[9]

This popular view of the inner city has manifested itself in 1995 crime legislation. Opinion polls showed crime to be the number one concern among Americans before the election of 1994 (Hull, 1994); the direction of this concern, at least as picked up in legislation at the national level and in the state of California, parallels strongly the view portrayed in shows like *Cops* and *America's Most Wanted*. First of all, the assumption is for the most part that crime is the consequence of not enough police and prisons. The majority of the money in the 1994 crime bill was dedicated to the funding of more police and the building of more prisons. Furthermore, although 7 billion of the 30 billion dollar crime bill was dedicated to crime prevention programmes, according to an article in the *New York Times*, the legislation 'does not guarantee that Congress will actually approve the outlays [for social programmes]' (Johnston and Holmes, 1994). By being concerned most with the enforcement of the law, rather than, at minimum, more job and recreation programmes for youth, the assumption is that criminals are inherently bad people.[10] An aspect of the crime bill where this viewpoint is echoed especially is in the expansion of the death penalty for some offences. The belief that someone should be put to death for a crime is the ultimate statement that this person is or has become an unreformable monster.

The expansion of the death penalty is particularly interesting here because two of the new crimes included in this expansion are connected to the narrative of isolation linked to the auto. First, killings associated with 'carjackings' are now punishable by death. By creating the image that criminals will be more deterred from attacking individuals in cars, the feeling of safety linked to being within a car is preserved. Second, murders resulting from drive-by shootings may also lead to execution. This directly parallels an initiative that was passed by an overwhelming majority in California calling for increased sentencing for 'second degree drive-by murder'. While the death penalty for carjacking plays off the desire to be protected within a car, the death penalty for drive-by shooting assures the desire to see the auto as containing and isolating a potentially dangerous person within it.

Both new applications of the death penalty imply a desire to be isolated and shielded from particular populations. The association of carjacking with people of colour was made clear in November 1994 when Susan Smith falsely accused a 'black man' of carjacking her and kidnapping her children, assuming people would be more likely to believe her story if the accused was black. Since gang members are most associated with 'drive-by killings', the creation of a crime for shooting from a vehicle is in part a measure to assure voters that new steps are being taken to control gangs and to protect people who live outside urban ghettos from the danger of these ghettos spreading.[11] Of course, the fact that the primary image of gang members is African-American and Latinos from the 'inner city' indicates the racial implications of these laws.

As was pointed out, support for the death penalty indicates a belief that criminals cannot be reformed or that they are naturally evil; and it is also worth noting, as Mumia Abu-Jamal (1995) has movingly recounted, the brutal racism of death row. The disproportionate application of the death penalty to blacks is just one of many disturbing aspects Abu-Jamal describes of this deeply racist institution. Equally important, because blacks are more likely to be tried for the death penalty, support for the death penalty implies that they are more likely to be unreformable or naturally evil. In fact, the connection between support for the death penalty and racial prejudice was made explicit in a study conducted by Adalberto Aguirre and David V. Baker. Their research shows 'white persons who choose to discriminate against Black persons are more likely to support the death penalty' (Aguirre and Baker, 1994: 152).

The freeway as racist institution

While the freeway is embodied in narratives which legitimate the socially segregated metropolis, significantly, the freeway also has historically played a role in creating this segregated metropolis. First of all, transportation has been central in many ways to creating the social and political divisions which exist between suburb and city. Suburbanization was aided greatly in the late nineteenth century by new transportation technologies such as the electric streetcar. But of those who still relied on the central city for business, only the wealthiest could afford to live in a large house on the urban fringe. Urban rail helped create the economically stratified metropolis where suburbs became more exclusive the further they were located from the city centre. When suburbs increasingly began to municipally separate themselves from the city in the 1920s, their exclusivity had serious consequences for the fiscal health of central cities. With autonomy they could, through zoning, require lot sizes that excluded low-cost housing, and as a separate municipality their taxes no longer had to fund the social and technical services of the central cities. Thus, because suburban residents continued to use the central city while no longer paying their share for this use, they contributed to the central city's decline. Sam Bass Warner describes the consequences for Boston: 'The growing parochialism and fragmentation resulted in a steady relative weakening of social agencies. Weakness, in turn, convinced more and more individuals that local community action was hopeless or irrelevant. From this conviction came the further weakening of the public agencies' (Warner, 1962: 160).

As southern blacks began to migrate to northern and western cities during and after the First World War, suburban exclusion became increasingly based on race as well as income. Restrictive covenants, which legally prohibited renting or selling to blacks, were common in the 1920s, when, for example, they covered 95 per cent of the homes in Los Angeles. Covenants were also sanctioned by an article in the National Association of Real Estate Brokers' code of ethics adopted in 1924 (Massey and Denton, 1993: 37). But this racial exclusion began to have its most severe consequences during the economic boom which followed the Second World War, when growing numbers of working- and middle-class whites were able to buy homes in the suburbs. This was possible in large part because the Federal Housing Administration, established in 1934, created federally insured, long-term amortized mortgages with low interest rates. The FHA favoured home purchases in the suburbs and helped assure that suburbs remained white by rejecting loans made in racially mixed neighbourhoods.[12] Although racial covenants were declared unenforceable by the Supreme Court in 1948, FHA policy and overt discrimination on the part of banks and real estate agents helped keep suburbs exclusively white up through the 1960s. The Fair Housing Act of 1968 made housing discrimination illegal, but because the Department of Housing and Urban Development was given little investigatory power, proving discrimination was difficult, so realtors and banks continued to routinely discriminate against blacks who tried to buy homes in white neighbourhoods (Massey and Denton, 1993: 195–200).

While earlier income-based suburban segregation was permitted by the streetcar, the post-Second World War racially exclusive suburbs were permitted by the automobile and freeway. The automobile dramatically increased the possibility of escaping the city because it permitted housing to be located at a distance from central transportation arteries. The 1956 Interstate Highway Act in particular benefited suburban residents by contributing 90 per cent of the costs of these suburban freeways. Thus, new roads and freeways in conjunction with federally subsidized mortgage insurance allowed many middle- and working-class whites to live in the suburbs: white suburban neighbourhoods increased their standard of living and enjoyed a wealth of new commodities aided by the equity acquired in their homes and by their ability to deduct mortgage interest and property tax from their income taxes. Without the benefits of home-ownership, black ghettos had less disposable income to sustain a neighbourhood economy or to buy automobiles to take advantage of the new freeways and roads. The declining central city tax base meant city services deteriorated, and federal aid for central city housing or public transport was not forthcoming to the extent that it had been for suburbs.

As John Mollenkopf (1983) has shown, the congressional coalition supporting aid to highways in the 1950s was the same group which opposed aid to the inner city in the form of low-income housing. While the 1956 Interstate Highway Act provided federal funds to build the largest public project in history, in the same period the 1954 Housing Act provided very limited funds for the construction of low income housing in the city. Equally important, the 1954 Housing Act allowed a significant amount of federal aid to be used for projects other than low-income housing (Mollenkopf, 1983: 116–22). According to John R. Logan and Harvey L. Molotch, 'less than 20% of all urban renewal land went to housing: over 80% went for developing commercial, industrial and public infrastructure' (1987: 168). These renewal projects disproportionately impacted African-American neighbourhoods, and, according to one estimate, '90% of low income housing destroyed by urban renewal was not replaced';[13] thus 'urban renewal' came to be understood as a euphemism for 'negro removal'. In short, federal aid was often used to make deteriorating downtowns more attractive to corporate office builders by demolishing older housing and replacing it with luxury condominiums, hotels and shopping malls (Kleniewski, 1984).

Freeways were an important component of this urban renewal because they could provide even more federal aid than the Housing Acts for purchasing and condemning large stretches of housing considered to be 'blighted'. In addition, the placement of urban freeways was controlled by local authorities and could be used to create a barrier between the downtown of corporate headquarters and the nearby urban ghettos. Mike Davis writes, 'It is not surprising that Los Angeles's Portman-built new downtown (like that of Detroit, or Houston) reproduces more or less exactly the besieged landscape of Peachtree Center [in Atlanta]: the new Figueroa and Bunker Hill complexes are formed in the same protective maze of freeways, moats, concrete parapets, and asphalt no-man's lands' (1992: 86). At the same time freeway construction, like urban renewal in general, by depleting the housing stock and in particular the amount of low-income housing, increased overcrowding and homelessness. Yet what made freeways especially damaging was not just their destruction of large numbers of housing units which were not replaced, but also the fact that they could create enormous concrete barriers within a formerly close-knit neighbourhood. This has consequences for the neighbourhood economy, since the local store that one might have been able to walk to in the past now requires a trip by automobile, perhaps making a large shopping mall more convenient.[14] Moreover, it could damage the sense of community as it became more difficult to see large parts of the neighbourhood.[15]

Just as the construction of freeways had important consequences for the post-Second World War form of housing and residency both in the suburbs and central cities, their construction also had an impact on the location of jobs in the postwar economy. Most important, freeways enabled new industries to locate in the suburbs. In the 1940s industries were attracted to the urban periphery by the ability to acquire large sections of land at low cost with access to the newly planned interstate highway system set in motion by the Highway Act of 1944. Suburbs used their ability to zone land near projected or existing interstate highways to attract industry. The fiscal inequalities discussed above which existed between suburbs and cities had consequences for the location of industry as well. Because of a stronger tax base and reduced need to support city services for the poor, suburbs were better able to compete for new industries (Gottdeiner, 1994: 250–4).

Like urban renewal, freeways could be used by central cities to encourage corporations to maintain their headquarters in the central city, first, by providing both convenient transportation access by private auto, allowing businessmen to avoid contact with inner city populations which might be on public transportation, and second, by creating a buffer zone against nearby ghettos. Moreover, the types of jobs these businesses provided were largely inaccessible to inner city blacks. While jobs for those with at least some college education increased in central cities, jobs for those with high school education or lower decreased (Kasarda, 1992: 622). While some inner city blacks were able to take advantage of the increase in jobs requiring higher education, many more were hurt by the decline in jobs requiring less formal education. At the same time, jobs which require less education increasingly became located in the suburbs, making it more difficult even for those inner city blacks that do have autos to reach these jobs. Perhaps most important for my argument, research shows that unemployed black males in major eastern cities frequently lack an automobile, thus directly implicating not just the location of low-skilled jobs in the suburbs but also the means of reaching these jobs – the freeway (Kasarda, 1992: 626).

In LA, where blacks are much more likely to have automobiles, this economic restructuring due to the freeway is especially evident. In the postwar period the LA region was the locus of tremendous industrial expansion. Most of these industries located in the suburbs amidst the newly constructed freeway networks. Significantly, blacks were largely excluded from this postwar boom. 'West of the Alameda "White Curtain" was the compacted Black ghetto, the third largest in the country, tantalizingly close to but increasingly distanced from the large pool of jobs to the east' (Soja, 1989: 197). This economic inequality only increased in the 1970s and 1980s as employment in heavy industry located near the central city dramatically declined while jobs in the high-tech industries expanded in the urban periphery, especially in Orange county (Soja, 1989: 197–217).

By the 1960s the civil rights movement and urban disorders throughout the US had made the consequences of urban segregation apparent to a large number of Americans, but a broad consensus failed to form behind a programme to change the conditions of the urban poor – perhaps, as I will suggest below, because of segregation. Contemporary racial politics can be traced back to this failed battle to end racial inequality in the 1960s. In order to better understand the racial politics which narratives around the freeway help to legitimize, it is useful to look at the evolution of these politics.

Beginning with the election of Richard Nixon as President in 1968, conservatives realized they could link the middle- and working-classes' experience of the rising cost of living with their discomfort around certain aspects of what Thomas and Mary Edsall call 'the rights revolution'. For example, while the majority of whites supported equality for blacks, they were less supportive of government intervention to assure this equality. This was particularly the case with integration of housing and schools. When civil rights leaders took their campaign north to desegregate schools and housing, they met violent resistance by traditionally Democratic constituencies. This helped to create a wedge within the Democratic Party, which was further brought out by the linking of welfare to higher taxes.

In the 1980s, the various resentments coalesced in the successful election of Reagan and Bush. Liberal Democrats came to be associated with government intervention for the benefit of 'special interests', seen as 'trade unionists, blacks, Hispanics, feminists, homosexuals, AIDS victims etc' (Edsall and Edsall, 1991: 203). As a result, popular opinion among middle- and working-class whites opposed the support of 'big government' with high taxes. Conservatives were able to harness this opinion for their direct benefit in two primary ways. First, the opposition to taxes benefited big business and the affluent as they had their taxes cut along with those on middle incomes (Edsall and Edsall, 1991: 168). Second, while middle- and working-class whites opposed government intervention on the local level in terms of enforced desegregation and affirmative action; their attitude helped to enable the critique of government regulation at the level of industry. This allowed, at least to some degree, a roll-back of intervention on the part of government agencies concerned with the protection of workers, consumers and the environment (Edsall and Edsall, 1991: 166). In sum, conservatives were able to form what Edsall and Edsall call a 'top-down coalition' which, 'with the interests, the will, and the cohesion to recast broad areas of federal policy, produced a substantial retrenchment of those redistributive policies that particularly benefit minorities' (Edsall and Edsall, 1991: 169).

While this top-down coalition was built in part by exploiting racist attitudes, these attitudes were themselves sustained by previous government policy. Much has been said, including in Edsall and Edsall's book, about how Republican campaigns in the 1980s used coded language to capitalize on resentment towards 'racial minorities': rather than seeing US economic decline linked to global restructuring, conservatives were able to link it to high union wages, regulation and welfare. However, it is equally important to see the role that segregation had to play in creating and sustaining racist attitudes. As Warner (1962) lamented many years back, the segregation of Boston's suburbs allowed for the ignorance of the problems of central city residences. And as individualist ideology enabled middle- and upper-class suburban residents to deny their need to support the city which they depended on for their wealth, they broke municipal ties and therefore any financial burden. As the conditions of the central city worsened, the middle class became afraid and dismayed by the inner city without recognizing that the structure of the suburbs was at fault.

> The conditions of the central city which so dismayed the middle class were the product of its failure to control the distribution of income, its failure to regulate housing and working conditions, its failure to develop an

adequate welfare program for the sick and unfortunate, and its failure to devise a community program for integrating the thousands of new citizens who every year moved to the metropolis.

(Warner, 1962: 163)

In a similar way, the extreme segregation of blacks supported by government policies and the auto has enabled their impoverishment and the simultaneous ignorance on the part of whites of this impoverishment. For example, because the history of FHA discrimination towards blacks is not well known, the inability of blacks to live in neighbourhoods with good housing is seen to be the fault of blacks. In fact, surveys have shown that a majority of whites believe that blacks are less likely to take good care of their house and yard (Massey and Denton, 1993: 94). More generally, the fact that blacks and whites live such highly segregated lives leads to what Edsall and Edsall call a 'screening effect'. Whites attribute only negative characteristics to blacks that they see on television and hear about on the news (Edsall and Edsall, 1991: 233–6). Because whites do experience the competition with blacks for jobs and education but have no direct knowledge of the continuing discrimination they face, they are unsympathetic to programmes such as affirmative action, which help blacks and appear to harm middle- and working-class whites.

The resentment towards African-Americans by middle-class whites comes from an inability to see their historical and geographical trajectory. Although traces of overt racism still exist, the majority of whites believe in civil rights for blacks, including the right to live where they want (Massey and Denton, 1993: 91). But because they cannot see the larger political and economic factors which caused many blacks to live in impoverished central cities, a large percentage of white Americans believe that blacks themselves are responsible for their conditions. White racism had a role to play in creating this condition, but government policies were important as well. FHA discrimination helped assure that blacks were excluded from living in suburbs, and before this, enormous discrimination in the workplace existed at the point when blacks first began to move to northern and western cities during the First World War. During the Great Depression the politics of the New Deal often did not aid blacks, as they were often the last to be hired for government work projects and in the case of unemployment insurance a majority were ineligible because domestic and farm labour were excluded from coverage. Labour unions also often excluded blacks up through the 1960s and discrimination existed within unions to ensure that blacks only received the lowest paying jobs. All these things went into the creation of what George Lipsitz (1995) has called a 'possessive investment in whiteness'; this meant that for those who could fit into the socially constructed category 'white', there were social benefits in maintaining a racial hierarchy. While a few whites may recognize these social benefits explicitly and want to maintain them, others may simply not be aware of institutional racism and its consequences. This could

be in part because the divisions and restrictions on mobility prevent the interaction between whites and blacks that might permit the learning of personal and
group histories. In the third section of this article I want to address the possibility
that the freeway – which historically promoted urban poverty and is now part of
narratives which help legitimate urban poverty – also hinders a shared discussion
of these narratives.

Freeway publics

In part what made the O. J. Simpson chase so fascinating was the apparent hear-
kening back to older forms of public interaction. As the *L.A. Times* reported,
'They cheered honked horns and lined the roadway waving – a scene more reminiscent of a parade or victory procession than a police pursuit of a murder
suspect' (Berman and Goldman, 1994). The description of the event as a parade
articulates the freeway into a discourse about traditional urban space as a place
of face-to-face contact. The space of the street has been and continues to be, in
cities like New York and Paris, a place for political manifestations. The street is
a place where those who historically have not had access to the exclusive bourgeois public sphere may gather and gain a voice.[16] Groups used the streets,
squares and parks to march and hold demonstrations, forming what Nancy Fraser
(1992) calls a 'counter-public' against the hegemonic elite. This type of protest
was partially made possible by the social space of the street, something which the
automobile helped to eliminate.[17]

Today, the urban space of the park, plaza or street has to some extent been
replaced by the freeway; the freeway has become a central part of the city in the
way a plaza was and provides similar possibilities for access: one need only head
for the nearest on-ramp to reach the space. The use of the freeway for a public
gathering in the O. J. event seems to counter the concern of many recent scholars
over the decline of urban public space and its replacement by privately controlled
'pseudo-public' space of shopping malls, hotel lobbies and corporate parks.[18] For
example, the freeway became a place of protest after the acquittal of the officers
who beat Rodney King when some 500 students sat in the middle of San Diego's
Interstate 5 and blocked traffic for more than an hour (Heard, 1993). Yet most
social contact that takes place on the freeway is separated by automobiles, so conversation among motorists is difficult. Thus the use of the freeway as a meeting
place may be more of an exception and very different from the everyday encounters which take place on pedestrian-dominated city streets.

In fact, the extraordinary character of the events surrounding the O. J. chase
precisely points to the power of the freeway to limit any type of random activity.
As Margaret Morse argues, the everyday experience of the freeway is the antithesis
of the experience of everyday life on pedestrian streets. Within the formal system
of the streets, Michel de Certeau (1984) argued, *space* may be created through

irregular disjunctive practices. According to Morse, the television, freeway and shopping mall prohibit these disjunctive practices by forming a *non-space* characterized by displacement from its surroundings, lack of location, and disengagement from face-to-face contact. Shopping malls present a controlled environment, a shelter from the hazards of the outside world[19] which transcends geographical location. Similarly, television has no geographical location, it is simultaneously broadcast everywhere and nowhere, and it creates a shelter by distancing the viewer from the external world. Finally, for Morse, the freeway is not considered a location but merely a vector between the non-space of television and shopping malls.

Morse argues that the television, freeway and mall simultaneously develop a sense of greater community integration and permit greater privatization and isolation. People come together in malls but only as consumers; freeways bring massive numbers of individuals together but they are separated by their cars; and television has a mass audience but is watched individually. For Morse, the drab realm of everyday work permits and leads to the need for a fantasy realm. This fantasy is of a timeless enclosed world found in front of the television, on the freeway and/or in the mall. Life is 'made easier', in that it becomes easier to live in this fantasy world. Products on television are found in the malls which are easily reached by freeway. Television programming is adapted to a common work schedule in order to make viewing compatible with the daily routine. Thus, the passage of time is not consciously experienced either on the freeway or in front of the television: it is experienced as voids of either driving time or viewing time. Morse characterizes this passage of time in non-space as 'distraction'.[20]

The events surrounding the O. J. chase challenge some elements of Morse's analysis while conforming to others. On the one hand, her notion of 'distraction' implies a certain passivity in the commensurate experience of shopping malls, televisions and freeways. Despite its exceptionality, the gathering that watched O. J. pass does indicate individuals' willingness to break out of the forced directionality of the freeway. In fact, smaller instances of the O. J. event take place on an everyday basis when individuals, 'looky-lous', slow for an accident. As Meaghan Morris (1990) argues, 'distraction' as a view towards the audience has been legitimately challenged both in its form as a female stereotype and in the way it collapses into the definition of consumers as 'cultural dopes'.[21]

On the other hand, Morse's description of the strange community in isolation seems at least partially apt for the watching of the O. J. event. Furthermore, the fact that every network television station was broadcasting the chase enhanced this sense of community. But how does this community relate to the more direct forms of public interaction?

Michael Warner (1992) argues that participation in an event such as this permits the viewer to be a part of a public in a way that is excluded by the construction of the traditional public sphere. He challenges the prototype of the public sphere established by Jürgen Habermas in his widely discussed book, *The*

Structural Transformation of the Public Sphere, in which Habermas described aristo-
crats and bourgeoisie conducting intellectual discussions in the neutral space of
a Paris salon, English coffee house or German tischengesellschaft. In criticizing
Habermas, Warner claims that the media today bring out the contradiction
between embodied and disembodied individuals which Habermas' bourgeois
public sphere tries to negate. The construction of the public sphere simultaneously included only those with certain social characteristics, mainly white
male property owners, and outwardly claimed to ignore social characteristics,
but the mass media makes this ignoring of social characteristics impossible. 'The
effect of disturbance in mass publicity is not a corruption introduced into the
public sphere by its colonization through mass media. It is the legacy of the bourgeois public sphere's founding logic, the contradictions of which become visible
whenever the public sphere can no longer turn a blind eye to its privileged bodies
(Warner, 1992: 397), 'for example when those bodies are displayed in the
media'. In other words, the corruption of the public sphere which Habermas sees
brought on by mass culture already existed in the attempt to construct a public
sphere which erased the privileges of certain subjects, and the mass media only
makes these contradictions more clear. Moreover, Warner argues, the mass
media can serve to enable a construction of subjectivity on the part of those who
have been excluded in the past. By permitting the mass identification with various
cultural artefacts and personalities, mass culture permits individuals to include
themselves within one of many possible mass publics. In particular, Warner
points out how the witnessing of a disaster permits one to become a disembodied mass witness. 'Disaster is popular because it is a way of making mass subjectivity available' (Warner, 1992: 392).

In a similar way, through identification with the O. J. chase, the viewer takes
on the publicity accorded the event, while at the same time distancing
him/herself from his/her own body. 'Resounding to an imminent contradiction
in the bourgeois public sphere, mass publicity promises a reconciliation between
embodiment and self abstraction' (Warner, 1992: 396). This suggests why witnessing the O. J. Simpson chase was so popular. Furthermore, the viewer not
only identifies with the O. J. event as a mass mediated object but also appropriates and manipulates this object/event. The viewing becomes a creative moment
as the viewer appropriates the text for future discussion or puts a spin on it, precisely as I have done in this article.

Yet several complications surround the notion that viewers of the O. J. chase
are members of a public. First, it is difficult to distinguish here between an 'audience' and a 'public'. A public usually implies a dialogue between members; in
this case, there does not appear to be a common forum through which the appropriation of the O. J. chase is expressed. Second, this notion of a public lacks a
clear connection to political decision-making. Celebrating the viewing of O. J.
being chased on the freeway is very different from debating public policy.
Looking at more details of the events surrounding the chase reveals how the auto

and freeway can play a role in creating contemporary forums for public expression and the political nature of that expression.

First, the event demonstrated the vitality of the radio as a public forum. People called into radio stations asking O. J. not to kill himself and to stop running from the police. In addition to providing a space for public appeals to O. J., the radio furnished information on the location of the chase. This allowed people who wished to avoid traffic jams to choose a different route, and, of course, it also gave directions to people who wanted to wave at O. J. or otherwise participate in the chase.

Significantly, talk radio is a forum which thrives on the auto and freeway. On the one hand, the extension of possible participants is much larger than in a public space like a plaza or park, especially when the programme is broadcast nationally such as Rush Limbaugh's show. On the other hand, the percentage of people who may actually have their voice heard is small in comparison to a gathering in a common space where many people may talk back and forth at the same time. This number becomes even smaller for those driving in cars, since many do not have car phones. Still, even those who are only listening are still participating; through their listening to the various programmes they help ensure that they stay on.

Although the ability of listeners to express their views on the radio may appear to make talk radio a model contemporary public sphere,[22] the model exposes problems with the ideal of a common forum for debate. As Nancy Fraser argues, there are always certain subjects, represented, for example, by their manner of expressing themselves, which are favoured over others in particular public spheres, and even when one is a 'disembodied voice' on the radio, cultural inequalities are revealed.[23] Equally important, the example of talk radio is a problem because rather than a single common audience, there are multiple radio stations and multiple audiences. Related to this, as Fraser argues, both historically and in the present, alternative publics have formed in response to the exclusions of the dominant bourgeois public sphere.[24] Although there is not necessarily a direct parallel between different publics and different radio stations, and members may shift between publics just as they shift between radio stations, the notion of a common forum for public dialogue is problematic.

Furthermore, Fraser's argument implies that not only do different forums for expression have different audiences, but some forums have greater prominence than others. For example, more people can listen to Rush Limbaugh than Gerry Brown and more can watch the *700 Club* than *Paper Tiger TV*.[25] Access to public forums with the largest audiences, including network television, is the most restricted, and the voices usually come from representatives of groups with the most power in society. The O. J. chase allowed momentary access to the largest possible audience by those who gathered on the freeway. In contrast to those who watched the event on television, the identification with the event was concrete. These spectators were simultaneously part of a public forum where they could speak face to face with others and part of a nationally broadcast forum. The first of these was largely a creation of the second, since not only did broadcasts help direct people to the chase, but they also showed the celebratory atmosphere and offered a chance to be on television. The voice these spectators received on a national forum was of course highly limited – at most a momentary glance of a sign saying 'We love the Juice'.

Returning to the second problem concerning the use of the term 'public', for the viewers of the O. J. chase, simply stating 'We love the Juice' or just being seen on the freeway appears to be unrelated to public debate on state policy. First, simply making oneself visible on such a broad spectrum is significant for those whose voice is usually excluded from the mainstream media. John Fiske argues with regard to those who looted during the 1992 uprising: 'Intentionally disruptive behaviour in public is . . . one of the most readily available, if not the only, means of access to the media for the most deprived and repressed segments of our society' (1994: 471). He argues that public places such as shopping centres are readily accessible to television, making them ideal locations for gaining visibility. The freeway, given its heavily monitored status, increases the potential for this visibility. At the same time, as Fiske cautions, 'any such access will always be on the media's own terms' (Fiske, 1994: 471). Thus, during the coverage of the chase and the nearly hour-long wait as Simpson stayed in the Bronco at his Brentwood estate, the networks were dominated by the voices of news reporters and anchormen describing the event. However, soon after Simpson was safely in gaol, spectators were interviewed, and their viewpoints became a central element of the story. In part to understand what they described as an 'Extraordinary Spectacle' and a 'Bizarre Chase', television and newspaper reporters gave voice to the spectators (Berman and Goldman, 1994; Pringle and Morgan, 1994).

Although the spectators and viewers of the O. J. chase may not have immediately related their discussions to matters of public policy, the debate surrounding the event soon had clear political implications. For example, an African-American woman who was interviewed on the night of the chase said, 'Everybody said that he killed two people. How do they know that the police and the D.A. didn't make all this evidence up to make him act the way he's acting?'[26] In other words, long before the revelations concerning Mark Fuhrman, this woman constructed Simpson's arrest and, even more specifically, the chase – 'the way he's acting' – into a narrative about police harassment. Because of the 'bizarre' nature of the event, residents of the city who are usually ignored by the mainstream media were given a voice, albeit limited. Furthermore, this viewpoint was radically different from that constructed by the dominant media which viewed his drive as an attempt to escape arrest. In dramatic contrast to a story of police harassment, front page stories in the *Los Angeles Times* and *San Diego Union Tribune* read 'LAPD Criticized for Leniency in Handling Case' and 'LAPD, DA take heat on actions', emphasizing what some viewed as the leniency of the LAPD (Ferrel and Malnic, 1994; Holland, 1994).

The quote of the woman above – 'How do they know that the police and the D.A. didn't make all this evidence up' – reveals a view of the criminal justice system which is linked to a view of the freeway as similarly unjust. That is, for people of colour the freeway can be a place of danger rather than a place of safety. The same isolation which may be a refuge for some can be hazardous for those who are pulled over: because of the disconnection from people passing in their cars at high speeds, police can more easily harass individuals. The beating of Rodney King was only the most publicized example of the common harassment experienced by black men in particular.[27] The multiple high-speed chases of undocumented immigrants in Southern California provide another example of how the freeway means something very different for people of colour. For all people with a dark complexion, driving from San Diego to Los Angeles on the freeway is a place of regular delay, at least, as they are stopped at checkpoints along the freeway and asked to open their trunks. But for the undocumented, it can be a space of terror as they try to outrun the border patrol. Between January and May of 1996 ten people died and forty-six were injured in accidents which resulted from the border patrol chasing suspected undocumented immigrants (Gross, 1996). Like Rodney King, these immigrants may have been motivated to flee from fear of being harassed and possibly beaten when they are pulled to the side of the road. The reality of this possibility was exposed to a broad audience on 1 April 1996 when a television news helicopter recorded the beating of two immigrants alongside the Pomona freeway in Riverside County. This incident re-affirms how the freeway can work as a public space, bringing visibility to those traditionally excluded from the dominant media. A protest following the beating drew 6,000 in LA, and received broad media coverage (Associated Press, 1996). The *Los Angeles Times* printed an article which focused on the experiences of the immigrants' flight from the police and included in-depth interviews with the immigrants (Boyer and Cox, 1996). Even the conservative *San Diego Union Tribune* began a series following the plight of a Mexican family from the economic difficulties they faced in Mexico to their multiple attempts to cross the border.

While the freeways' connection to the media enables a visibility from which can come voices challenging a dominant narrative surrounding the freeway – a narrative which merely demonizes poor people of colour – the voices of challenge remain small among prevailing media images. For example, the dominant construction of immigrants being chased on the freeway, as reflected in the pages of the *Union Tribune*, remained one that blamed them for their problems and reiterated their 'illegal' status (Callahan and Petrillo, 1996; Leffert, 1996; Webb, 1996).[28] Not only does the dominant construction of the freeway and events which take place on it receive more space in the media, but ultimately it is this viewpoint which has more influence on public policy. Debate among public officials focuses on the treatment of 'illegals' after they have arrived in the US, but there was little opposition among these officials towards 'Operation Gatekeeper', the increased militarization of the border instituted in late 1994.[29] Another element of the traditional public sphere is the ability of members to influence the issues which they debate. For undocumented immigrants, their exclusion from the dominant media forums coincides with little political influence over decisions which impact on them since they lack voting rights. Although African-American residents of the central city are more likely to have voting rights, their limited voice in the major media also corresponds to little political influence, especially at the national level.

Conclusion

The contrasting experiences that whites and people of colour have on freeways translates into different political attitudes. The experience of whites undergirds the popular support for stronger penalties to fight crime. The experience of people of colour leads to a deep belief in the continuing injustices of government institutions. These contrasting attitudes are expressed through multiple forums, from talk radio to rap music, but the expressions remain largely segregated, and this segregation has a hierarchy, both in how far the forums reach and how much power, economic and political, members of the forum or public have. The segregation of these publics roughly parallels the segregation of the suburbs and cities which was outlined in the first two sections of this article. In other words, the residents of mostly white middle-class suburbs who may have forums for discussion among themselves rarely benefit from dialogue with the black and Latino residents of segregated urban neighbourhoods. This segregation of public debate was revealed in the interpretation of the O. J. event: a poll taken soon after the case found that while 77 per cent of whites believed O. J. should stand trial, only one-third of blacks believed he should (Associated Press, 1994).

While Morse perhaps overemphasizes the passivity of contemporary freeway drivers and the empty social isolation of individual experience around the freeway, the social interaction which she fails to see may ultimately have passive consequences. Because it is a largely segregated interaction, white suburbanites are hindered from recognizing the need for social change. While the freeway, in conjunction with the television and radio, may at times undermine this segregation by bringing usually excluded voices to a broad audience, the freeway, television and radio also create a mediated forum for public discussion which facilitates this segregation. This is not to romanticize a public sphere which existed before the development of contemporary media. Older mediated technologies, journals and newspapers were and are segregated and exclusionary in terms of who may have their voice heard. Equally important, as Warner and Fraser point out, the construction of an ideal public sphere erases the social hierarchies that exist in actual public discussions. However, the face-to-face contact which takes place in older cities and is prevented by the automobile and freeway form of transportation does have potential for dialogue across publics. This is not because there is more hope of eliminating inequalities; rather, it is simply because the contact which takes place in common space is more random and less selective. Whereas the voices which can be heard on television or the radio are very limited, simply being in a space which other people share means having access to that public forum, and if it is a space such as a public bus which people of diverse social backgrounds are forced to share, there is potential for discussion among geographically segregated groups. Obviously there is no necessity that this potential becomes actualized, but it is significant that this potential is seriously reduced by the auto and freeway.

Finally, urban transportation forms have material consequences in the way they shape everyday understandings of the world. Wolfgang Schivelbusch (1986) describes how rail travel worked subtly to condition the body to approach the world in multiple new ways.[30] Similarly, Morse's essay is perceptive in articulating the impact which freeway driving has on everyday experience. But whereas Morse emphasizes the freeway's erasure of texts, I wish to assert that local stories are everywhere and are always being read in urban space. The urban landscape is continually reminding those who pass through it of personal and public narratives. For example, a particular park or parks in general can be a symbol of family picnics and childhood recreation or of homelessness and 'perversion', and each of these symbols is an element in multiple discourses about the city, contemporary politics, race, etc. Thus, while the freeway may shape a particular distracted experience of everyday life, it is also a symbol of isolation and isolatability, images which further shape the driving experience but which also, by fitting readily into racialized stories of the city, have consequences for popular politics. The challenge for those of us who wish to struggle against dominant narratives which blame urban poverty on 'declining cultural mores' is to fill the landscape with rich historical narratives that undermine the innocence of urban forms; in other words, to show how these forms were political, not natural, creations which benefited some groups and harmed others.

Notes

1   Douglas Massey and Nancy Denton (1993: 67–74) show how African-Americans who live in the suburbs remain highly segregated. For several excellent case studies see Bullard *et al.*, 1994.

2   Evidence of the desire to avoid the problem of contact with people of colour on public transport exists not just in the Jim Crow south, where blacks were forced to sit in the back of the bus, but also in LA, where the Pacific Electric refused to serve blacks until the Second World War required their labour (Collins, 1980: 42).

3   In actuality there are many ways drivers and others can be impacted by another driver; for example, if s/he is driving drunk or reckless. The fear of this happening is partly contained by the belief that because one is driving onself, one

is in control of one's own destiny. Moreover, because these types of accidents are so common and do not harm large numbers of people simultaneously, they do not receive the same publicity as an event that takes place on public transit. In short, the freeway and automobile give an image of their safety where one is simultaneously protected by one's own car and other drivers are contained within theirs.

4   Mike Davis (1992) describes the high-tech militarization of the LAPD including infra-red helicopter cameras and high-powered spotlights. Television has brought this intense police surveillance to viewers.

5   The shopping mall tries to replicate the city while erasing any signs of its social character, in part with elaborate surveillance and security systems and by selecting shops which cater to a particular clientele.

6   This construction of O. J. may be made problematic by the fact that O. J. is a sports celebrity, but race still clearly plays a role in how O. J. was perceived. Evidence of this comes from surveys which indicated that opinions on the O. J. trial varied greatly by race (Associated Press, 1994).

7   Significantly, the driver being hijacked was African-American. The driver is at first annoyed by the trouble caused him by the white officer but eventually is endeared to him, since after all he is serving a 'higher purpose'. Thus, the scene mocks the history of police harassment which blacks have faced in LA.

8   It is also interesting to note how the fact that the bus carries many people, meaning it is 'mass' transit, is crucial to enable the character played by Dennis Hopper to make his demands: if one person is rescued, he still holds the rest of the people on the bus to ransom.

9   Steinberg notes how widespread this stereotype is in the media (Steinberg, 1989: 281–2).

10   As Thomas Dumm writes, 'There is less effort than ever to engage in the discipline of an earlier era, in what was once called "rehabilitation". . . . Once such a fundamental theological category as wickedness is reintroduced to provide a justification for the infliction of punishment on "abnormal others," the normalized community has moved into an ominous zone, where lives might collectively be condemned as wicked and eventually be taken, all in the name of justice' (1993: 191).

11   Dumm (1993) makes a similar point, arguing that this fear on the part of suburban whites helps to explain the acquittal of the officers who beat Rodney King.

12   'Federal subsidy and the suburban dream: how Washington changed the American housing market' (Chapter 11 of Crabgrass Frontier) is probably one of the most important historical works for understanding contemporary racial inequality in the US (Jackson, 1985: 190–218).

13   Roger Friedland, quoted in Logan and Molotch (1987: 169).

14   James Flink notes how the auto encouraged the decline of local general stores due to the economies of scale and free parking which supermarkets and shopping centres could offer (Flink, 1988: 155, 164–5).

15   In Saint Paul, the African-American community of Rondo was destroyed in 1956 as interstate 94 required the removal of 650 families. A resident of the neighbourhood powerfully described the impact:

> As a community we had a geographical bond. Rondo was the thoroughfare, the main drag, the main contributory, the focal point, the center, the epic center, the nexus. . . . When you walked down that street you walked past people you knew, places you ate, places you partied at, and everybody knew you. A common thread ran through everyone and when they tore that street up. It was like ripping your arm off. People were floundering. We were castaways. Where was our Rondo?
>
> (Anderson, 1995: 26)

16   Mary P. Ryan (1992) discusses the importance of urban space for nineteenth-century American women's protest. Susan Davis (1988) emphasizes the important political role the space of the street could play, as workers or other groups could quickly gather and march through the city to have their complaint heard. And Richard Sennet (1990) discusses the role of the street in political protest historically and up to the present.

17   Gunther Barth describes the liveliness of US city streets in the nineteenth century and their central role in daily work – going shopping, running errands – and in play – in baseball and other street games (Barth, 1980: 9–10, 176–7). As streets became places only for transportation, especially after the Second World War, their role in this type of public gathering declined.

18   See e.g. Schiller (1989); Davis (1992), and Sorkin (1992).

19   The temperature is controlled at a comfortable level and soothing music is sent continuously through the air. The mall is also socially controlled by elaborate surveillance and security systems and by its catering to particular clientele.

20   Distraction, for Morse, involves the interplay between seeing the external world as real and seeing it idealized. It thus requires a screen or a window to distance the viewer from the outside. At one level, the individual experiences him/herself in the car, watching television or in the mall, and at another level s/he experiences the horizon passing by in the car window, the world displayed on television or the life embodied in the ownership of the various commodities displayed in the mall. 'Distraction as a dual state of mind depends on an incomplete process of spatial and temporal separation and interiorization' (Morse, 1990: 202). Morse builds on the duality of distraction to say that the experience of the self is not static but involves a mobile subjectivity. 'Because the interior of the auto is disconnected and set in the midst of a new kind of theater of derealized space, the experience of self-awareness in a here and now – becomes one of unanchored mobility' (p. 204). In the car the experience of the 'here and now' is at the same time the experience of movement. The mobile subject also implies freedom both in terms of changing location and social advancement. Both of these are embodied in the suburban life-style: the freeway makes living in the suburbs convenient and moving to the suburbs can imply an improved social status. The subject also experiences movement in the shopping mall through the constant change in product lines and in the continual changing and remodelling of department stores' interior designs.

21   Morris attacks the distraction hypothesis in her criticism of popular culture theorists like Ian Chambers for failing to present a more theoretical discussion

of pop culture texts. 'Here, I want to suggest that an image of the subject of pop epistemology as casual and "distracted" obliquely entails a revival of the figure that Andreas Huyssen, Tania Modleski, and Patrice Petro have described in various contexts as "mass culture as woman" . . . a stylistic enactment of the "popular" as essentially distracted, scanning the surface, and short on attention span, performs a retrieval, at the level of enunciative practice, of the thesis of "cultural dopes"' (1990: 23–4).

22   To some extent talk radio appears to match Nicholas Garnham's (1992) pre-scription for bringing Habermas' enlightenment project into the realm of the media, specifically by constructing 'systems of democratic accountability inte-grated with media systems of matching scale that occupy the same social space as that over which economic or political decisions will impact' (p. 371). However, the use of American talk radio as a model for Garnham is made prob-lematic by the commercial status of most talk radio programmes since he sees commercial funding of the media constraining public debate. Similarly, critics of conservative talk radio programmes echo this argument by pointing to the corporate ownership of the media. 'Corporate ownership and sponsorship of American broadcasting is a major factor behind the limited political spectrum among talk show hosts and pundits – a spectrum that seems to extend from GE to GM' (Rendall et al., 1995: 115). They also point out that although hosts like Rush Limbaugh claim to encourage diverse views, in reality they screen out callers that disagree with their politics (Rendall et al., 1995: 100).

23   'Public spheres themselves are not spaces of zero-degree culture, equally hos-pitable to any possible form of cultural expression' (Fraser, 1992: 126).

24   'In fact, the historiography of Ryan and others demonstrates that the bourgeois public was never the public. On the contrary, virtually contemporaneous with the bourgeois public there arose a host of competing counterpublics, including nationalist publics, popular peasant publics, elite women's publics, and working-class publics' (Fraser, 1992: 116). Rap music is an excellent example of a contemporary alternative public sphere. As Tricia Rose writes, 'rap music is also Black American TV, a public and highly accessible place, where black meanings and perspectives – even as they are manipulated by corporate con-cerns – can be shared and validated among black people' (1994: 17).

25   Paper Tiger TV is a volunteer collective that produces programmes for public access stations in New York and San Francisco.

26   KABC, Los Angeles, 17 June 1994.

27   For documentation of the continued harassment which blacks face in the US today including being frequently pulled over by officers without explanation see Feagin (1991).

28   Border patrol agents were given a significant amount of space in Union Tribune articles on the 'border saga', and they were quick to blame the Mexican smugglers, calling them 'parasites' and 'villains' (Callahan and Petrillo, 1996; Webb, 1996).

29   While California Governor Pete Wilson supported denying medical aid and education to undocumented workers while Diane Feinstein opposed it, both

favoured increasing the amount spent on preventing undocumented migrants from crossing the border.

30   He writes, for example, 'To adapt to the conditions of rail travel, a process of deconcentration, or dispersal of attention, took place in reading as well as in the traveler's perception of the landscape outside' (p. 69).

References

Abu-Jamal, Mumia (1995) *Live From Death Row*, Reading, MA: Addison Wesley Publishing.

Aguirre, Adalberto and Baker, David V. (1994) 'Racial prejudice and the death penalty: a research note', *Social Justice*, 20 (1–2): 150–5.

Allen, Jane (1996) '2 named in L.A. freeway attacks', *San Diego Union Tribune*, 11 October: A3.

Anderson, Roger (1995) 'Profile of a visionary: interview with Roger Anderson', in Vikki Sanders (ed.) *Remember Rondo: A Tradition of Excellence*, a publication of the Remember Rondo Committee.

Associated Press (1994) 'O. J. poll – study in black and white', *San Diego Union Tribune*, 10 July: A3.

—— (1996) '6,000 in L.A. protest video beatings', *San Diego Union Tribune*, 7 April: A3.

Barth, Gunther (1980) *City People: The Rise of Modern City Culture in Nineteenth Century America*, New York: Oxford University Press.

Benjamin, Walter (1969) *Illuminations*, New York: Schocken.

Berman, Art and Goldman, John J. (1994) 'Nation transfixed by extraordinary spectacle', *Los Angeles Times*, 18 June: A1.

Boyer, Edward and Cox, John (1996) 'Migrants tell of harrowing flight from authorities', *Los Angeles Times*, 5 April: A1.

Bullard, Robert D., Grisby, J. Eugene and Lee, Charles (eds) (1994) *Residential Apartheid: The American Legacy*, Los Angeles: CAAS Publications.

Callahan, Bill and Petrillo, Lisa (1996) '7 immigrants killed in wreck', *San Diego Union Tribune*, 7 April: A1.

Collins, Keith E. (1980) *Black Los Angeles: The Maturing of the Ghetto, 1940–1950*, Saratoga CA: Century Twenty One Publishing.

Davis, Mike (1992) *City of Quartz: Excavating the Future in Los Angeles*, New York: Vintage.

Davis, Susan G. (1988) *Parades and Power: Street Theater in Nineteenth-Century Philadelphia*, Berkeley: University of California Press.

de Certeau, Michel (1984) *The Practice of Everyday Life*, Berkeley: University of California Press.

Dumm, Thomas L. (1993) 'The new enclosures: racism in the normalized community', in Robert Gooding-Williams (ed.) *Reading Rodney King: Reading Urban Uprising*, New York: Routledge.

Edsall, Thomas and Edsall, Mary (1991) *Chain Reaction: The Impact of Race, Rights, and Taxes on American Politics*, New York: W. W. Norton & Co.

Faison, Seth (1993) 'Gunman kills 5 on L.I.R.R. train: 19 are wounded', *New York Times*, 8 December: A1.

Feagin, Joe R. (1991) 'The continuing significance of race: anti-black discrimination in public places', *American Sociological Review*, 56(1), February.

Ferrel, David and Malnic, Eric (1994) 'LAPD criticized for leniency in handling case', *Los Angeles Times*, 18 June: A1.

Fiske, John (1994) 'Radical shopping in Los Angeles: race, media and the sphere of consumption', *Media, Culture and Society*, 16: 469–86.

Flink, James J. (1988) *The Automobile Age*, Cambridge, MA: MIT Press.

Fraser, Nancy (1992) 'Rethinking the public sphere: a contribution to the critique of actually existing democracy', in Craig Calhoun (ed.) *Habermas and the Public Sphere*, Cambridge, MA: MIT Press.

Garnham, Nicholas (1992) 'The media and the public sphere', in Craig Calhoun (ed.) *Habermas and the Public Sphere*, Cambridge, MA: MIT Press.

Goddard, Stephen B. (1994) *Getting There: The Epic Struggle between Road and Rail in the American Century*, New York: Basic Books.

Gottdeiner, M. (1994) *The Social Production of Urban Space*, 2nd edn, Austin: University of Texas Press.

Gross, Gregory (1996) 'Shifting to the East', *San Diego Union Tribune*, 5 May: A1.

Heard, Mary Betty (1993) 'Chancellor complies with two demands after I-5 is occupied', *UCSD Guardian*, 4 May 1992: 1.

Holland, Gale (1994) 'LAPD, DA take heat on actions', *San Diego Union Tribune*, 18 June: A1.

Hull, Jon D. (1994) 'Anger from the grass roots', *Time*, 29 August: 38–9.

Jackson, Kenneth (1985) *Crabgrass Frontier: The Suburbanization of the United States*, New York: Oxford University Press.

Johnston, David and Holmes, Steven A. (1994) 'Experts doubt effectiveness of crime bill', *New York Times*, 14 September: A1.

Kasarda, John D. (1992) 'Urban employment change and minority skills mismatch', in Dennis Judd and Paul Kantor (eds) *Enduring Tensions in Urban Politics*, New York: Macmillan.

Kleniewski, Nancy (1984) 'From industrial to corporate city: the role of urban renewal', in William K. Tabb and Larry Sawers (eds) *Marxism and the Metropolis: New Perspectives in Urban Political Economy*, 2nd edn, New York: Oxford University Press.

Lacy, Dan (1972) *The White Use of Blacks in America*, New York: McGraw-Hill.

Leffert, Dennis J. (1996) 'Pursue all criminals, including the illegal border crossers' (Letter to the Editor), *San Diego Union Tribune*, 3 May.

Lipsitz, George (1995) 'The possessive investment in whiteness: racialized social democracy and the "white" problem in Amerian studies', *American Quarterly*, 47(3): 369–87.

Lo, Clarence (1990) *Small Property Versus Big Government: Social Origins of the Property Tax Revolt*, Berkeley: University of California Press.

Logan, John R. and Molotch, Harvey L. (1987) *Urban Fortunes: The Political Economy of Place*, Berkeley: University of California Press.

Marsh, Margaret (1990) *Suburban Lives*, New Brunswick: Rutgers University Press.

Massey, Douglas S. and Denton, Nancy A. (1993) *American Apartheid: Segregation and the Making of the Underclass*, Cambridge, MA: Harvard University Press.

Mollenkopf, John H. (1983) *The Contested City*, Princeton, NJ: Princeton University Press.

Morris, Meaghen (1990) 'Banality in cultural studies', in Patricia Mellencamp (ed.) *Logics of Television*, Bloomington: Indiana University Press.

Morse, Margaret (1990) 'The ontology of everyday distraction', in Patricia Mellencamp (ed.) *Logics of Television*, Bloomington: Indiana University Press.

Pringle, Paul (1996) 'Freeways in L.A. are safer than you think', *San Diego Union Tribune*, 13 October: A3.

Pringle, Paul and Morgan, Shanté (1994) 'O. J. in custody, at last: bizarre chase ends in standoff at estate', *San Diego Union Tribune*, 18 June: A1.

Rendall, Steven, Naureckas, Jim and Cohen, Jeff (1995) *The Way Things Aren't: Rush Limbaugh's Reign of Error*, New York: The New Press.

Rose, Tricia (1994) *Black Noise: Rap Music and Black Culture in Contemporary America*, Hanover, NH: Wesleyan University Press.

Ryan, Mary P. (1992) 'Gender and public access: women's politics in nineteenth-century America', in Craig Calhoun (ed.) *Habermas and the Public Sphere*, Cambridge, MA: MIT Press.

Saxton, Alexander (1990) *The Rise and Fall of the White Republic: Class Politics and Mass Culture in Nineteenth-Century America*, New York: Verso.

Schiller, Herbert I. (1989) *Culture Inc.: The Corporate Takeover of Public Expression*, New York: Oxford University Press.

Schivelbusch, Wolfgang (1986) *The Railway Journey: The Industrialization of Time and Space in the 19th Century*, Berkeley, CA: University of California Press.

Sennet, Richard (1990) *The Conscience of the Eye: The Design and Social Life of Cities*, New York: Knopf.

Sharpe, William and Wallock, Leonard (1994) 'Bold new city or built-up burb? Redefining contemporary suburbia', *American Quarterly*, 46(1): 1–30.

Smith, Gordon (1996) 'Pall hangs over Riverside after high-profile beatings', *San Diego Union Tribune*, 7 April: A3.

Soja, Edward W. (1989) *Postmodern Geographies: The Reassertion of Space in Critical Social Theory*, New York: Verso.

Sorkin, Michael (ed.) (1992) *Variations on a Theme Park: The New American City and the End of Public Space*, New York: The Noonday Press.

Steinberg, Stephen (1989) *The Ethnic Myth: Race Ethnicity and Class in America*, Boston, MA: Beacon Press.

Warner, Michael (1992) 'The mass public and the mass subject', in Craig Calhoun (ed.) *Habermas and the Public Sphere*, Cambridge, MA: MIT Press.

Warner, Sam Bass (1962) *Streetcar Suburbs: The Process of Growth in Boston, 1870–1900*, Cambridge, MA: Harvard University Press.

Webb, Michael (border patrol agent) (1996) 'Smugglers of illegal immigrants are villains in the border saga' (Editorial), *San Diego Union Tribune*, 21 December: B11.

Andrew Cowell

THE APOCALYPSE OF PARADISE AND THE SALVATION OF THE WEST: NIGHTMARE VISIONS OF THE FUTURE IN THE PACIFIC EDEN

Abstract

This article examines representations of the Pacific in the film *Rapa Nui*, in articles from *National Geographic*, and in the academic debate on cannibalism as epitomized by Marshall Sahlins' and Gananath Obeyesekere's discussion of Cook's fate in Hawaii. While the area is typically the location of an Edenic paradise, in these texts it becomes the locus of apocalypse ending in cannibalism. Furthermore, rather than being radically 'other', the Pacific becomes a paradise whose virtues are those of the West as well, but whose very virtues lead to its destruction. The article argues that these texts use the 'apocalypse of paradise' as an allegory for the economic history and destiny of the West, such that cannibalism becomes a quintessentially Western practice. But the texts also contain mechanisms for the construction of a critical consciousness centred on Nature which is denied to the islanders themselves, and which serves in classic colonial style to institute a future alterity which will redeem the West from apocalypse.

The texts' use and subsequent undermining of the more typical paradise images, many of which can be localized in the post-Second World War era, can finally be read in the light of a late twentieth-century, leftist socio-environmental critique of the economic, political and environmental legacy of postwar America. However, the texts betray a more postmodernist sense of doubt about the reality of a rational critical consciousness. They raise important issues regarding the liminal space between self and other, threatening as they do to dissolve this distinction. But they all attempt to use cannibalism as a last bulwark for the construction of a privileged, natural discourse which combines environmentalism, colonialism and classical humanism while resisting the full implications and limitations of postmodernism.

Keywords

Pacific; cannibalism; Nature; alterity; environmentalism; colonialism

THE ROLE OF THE PACIFIC, and especially Polynesia, as one of the archetypal locales for the Western representation of paradise is well known. It is the place where Western representations have consistently located not just an other, but a seemingly better and more perfect other. It has been the place that can perhaps save the West ('First World' western Europe and North America), as epitomized by Paul Gauguin's desire to find in Tahiti those elements of the good life which were missing from industrial France. In this article, however, I would like to look at representations of the Pacific which find in this region not paradise but decay, failure and even apocalypse. These texts include the recent film *Rapa Nui*, certain articles from the magazine *National Geographic*, the Sahlins-Obeyesekere academic debate regarding Hawaiian cannibalism and Captain Cook, and a brief excursus on Denis de Diderot's Enlightenment vision of Tahiti, the *Supplément au Voyage de Bougainville*. All these texts feature to one extent or another the fall of paradise. Most interestingly however, that fall is depicted as being the result of the very nature of paradise itself.

In contrast to the images of paradise, there is also a long tradition of finding in the Pacific a poorer, inferior other, to be colonized and missionized by the West, and to serve as the negative model for the West's own representation of its cultural superiority. In fact, the 'paradise' image of Polynesia had its heyday for a brief period in the late eighteenth century, before being challenged by the evangelical discourse of the 'ignoble savage' and the romantic discourse of the 'primitive savage', as well as by the unpleasant realities of the deaths of Captain Cook and others.[1] But whether it is saviour or servant, the Pacific is typically imagined as radically different from the West.

Yet the depictions of a Pacific apocalypse to be considered here are striking in that they frame the positive and negative sides of paradise not in terms of some distant other, but in terms of Western society itself. Unlike either the missionary/colonial or utopian/paradise representations of Polynesia, these texts either weaken or abolish the differences between the region and the West, and the destruction of paradise can be read as a warning of the danger to the West itself of its own negative tendencies. The texts in question are thus emblematic of a more general enactment of the 'sacrifice' of paradise in order to encourage the redemption of a Western society whose faults are exactly those of paradise.[2]

The redemption, in fact, lies in a recognition of sameness. This recognition then allows for salvation in a future alterity based on a critical consciousness denied to the actual inhabitants of paradise. It is this sacrifice and its redemptive qualities which I will emphasize in this article. More particularly, I will argue that this redemption is tied to particular Western models of Nature and critical consciousness which are intimately linked to both contemporary leftist economic and environmental critiques and to certain classic features of colonialism. The Pacific Eden becomes the site of confluence for a unique, late twentieth-century Western combination of environmentalism, colonialism and the popular iconography of paradise.

Finally, that most horrific of apocalypses – cannibalism – will be examined in the various texts. As with paradise and its decline, cannibalism turns out to be not an icon of alterity, but a specifically Western practice. Its representation in conjunction with the Pacific allows for a postmodern critique of Hollywood films, *National Geographic*, and the contemporary academic debate over the subject in terms of their relationship to this practice. While I will carefully examine the conditions of textual production and reception of each of these discursive milieux separately, they turn out to reveal interesting contiguities to one another in their suggestion of where paradise may lie and what its future may actually be. The sacrifice of paradise and the (attempted) redemption of the West can be read as one response to an American, left–centre political and cultural sense of both future uncertainty, and criticism of America's own recent past from the Second World War to the 1970s – the era whose images of paradise are disrupted in the texts to be examined here.

The autumn 1994 release of the Kevin Reynolds/Kevin Costner film *Rapa Nui* (the Polynesian name for Easter Island) marked one of the latest instalments in the West's (and Hollywood's) fascination with Polynesia as a locus of desires for paradise. The opening scenes of the film feature many of the now standard motifs of the Polynesian fantasy – a scenically spectacular island rising from the ocean, surrounded by pounding surf in which bronzed young men happily swim and cavort, bare-breasted women dancing about a bonfire as part of a 'primitive' festival or ritual, and the complex-free satisfaction of sexual desire on the part of the film's male and female hero and heroine (played by Jason Scott Lee and Sandrine Holt) in a setting of pure nature on a grassy hillside above the ocean. To this point, the film resonates most strongly with the images of *South Pacific*, or James Michener's *Hawaii*. However, the use of Easter Island introduces, for the typical American viewer, a second set of images which work in two opposite directions. For Easter Island is also famous as the site of the giant sculpted heads known as 'Moai', associated with mystery, magical power, and even extra-terrestrial visits (in Erich von Daniken's *Chariots of the Gods?*). The larger region, including Pitcairn Island (which appears in the movie) would also generally be associated with the various written and film versions of *Mutiny on the Bounty*, and older viewers would possibly

remember Thor Heyerdahl's books *Kon-Tiki* and *Aku-Aku*, claiming that Easter
Island was the site of settlement from South America in pre-historic times. The sum
total of these associations works to increase the sense of otherness and alien-ness of
Easter Island, but at the same time it introduces elements which tend to counter-
act the sense of pure, easy pleasure which tourist-poster images of Hawaiian
beaches, for example, are supposed to evoke. If it is possible to suggest a generalized American cultural horizon of expectations for the film, it would be characterized by the contradictory tendencies of Pacific paradise and a mysterious, vaguely
disquieting sense that something else is up as well. Thus Easter Island is particularly
well suited for a representation of Polynesian paradise turning into apocalypse.

Indeed, this seeming paradise rapidly reveals itself to be a hellish world apart
– food is short, the island is riven by conflict between its two tribes, the 'Long-
ears' and the socially inferior 'Short-ears'. The society is dominated by tyranni-
cal priest-kings who rule through taboos, as demonstrated graphically in a scene
where one priest kills an old man for being caught with a taboo fish. The young
couple, who resemble most closely Romeo and Juliet (since the woman is a
member of the Short-ears, while the man is a Long-ear), find great obstacles
placed in the path of their love and desire to marry. Yet the central focus of the
social crisis turns out to be the problem of over-population and diminishing
resources, which lie at the root of the many other problems mentioned above.
The islanders are literally eating and reproducing themselves out of house and
home, even as their befuddled, religiously blinded leader urges them to have
more children. It is this resource shortage, combined with supposedly inflexible
and unchanging modes of thought which are blind to the need for change, which
bring the social crisis to a boil. The result is the revolt of the Short-ears, the deci-
mation of the last remaining coconut groves on the island (symbolic both in the
film and in Polynesian mythology of fertility), and finally the killing and eating
of the Long-ears by the Short-ears, as the film ends in an orgy of cannibalism,
exhaustion of resources, and the escape of the two lovers to colonize (it is suggested) the island of Pitcairn – perhaps only to begin the cycle anew.[3] They leave
the Short-Ears behind to feast on the charred remains of the Long-Ears.

As is typical of the 'Polynesian paradise' myth, it is sex, feasting, ritual and a
timelessness which refuses to evolve towards the modern world that constitute
the paradisaical nature of the island. They are emblematic of a larger practice of
free indulgence of desire within the confines of an absolute, unchanging, and
therefore unproblematic and unanalysed system of constraints. Ironically, such a
world mirrors the Garden of Eden with its absolute freedom, constrained only
by the unexplained taboo of the Tree of Knowledge. Yet even more ironically, it
is the garden itself which is its own downfall in this case. It is sex, feasting and
unchanging ritual which lead ultimately to the destruction of the paradise which
once existed on the island, in the form of the overindulgence and over-population which cause the final catastrophe in the film. The inhabitants of paradise
literally consume it and themselves.

This discourse of self-consumption, turning paradise into apocalypse, occurs widely in contemporary American culture, and certainly not just in film. Cynthia Deitering, writing on 'postnatural' novels such as Don DeLillo's *White Noise* and John Updike's *Rabbit at Rest*, speaks of a 'toxic consciousness' which 'transmogrifies one's experience of the earth as a primal home' and confronts 'a generation poised on the precipice of epistemic rupture – between knowing the earth as ". . . the home in which life is set" and knowing it as toxic riskscape'.[4] Bill McKibben's *The End of Nature* likewise suggests that Nature, once a force independent of humanity, has been subsumed, if not consumed, by humans. In subsuming that which lies at our origins, we subsume ourselves as well.

Given the liberal/environmental leanings of much of the movie world in general, and of Kevin Costner in particular, *Rapa Nui* could certainly be read as a microcosm of the environmental catastrophe which potentially awaits the larger world as a whole in the face of inferior leadership blind to the need for change, and in the face of over-population and excess resource consumption. Two of Costner's subsequent films, *Waterworld* (also filmed in the Pacific), and *The Postman,* continue with themes of apocalyptic and post-apocalyptic visions. This reading is enhanced by *Rapa Nui*'s opening, which features a giant rotating globe suspended in space as the outlines of the Easter Island myth are narrated by a disembodied voice. The image of the rotating globe and the voice-over, with what at first seem like low-quality production values, in fact serve to recall the use of the same image in classic 1950s apocalyptic visions of warning such as *The Day the Earth Stood Still*. Costner himself is quoted in a review that the film seeks to emphasize a more general social message about 'this little time we occupy the planet' and the need – 'as bad as we are' – for responsibility towards it (Maslin, 1994). Thus the film can be inserted, on a metaphorical plane, into a much broader, generally leftist discourse on the environment, consumer capitalism, and most generally on Nature and our relation to it. The fundamental message of the film, from this standpoint, is twofold: first, that the behaviours of 'blind indulgence' which seem so 'natural' and emblematic of paradise are actually not natural at all, because they lead to the destruction of paradise, Nature and humanity. Or more precisely, the behaviours, untempered by a sense of critical awareness, are unnatural. Thus a true connection to Nature, and a true naturalness, is intimately tied to critical consciousness (a point to which I shall return). Second, our own superficially appealing post-industrial life-style is equally blind and dangerous, and fundamentally opposed to Nature. In using a typical Polynesian paradise – a classic emblem of the 'natural' – and having it devolve into cannibalistic self-destruction and self-consumption, the film fits perfectly into the representations of 'epistemic rupture' of which Deitering speaks, with cannibalism replacing toxicity.

The confrontation of Nature with cannibalistic destruction is enacted most powerfully in perhaps the central image of the film: the lone remaining coconut grove on the island, which is clearly a totem of fertility, reproduction and hope for the future. This is the place where the two young lovers agree to undergo the trials necessary to allow their marriage, this is the place where pictographs representing the islanders' cultural heritage and continuity are inscribed, and it is this grove which the hero (who also argues for population limitation) tries to protect. It is the cutting down of the last of these trees – the castration of the fertility totem, one might say – in order to use them as rollers to transport the fetishized sculpted heads known as 'Moai' to their proper place near the ocean which presages the doom of the island's civilization.

This fetishized production includes within it the need for both the food and the worker population which the island can no longer sufficiently produce and support, and is itself the product of the ritualistic religion which dominates the island. The focus of this religion is the idea that the 'ancestors' will arrive with a white canoe to rescue the islanders from their speck of land – the last bit of earth remaining above the waters, according to the legend narrated in the film. But the production of the Moai is necessary to ensure this. The sculptures can thus be read in the film as both the expression of, and the doom of, the island's culture – as another aspect of the self-destructive tendency of paradise. They embody an attempt to rescue the island through a process of production which both emblematizes the island's political and sexual economy and hastens its demise.

In fact, in Marxist terms, one could say that the Moai are the reification of both the mode of production and relations of production on the island, and that their production, like that of capitalism itself, carries within it the seeds of its own destruction. This broadly Marxist echo is not part of an attempt to formulate any narrowly orthodox economic critique in the film, however, but simply reflects the diffusion of such ideas into what could be termed popular leftist economics. The main point here is that the film evokes for the typical liberal/environmentally conscious viewer an easily graspable series of analogies to the current environmentalist critique of 'capitalism' broadly conceived.[5]

More specifically, in the fetishized production which is at the same time a castration of true fertility, the film addresses a central current concern. It can be viewed in the long line of Western critiques of the 'technological solution' – the idea that technology can rescue humanity from the crises which technology itself has produced – pollution, over-population, nuclear holocaust and so forth. Thus the most potent symbol of the native culture of Rapa Nui, the Moai, is appropriated by the film as a symbol of Western-style industrial production. More generally, the culture of Easter Island becomes the stage for the representation of the Western post-industrial nightmare. We too, the film suggests, threaten to over-populate our world and exhaust its resources, and our own fetishizing of technology and large-scale production may be not the solution, but rather the embodiment and root cause of our own predicament. The self-contradictory and ultimately self-destructive culture of 'paradise' is only a metaphor for what Western culture may ultimately become, and the destruction of paradise is really a warning to the late twentieth-century post-industrial West of the danger of its

own destruction. In a final ironic twist, Polynesia becomes redefined and appropriated as the site of apocalypse, and the wisdom of self-preservation is left
implicitly to the West – a culture (hopefully, according to the film) less blind to
the need for cultural change.

This final twist – the implicit construction of a moment of redemptive vision
in the viewer – is of course vital to the film's message. This construction suc-
ceeds because it draws simultaneously on the cinematic expectations of paradise
and of the ignoble (cannibalistic) savage. Both of these, in cinematic terms, are
historically emblems of alterity. They thus allow the Western viewer to recover
a sense of difference from – and superiority to – the 'innocent' subjects of the
film. In other words, the allegory of potential sameness is conveniently presented
in an iconography which allows for the construction of a critical distance from
the characters and situation depicted in the film, and consequently a critical
awareness regarding the film itself. It is this distance which makes possible an
appreciation of the allegorical message of the film, and which also allows a (hopefully leftist) sociopolitical response on the part of the audience.

Cannibalism in particular, in the 'popular imagination', is an eternal emblem
of difference. But for *Rapa Nui* to 'work', its audience must recognize the metaphorical power of cannibalism as a point of sameness, while still retaining a
horror of the actual practice as stereotypically 'different'. Correctly reading the
metaphor is fundamental to the construction of a model of critical sociopolitical
consciousness: one must simultaneously grasp the metaphor of similitude while
recoiling from the practice. In the space between metaphor and practice is
redemptive vision. If there is to be difference, it is finally up to Western textual
consumers to reinstitute that difference in the future by stepping back, at the last
moment, from their impending self-destruction. The step back (symbolically
enacted in the reading of the metaphor), marking as it does an objectivity about
present and potential future sameness which is denied to the native, becomes the
differing step.[6] It locates alterity in consciousness rather than in any specific social
practice, and it locates it in the future. (See Harris (1977: xi) for a very similar
take on explaining cannibalism, and the ability of this explanation to help us avoid
'a blind form of determinism'.)

In the end, it becomes apparent that the efficacy of the film's leftist econo-
environmental message rests on a basis of classic colonialism. In using Easter
Island as an allegory of Western economic history, the film relies on a constant
tension between recognized sameness and a culturally conditioned sense of
otherness. This recognition of otherness is what constitutes the critical distance
from the other – and the subsequent critical awareness of oneself in relation to
the other – that is fundamental to the supposed superior Western consciousness.
Clearly, such allegories must always impose their familiar Western discourse on
to targets which the viewer is culturally conditioned to see as radically other, for
only in this way can the critical distance be achieved – thus the choice of a region
like the Pacific. In addition, the greater the initial expectation of difference on

the part of the audience, the more effective the recognition of metaphorical sameness becomes. Second, the greater the distance between the two different poles of alterity, the more effective the film's message. Thus Easter Island, located between Polynesian paradise and cannibalistic apocalypse, provides access to two of the most otherly – and most mutually exclusive – icons of Western popular imagination.

This post-colonialist critique opens the possibility of a Modernist critique of the film's construction of critical consciousness as well. Potentially, the spectator's final interpretation of the film could be construed as a warning of danger, but at the same time it could be seen as the construction of a point of knowledge which effectively assures him or her that the danger is not a real threat since he or she is already at the point necessary to avoid such a catastrophe. We may recall Theodor Adorno's assertion that the cultural critic actually collaborates with his own culture by helping to lend it the pretension of 'distance' and an ability to know and critique itself, thus simply validating that culture (Adorno, 1955/1981: 20). Certainly the fact that *Rapa Nui*'s environmental awareness contains within it such a colonial blindness would tend to support such a view. In fact, according to reports from Easter Island itself, the degradation of paradise seems quite literally to have occurred at least to some extent in the making of the film *Rapa Nui*, as vast amounts of trash were left behind and island life disrupted. The filming of the movie on location could be seen as simply an explicit physical realization of the implicit visiting of Western vision and destruction on to 'paradise' as discussed above. And a second allegorical reading of the film, again from a post-colonialist perspective, would be to see it as enacting discursively the historical process of Western capitalism's self-imposition on to non-capitalist, kin- or distribution-based cultures (see Wolf, 1982). Historically, Easter Island was certainly not a capitalistic society when it constructed the Moai. The film's representation essentially misappropriates a vaguely Marxist discourse of capitalist critique and imposes it on to what was probably a distribution-based economy, just as the making of the film imposed an American capitalist model of production on to a clearly 'peripheral' and colonized area.

Tens of millions of Americans are at least vaguely aware of the depictions of Polynesia and Micronesia in *National Geographic* magazine. This magazine is in fact probably more responsible for the contemporary American view of the Pacific as the locale of a kind of paradisaical otherness than any other single source. In fact, in a 1946 article on Bikini Atoll, the writer describes his view as he approaches in terms quite similar to the presentation of Rapa Nui: palm trees, beaches, lagoons, outrigger canoes and boys playing in the shallows. He then writes: 'When I commented that the setting might have come out of Nordhoff and Hall's stories about the South Seas, one of the sailors in the whaleboat alongside said, "Naw, you mean the *National Geographic*"' (Markwith, 1946: 97).

Yet more recently, the images have been less sanguine. This is a topic which has been explored in the book *Reading National Geographic* (Lutz and Collins, 1993). The book as a whole emphasizes a recent tendency of the photos in the magazine to ultimately abolish a clear otherness in favour of a subtle identity between observer and observed which nevertheless clearly preserves for the observer the place of dominance: a process which replicates that which I have discussed above. In a section on Micronesia, the authors stress the ways in which the magazine emphasizes the alterity of this region in terms of the traditional Pacific paradise (pp. 133–44). They also trace what they see as a noticeable decline in this representational tendency into the 1980s, as what was once a friendly (if still 'other') paradise becomes a more politically, socially and environmentally polluted and hostile region for Americans – another 'toxic riskscape'. While, in stories from the 1960s, smiling American paternalism and influence is pervasive, in stories and photos from the 1980s, contact between Americans and Micronesians lessens, and the new climate makes for 'a photographic response in which it is declared that, should we lose Micronesia, it would not have been worth having' (p. 144). A photo reproduced in the book, for example, shows a beach almost entirely covered with rusting scrap metal and other detritus, with not a palm tree in sight.

The vision of the treeless beach recalls Andrew Ross' evocation of the 'Christian logic of destroying groves sacred to pagan rituals', which he links with capitalist impulses to forest destruction, all part of a Western attitude that has come back to haunt us in the form of global warming (Ross, 1991: 224). (Recall also the sacred grove of trees on Easter Island, whose destruction *Rapa Nui* enacts.) But in Ross' case, it is clearly us destroying pagan groves populated by a pristine other. In this sense, his viewpoint is typical of a Western discourse which locates in the primitive paradise and its inhabitants – in their radical otherness (whether real or constructed) – an alternative to our problems.

In the Micronesian case on the other hand, it seems that something more subtle and insidious is occurring. What is happening is that the Micronesian other is becoming increasingly us – the beach is after all littered with Western industrial detritus, acquired by newly acquisitive-minded consumers not so different from us. It is we who have implicitly sacrificed paradise, through the person of the Micronesians who, as a key 1960s article makes abundantly clear, are our own sociocultural protégés in many ways (its title is 'The Americanization of Micronesia'). A later article on Micronesia (October 1986) actually alternates between classic 'paradise' images – bounteous fruits, lush green islands in a sparkling ocean and bare-breasted maidens – and images which mark the assimilation of the Micronesians to Western socioeconomic patterns – overdeveloped islets, grandiose development schemes, and the unloading of massive quantities of consumer items (in this case beer).

A comparison of the two articles from 1967 and 1986 clearly suggests that the decay of paradise comes specifically from the willingness of its citizens to be just like us. But this welcoming openness is the very component of the Pacific paradise which has so fascinated Westerners, particularly in its sexual expression. In the end, the two *National Geographic* articles seem to suggest, it is the very openness and friendliness of the Pacific Islanders themselves – an aspect emphasized over and over again in descriptions of the region, including the 1967 article – which has led to the region's assimilation of the mechanisms of its destruction.

But of course *National Geographic* itself is premised on the openness and friendliness of the West – both to others and to its own innovations and progress. If the article locates the fall of Micronesia in the islanders' desire and willingness to be like us, it also implicitly poses the question of whether we will ultimately choose to be just like them – just as open to the mechanisms of our own destruction. The articles reveal the magazine's own ambivalence about the universal humanism which is otherwise its guiding principle. Humanism resists the fundamental implications of alterity in favour of a universal sameness, yet this is just what seems to worry the producers of *National Geographic* in this case.

Read in their larger temporal context, these articles have further resonance on the American cultural scene. The 1967 article obviously occurs at the time of the Vietnam War – an event which *National Geographic* itself covered in several articles. The even larger context is the cold war, and the effort to 'win over' the various peoples of the world. *National Geographic* has of course always been a notoriously conservative publication, and throughout the 1940s, 1950s and 1960s provided highly patriotic support for overseas war efforts.[7] Of particular strategic importance in the cold war was Micronesia, with its atomic and missile test sites at Bikini and Kwajalein Atolls. Thus behind the smiling paradise images of 1967 lies the ultimate subtext of Western self-consumption – nuclear annihilation. The representational evolution which I have been discussing is in fact closely replicated in two articles on Bikini Atoll, the first from July 1946, the second from June 1986. In 1946, the Bikinians are clearly other, but at the same time they are our friendly, welcoming allies. By 1986, the article suggests, we have consumed this island paradise, our allies, and ultimately a part of ourselves in the nuclear pursuits of the cold war that was meant to save us. (For more on Bikini, nuclear testing and the sexual paradise epitomized by the bikini, see Teaiwa, 1994.)

The juxtaposition of paradise and annihilation recalls similar images of the Pacific which flooded the US during the Second World War – of horrific battles on beautiful islands, especially as captured in documentaries like the 1943 *Battle of the Beaches* (see Griffith *et al.*, 1981: 374–5), as well as numerous fictional war films. As with the choice of Easter Island, the use of the Pacific again seems especially appropriate for meditations on our own future. The huge distance between the alternative poles of cultural expectation for the region serve perfectly in this regard. This is one factor which helps explain *NG*'s love of photos of rusting Japanese planes and sunken Second World War ships now covered by lush jungle and encrusted in spectacularly beautiful coral. In the 1967 article, however, the two realms remain absolutely separate. 'Our' American paradise can still be paradise. On the other hand, the 1986 article came at a time when Micronesia was gaining an increased measure of autonomy from the US in the form of a Compact of Free Association. This was perhaps due in part, as Lutz and Collins suggest, to the fact that it was 'not worth having' any more – at least not in the form of a very closely held area which was conceived of as potentially becoming another 'America in the Pacific' on the model of Hawaii. The NGS itself had also become somewhat more open to questioning and critical examinations of political issues (Bryan, 1987: 381ff). By this time, as the juxtaposition of Western-style development and tropical fruits from photo to photo illustrates, an epistemic shift has occurred. The larger sense of the articles could be taken as a meditation on the era of the Vietnam War itself and the height of the cold war, and on whether the US partially 'consumed itself' in the fighting of this war, or whether there was in some sense a lack of critical national (or editorial!) awareness.[8] While the 1967 article is entitled 'The Americanization of Microne-sia', the 1986 article reveals that Americanizing led ironically to both scenic and economic 'contamination' and political loss. The articles enact, over the course of nineteen years, what *Rapa Nui* enacts in the confines of its running time. What we like about paradise is the part of it that likes and replicates us, but this is the part that led to its – and potentially our – destruction.

Of course, *National Geographic*'s views of the Pacific enact a relatively main-stream form of national self-awareness and ambivalence, in contrast to *Rapa Nui*'s more critical attitude which seems to call for the implementation of an alternative. Both do however contain within them the construction of critical consciousness: in *Rapa Nui*'s case, in the reading of cannibalism, in *National Geographic*, the juxtaposition over time, as well as the photographic juxtapositions within the 1986 article which allow the viewer a sense of critical awareness again denied to the 'natives'. The key to both texts' construction of a point of departure for a future of alterity is the confrontation of culturally determined icons of the very positive and very negative. This confrontation must be readable as an allegory of similitude, whose trajectory is from the positive to the negative, and whose intertext is an imposed discourse of Western socioeconomic evolution. Yet the icons nevertheless retain their culturally established history of radical otherness, thus allowing the critical distance which provides an escape from the endpoint of the allegory.

Clearly, the concept of 'The other as us', particularly for self-criticism, is not restricted to the Pacific. Social critics from Edward Said onwards have argued that the other is finally always a construction internal to its own constructors, and a vehicle for retrospectively defining the constructing agency through its construct. It is the Pacific's cultural history within American representational contexts as a place that is radically other in both very positive and very negative senses which makes it especially privileged for such constructions. (One could also add that for various reasons – political, demographic, geographic – the

Pacific has until recently been able to generate less resistance to these constructions than some other regions of the world.) Bikini in fact, with its two associations of Eden and nuclear holocaust, is perhaps the most privileged place on the
planet for such constructions.

I would now like to make a brief excursus to the origins of the Polynesian paradise myth in the Enlightenment. I do this in order to suggest certain cultural
continuities between that era and our own in their use of Polynesia, Nature and
cannibalism as emblems for the construction of critical consciousness. With this
analysis in mind, we will see that cannibalism in particular tends to become a last
bulwark of Enlightenment humanism seeking to resist the postmodern dilemma
of absolute alterity and the loss of any 'natural' position which would offer the
opportunity for a social critique.

The explosion of the Polynesian myth in the West dates most strongly from
Bougainville's report of his voyage to Tahiti which was published in Paris in 1771.
Yet the apocalypse of *Rapa Nui* finds its Enlightenment parallel in Diderot's literary response to Bougainville's report, his *Supplément au voyage de Bougainville*, published posthumously.[9] This text purports to be a conversation between a French
priest and a Tahitian sage, who makes a series of parallels which serve to suggest
that European society was corrupt and decadent in comparison to the State of
Nature in which Tahiti found itself.

Yet especially when considered in the context of the introduction and conclusion which frame it, Diderot's text actually anticipates *Rapa Nui*. A close
reading of the Tahitian sage reveals that it is not really pleasure and free love
which govern the society, but a utilitarian form of social engineering that seeks
to maximize population and agricultural productivity.[10] For example, sex is
encouraged simply because it produces more children to work the land.

But this reading only masks a greater irony. Ultimately, Diderot's Tahiti is
merely a reflection of his own and others' (particularly the Physiocrats') ideas for
socioeconomic reform in Enlightenment France. Tahiti is not only a return to the
state of pure Nature, but an ideal model for future European economic and sexual
reform.[11] Many of the social reforms proposed by the philosophes in the *Encyclopédie*, such as their critique of celibacy and their support for divorce, as well
as their fear of the 'unhealthy' cities which disfavoured stable sexual relations and
the raising of healthy families (commerce, for example, 'depopulates the
countryside' (Lough, 1971: xiii.101a)), can be seen in the light of this desire for
a utilitarian social organization which would maximize agricultural reproduction.[12] Tahiti is in many ways simply the incarnation of the physiocratic reform
ideas taken to their ultimate conclusion, and Diderot's desire for Tahiti is the pro-
jection of his own philosophic speculations on to that unsuspecting island.

Yet there is clearly a dehumanizing aspect to this idealistic imposition. In fact,
humans are reduced in Tahiti to pure economic capital.[13] Diderot himself was
quite ambiguous on the question of marriage: in the eighteenth-century

sentimentalist sensibility, he recognized the limits of pure utilitarianism: 'We are no longer in the state of savage nature where all women belonged to all the men . . . our faculties have becomes perfected, we feel with more delicateness' (Ency viii.701b). While Tahiti may have reduced women to the status of capital and removed any sentimentality from human relations, Diderot privileges this same sentimentality as a mark of European 'improvement'. Thus Diderot, after having imposed an ideal reformist vision of European origin on to Tahiti, uses Tahiti itself to undermine that very vision, while reserving to France, and particularly to himself, the wisdom of having both surpassed the state of pure (utilitarian) nature, and the reason necessary to question a return to that state via ideal future reforms.[14]

The most striking aspect of the *Supplément* is the introduction. Diderot opens with a general enquiry on the arrival of humans on the islands in the middle of the Pacific, which could itself be read as a more general meditation on the arrival of humans in our own world, an island in the sea of space as depicted in the opening of the film *Rapa Nui*. Speaking of one particular island near Tahiti, which differs primarily in size, so that the Tahitian reproductive policy has reached its logical conclusion there, his fictive interlocutors ask:

B. What happens to the inhabitants as they multiply on a space no bigger than one league in diameter?

A. They exterminate themselves by eating each other; and this is perhaps a first, very ancient and natural epoch of cannibalism, which originated on islands.

B. Or multiplication is limited by some superstitious law; the child is crushed in the womb of his mother thrown under the feet of a priestess.

A. Or men with their throats slashed die under the knife of a priest; or they have recourse to castration.

(p. 460)

These remarks, which immediately follow the discussion of the arrival of animal species on isolated islands, suggest that the *terminus ad quem* of Tahiti can scarcely be different from that of the particular island here in question, the Ile des Lanciers in the Tuamotus, or from Easter Island as well.

The ultimate result of reason, utilitarian order and utopia – both Tahitian and physiocratic – is potentially catastrophic. Human reifications of their own desires threaten Hell, castration and cannibalistic self-destruction. This proto-Malthusian argument of course finds interesting echoes today not just in the words of Kevin Costner, but more generally in the environmental movement in the US, and most particularly in the question of 'limits' and the discourse of eco-logical catastrophe (see especially Ross, 1991 and Lasch, 1991). Fittingly, one important critique of the Enlightenment by thinkers such as Theodor Adorno was its alienation from Nature (for much more on this, see Hochman, 1997). Of course, Diderot criticized his utopian ideals for being all too 'natural', but his critique of this utopia due to its pure utility suggests a deeper vision of a truer sentimentalist, romantic nature on his part which corresponds in many ways to that of many modern environmentalists. The physiocrats are in fact 'unnatural', and Nature becomes the realm of 'wisdom', or, in the terms of this article, of critical consciousness. As such, Diderot's text and Costner's film suggest that Nature and its higher dictates can offer an escape from the techno-industrial, utilitarian society which both pre- and (some) post-modernists fear. Of course, Diderot speaks from the position of a late-Enlightenment sentimentalist and pre-capitalist, falling back on essentially classical and agrarian concepts of nature, while Costner and Reynolds speak from the standpoint of late-capitalist, leftist critics relying on a vision of Nature formed by the American tradition of Thoreau, John Muir and Aldo Leopold.[15] Yet both share a certain rational, humanist viewpoint which is also essentially that of *National Geographic*, and whose origin is often located in the Enlightenment.

Of course, the people who can supposedly grasp Nature as a saviour are ironically not the people living closest to the natural world, in their Polynesian paradises, but Diderot's Europeans and Costner's post-industrial Westerners. The inhabitants of paradise are engaged in 'unnatural acts'. More precisely, their acts become unnatural and destructive because of the failure to temper them with a critical vision or awareness. It would be harder to find a clearer (implicit) admission that 'Nature' as a source of salvation is a construct of Western culture for itself than this ironic situation. And indeed, Nature, since the Enlightenment, is at least partially an emblem of the Western tendency to cultivate a conscious position of observation. Nature is to be studied, described, preserved, measured and catalogued. It is one of the privileged objects of the Western cultivation of the consciousness of being an observer.[16] Thus Costner and Diderot are in a sense true to their own textual logic in presenting Nature as a cultural construct more accessible to them than to the Polynesians they describe, and in locating it as the source of salvation from the blind consumption to which the Easter Islanders and Tahitians must eventually succumb. More generally, virtually all Western representations of the Polynesian Eden, no matter how plenitudinal, subtly reveal not only that this paradise is a Western representation, but that it is finally inferior to the true 'best of all possible worlds' (if not paradise itself) – the West. Nature as an entity distinct from culture is the mark of a consciousness which can at least potentially save this best of all possible worlds from its own cannibalistic cultural tendencies.

To return to an earlier point, it becomes apparent that environmental awareness of the type offered by *Rapa Nui* and *National Geographic* must necessarily be linked to colonial blindness. For Nature is virtually equivalent to critical consciousness in this discourse, and is thus intimately connected to the colonial construction of that consciousness. Environmental awareness and colonialism, in the context of these texts, are one and the same. And both Nature and Western colonial superiority can be saved by the identical gesture. That is, by positing the endpoint of paradise's evolution as cannibalism, the texts underline the unnaturalness of the acts which lead to that endpoint. Thus the break from cannibalism, toxicity and self-consumption, which serves to establish a point of superior consciousness, also simultaneously defines the Western viewpoint as the 'natural' (anti-cannibalistic) one. All the texts examined here resist the step into the 'postnatural' and more generally, into the postmodern. Nature can still be rescued.

In closing, I would like to shift my analysis somewhat, towards the academic. Having considered both the import of *Rapa Nui* and *National Geographic* for their own generalized audiences, and critiqued these texts from what could be termed an academic standpoint, I would like to consider what the texts have to say to a specifically academic audience.

I would suggest that the fundamental image of horror, in Diderot and *Rapa Nui*, is that of cannibalism, while in *National Geographic*, the subtext of the atomic age introduces a metaphorical equivalent of this. Cannibalism's use as a point of horror, and as a mechanism for constructing consciousness, could in fact be traced at least back to the Renaissance in the form of Montaigne's 'Des Cannibales'.[17] More generally, the topic of cannibalism has generated enormous academic debate in recent years (for a general summary of this debate, see Osborne, 1997). One particular nexus of this debate has been the argument between Marshall Sahlins and Gananath Obeyesekere over the fate of that most famous of European visitors to the Polynesian paradise, Captain James Cook. The central focus of that argument is whether Cook was in fact deified by the Hawaiians as the God Lono. A subsidiary question involves whether the Hawaiians – and the Polynesians in general – were cannibals, and if so, what were the reasons for this, and specifically whether Cook himself might have potentially been eaten by the Hawaiians, as he himself had concluded that they sometimes did with their enemies.[18]

The larger debate between these two scholars could be understood as a debate on the 'difference' of the Hawaiians, and even more generally, on the concept of difference itself. Obeyesekere suggests that cannibalism was in large part a British imposition on to both Hawaiians and Maoris (for whom it is better documented: 1992b), and he seeks to underline the 'violent, irrational' – savage, one might say – side of Cook in his work (1992a: 8), ironically (and purposefully) assimilating him to traditional visions of 'natives'. Sahlins meanwhile accuses Obeyesekere of turning the Hawaiians into 'bourgeois realists' (1995: ix) and excessively relying on a common humanity in which all natives are alike – a humanity which erases fundamental cultural differences (1995: 4–5). As such, the debate touches on the liminal space which this article has sought to examine.

Sahlins' argument, in this debate, is really an argument for profound differ-ence, while Obeyesekere argues for a unilaterally constructed difference which can finally be transcended through a common humanity. But both sides locate the point of debate as the potential cannibalism, which either is or is not practised by the Polynesians. The argument starts with an assumption that cannibalism is other, then goes on to argue whether either cannibalism or its associated other-ness are fundamental realities. In other words, if cannibalism exists, then other-ness exists, and if a culture has engaged in cannibalism, then it is irredeemably other. Cannibalism is, for the West, an emblem of absolute difference, it has been argued (Kilgour, 1997: 20–1. See also Kilgour, 1990: 7). Yet once again, to repeat my previous point, the other is us. It is really we who, metaphorically, stand accused of eating Captain Cook in the larger scheme of things. That is, it is the West itself which faces the possibility of ruining – and consuming – itself, the texts discussed in this article suggest. Metaphorically, cannibalism – or at least the potential of cannibalism which *Rapa Nui*, *National Geographic*, the postnatural novel, Diderot and Montaigne all suggest – can be read in this context as a quin-tessentially Western practice. The texts discussed above thus reverse the terms of the Sahlins-Obeyesekere debate: the case for cannibalism, at least in the context of the Polynesian apocalypse, is the case for sameness, not difference. The representation of cannibalism is the enactment of our own demise, and it has far less to do with difference than it would initially appear.

Of course, in a sense Obeyesekere is thus correct in his claim that cannibal-ism is a representation whose origins lie in the West, and that the Pacific is the field for this and other representational gestures. This same point is one of the central ideas which I have stressed here. But, as Sahlins points out, Obeyesekere's granting of a universal, practical rationality to the Pacific (in the process of denying its practising of cannibalism) is simply another such gesture. His attempt to remove the blemish of cannibalism from the Pacific reveals his own implication in the dualities of self and other which he seeks to overcome, since it suggests that cannibalism is part of a truly 'essential' otherness which must be denied in order for the Pacific 'natives' to be as rational as us.

Sahlins, meanwhile, chooses the most 'unnatural' of practices to establish a basis for essential otherness. This is a choice that implicates him in a discourse which, while claiming to be about a kind of alterity located all on a single plain without hierarchies, nevertheless leaves the Western academic discursant in the 'natural', non-cannibalism-practising position. His own discourse cannot escape the cultural determinations which cannibalism imposes on it.

The entire anthropological debate in fact replicates this conundrum. Obeye-sekere's argument that cannibalism is a unilateral imposition by the West echoes William Aren's oft-discussed claims that cannibalism does not exist, and is merely a rhetorical device for asserting moral superiority over the accused (Arens, 1979). In rightly castigating Western anthropologists for ignoring contrary evi-dence, Arens nevertheless seems to over-reach in disturbing ways. He ironically ends up denying a voice, or the potential of true difference, to the entirety of non-Western culture, whose historical past is reduced to nothing but a series of Western overdeterminations, and whose own claims about cannibalism are all just as false as our own, and motivated by just the same self-aggrandizing desires (1979: 145). It is the sweeping certainty with which Obeyesekere and Arens argue for an identity between us and them which gives one pause and suggests a larger agenda to deny even the possibility of difference.

On the other hand, Sahlin's argument is part of the response from a number of primarily symbolic anthropologists, notably Peggy Sanday (1986), who argue that cannibalism is simply an alternative system of formulating cultural myths and rituals of renewal and reproduction (see also Brown and Tuzin, 1983). But the cannibalistic system is characteristic of societies most concerned with domination and control, Sanday argues (1986: 26), and is absent from societies characterized by accommodation and integration – a viewpoint which conveniently leaves cannibalism as a rather unenviable form of social reproduction. The favourable position turns out once again to be the non-cannibalistic one.

One also suspects that much of the resistance to earlier materialist (Harris, 1977) and psychological (Sagan, 1974) explanations of cannibalism is due to the fact that they bring it too close to home. Eli Sagan argues that cannibalism may arise as a result of the decay of advanced societies, including Nazi Germany (Sagan, 1974: 141; see also Sanday, 1986: 10–11). Sahlins and Sanday criticize Marvin Harris for explaining Aztec cannibalism as a natural outgrowth of a 'western business mentality' (Sanday, 1986: 18, see also Arens, 1979: 168). The resistance to these explanations ironically echoes the New Guinea Arapesh's refusal to admit that Japanese cannibalism of the Second World War against the former allies of Japanese the Arapesh themselves, was motivated by hunger. To do so, one anthropologist suggests, would have been for the Arapesh to admit that they themselves, like their Japanese friends, were capable of descending to such deeds, and that such behaviour was 'natural'. Rather, they claimed that the Japanese were 'deranged' by the fear of their impending defeat and driven to madness – another form of alterity (Tuzin, 1983: 63). The 'naturalness' of cannibalism must always be hidden and denied, it seems.

In this light, both Sahlins and Obeyesekere, in positing cannibalism as the most 'otherly' practice imaginable, and implicitly as the most unnatural practice, participate in a lack of vision related to that of the popular texts we have examined. Their establishment of their own positions as the 'natural' one reveals a blindness to the fundamental self-cannibalism of the West which the popular texts expose. Indeed, the Western fascination with cannibalism in popular culture (as opposed to academic) is in large part with the way in which we are capable of this practice – Western American examples such as the Donner Party or Colorado's Alferd Packer come quickly to mind, as well as books like Piers Paul Read's *Alive*, and cannibalism has become a popular Hollywood metaphor for consumer culture (see Kilgour, 1997). While I will not seek to adjudicate the question of whether cannibalism 'actually' occurred in Hawaii in 1778, I would suggest that the entire terms of much of the debate on the existence of cannibalism as a practice, anywhere in the world, participate in a form of academic colonialism and the construction of positions of critical consciousness which belie much of the rhetoric of the debate. Arens notes that 'anthropology has a clear-cut vested interest in maintaining some crucial cultural boundaries – of which the cannibalistic boundary is one – and constantly reinforcing subjective conclusions about the civilized and the savage' (1979: 170–1). Yet while he recognizes that this usage is not unique to the West (1979: 145), it is specifically Western anthropologists who are taken to task for their construction of a 'we–they dichotomy' to which they at least, if not the less 'complex' societies which they study, should be immune (1979: 169). Thus while Sahlins and Sanday use cannibalism as a marker of (unequal) difference, Arens and Obeyesekere use the refusal of cannibalism's existence as a marker of critical superiority.

This article has tried to show how images of Polynesia and Micronesia interact with larger issues concerning cannibalism, Nature, colonialism, leftist economic and environmental critiques, critical consciousness, and the epistemic breaks between rational humanism, modernism and postmodernism which are characteristic of late twentieth-century America. Certainly none of these interactions is independently surprising. For example, the imposition of Western intertexts on to the Pacific is relatively obvious and widespread: Peter Brooks has recently illustrated how Gauguin imposed Western pictorial intertexts on to Tahiti in his paintings, and certainly the examples could be multiplied many-fold, as Bernard Smith's more sweeping studies find in the Pacific replications of Western neo-classical and romantic aesthetics (Brooks, 1993; Smith, 1985, 1992). And no one needs to be told that the Pacific has been a heavily colonized area. But the sum total of the interactions depicted here, which serve to sacrifice paradise for the sake of the West, have their own peculiar specificity and efficacity. This specificity lies particularly in the status of Polynesia (and Micronesia to a lesser extent) as the site of an Edenic paradise in the general Western (and particularly American) cultural imagination, and even more specifically in the American imagination of the post Second World War era. The true efficacy of these texts as rationalist, critical vehicles lies in their suggestion that if even paradise is vulnerable, then everything is vulnerable, especially since this paradise is an 'artificial paradise' (to quote Baudelaire) which all too closely resembles our own comfortable Western world. And what is finally most striking about the representations examined, I believe, is their destruction of paradise specifically in terms of the very features of paradise itself.

But despite – or more precisely because of – the postmodernist critiques which can be made of these texts, they betray a moment of doubt which is itself in many ways postmodern in its questioning of the possibility of escaping from a systemic blindness which could be, some might argue, apocalyptic. In allegorically deconstructing the recent American past and particularly one of its most cherished Edenic images, the texts attempt to recuperate the critical awareness that they suggest was missing from the postwar past that constructed those images of paradise. Yet they are faced with the postmodern dilemma that our own era may be no more able to achieve such a critical vision than was that which preceded it. In other words, they are faced with a metatextual version of that same crisis of 'sameness' which the texts examined here enact in the confines of their representations. All the discourses, both popular and academic, turn finally to the far extremes of alterity – to the most 'natural' Eden and especially to that most 'unnatural' cannibalism – to rescue the environment, post-industrial late capitalism and the West from the postmodern and the postnatural. In uniting these two extremes of stereotypical representation, they make the Pacific a sacrificial locus for the construction of a Western salvation.[19]

Notes

1   I borrow these concepts from Bernard Smith. For more on these two discourses, see especially 1985: 144ff, 318ff (on the evangelical) and 1985: 326ff (on the romantic).

2   Certainly such a sacrifice can be read partially in terms of the Christian discourse which has seen in Polynesia an emblem of the decline and ultimate transitoriness of golden ages and earthly life – a moralistic object lesson corresponding to Chateaubriand's use of Tahiti in his *Génie du Christianisme* (see Smith, 1985: 44ff, 153). Yet the force of the object lesson here rests not so much on the tempting but illusory perfection of the object as the actual correspondence between subject and object, us and them. It is not the desire for an illusion which is dangerous, but the fact that we and the object of danger are one and the same.

3   This event replicates the trajectory of *Mutiny on the Bounty*, which also ends with a flight to Pitcairn.

4   See Deitering 1996:200. She cites specifically John Updike's *Rabbit at Rest* as 'the story of an empire voraciously consuming itself'. See p. 199 and the accompanying notes and citations on the novel as 'the story of a stomach'.

5   It is interesting to note in the film, however, a number of other features of a potential Marxist allegory of the historical development of capitalism. Among these are: the fetishization of both labour and the commodities it produces; the increasing alienation from Nature; the fact that the entire process is governed by a religiously oriented ideology; the class-based society of short-eared workers and long-eared 'bourgeois'; a terminal crisis of overproduction; and an economic system which includes the causes of its own demise. Of course, other requisite features are lacking (the pressure towards technological innovation typical of capitalism, the accumulation of monetary capital, and money

itself, for that matter). And to repeat, the film is clearly not an attempt at narrowly orthodox Marxism.

6   See Maggie Kilgour's argument (1990: 7) that the 'product of that victory [of cannibalism over communion] is the identity of the modern subject or individual'. The conflict between the two is that 'between identification and the division that creates power over another' (1990: 7).

7   See Bryan, 1987. Even in the mid-1970s, an effort to present a 'balanced' portrayal of Cuba led to threats and recriminations from the NGS's board of trustees (p. 389ff).

8   See Kluge (1991) for a similar analysis of Micronesia, especially with regard to the optimism and confidence of the early Peace Corps.

9   See Diderot, 1964 (Vernière): 445–516. I have previously written in detail on the distopian character of Diderot's *Supplément* (Cowell, 1995), and what I will say here is a shorter version of those remarks. Translations into English are my own.

10   He states: 'Do you wish to know at all times and in all places what is good and bad? Address yourself to the nature of objects and actions, to your relations with your fellow man, to the influence of your conduct on your own personal utility and the general good' (p. 482). The Tahitians provide welfare for the aged specifically because they help care for the young (p. 485); new children constitute both a 'domestic and public joy' (p. 485); women's beauty is evaluated according to their utility, and in particular according to whether they 'promise many children' (p. 488); on the other hand, old women no longer able to bear children are condemned for engaging in sexual relations (p. 488), since this siphons sexual energy away from reproduction, and celibacy is likewise condemned; indeed Orou suggests that those who are too old or sick might reasonably be killed off (p. 502).

11   In particular, the 'Tahitian' idea that population constitutes the source of wealth parallels the doctrines of the Enlightenment philosophers and reformers known as the 'physiocrats'. These thinkers, who exercised an important influence on Diderot, believed that agriculture was the only reliable source of national wealth, and that given the then current labour-intensive nature of agriculture in France, only maximum human resources could produce maximum wealth ('there is no true wealth except men and the land' writes Diderot in the *Encyclopédie* (viii.278b)). (Citations from the *Encyclopédie* are taken from Lough, 1971. Translations are my own.)

12   Thus in criticizing the prohibition of divorce they write that 'if one of the two [persons] is not fit for generation, then the generative ability of the other is nullified and is a pure loss to society' (*Encyclopédie* xiii.92a).

13   This is not surprising, since the physiocrats' other principal reform proposal, after the freer exercise of sexual desire, was the free circulation of capital for the benefit of agricultural investment. The Tahitians likewise note that 'our daughters and our wives are common to us all' (p. 467) and criticize the 'tyranny of the man who converts the [sexual] possession of women into a property right' (p. 509). In other words, marriage inhibits the free circulation of human capital.

14   See the philosophical discussion which concludes the *Supplément*. 'A' notes that it is easier for the Tahitian to escape his excess 'rusticity' than for modern Frenchmen to go backwards in order to reform their abuses, to which B responds 'especially [for] those who believe in the union between man and woman' (pp. 505–6). Diderot is in effect using Tahiti to explore the limits of his own utilitarian and reforming vision. The dehumanizing perfection of a future 'paradise' ironically validates the inconsistent but sentimental nature of the Enlightenment present.

15   In fact, the position which I have elaborated for him corresponds in certain ways to that of Fredric Jameson (1991: 46), in particular for his critique of the postmodern embrace of 'salvational' technology. But *Rapa Nui* remains fundamentally humanist/pre-modernist in its apparent discursive intentions, even if its use of Nature can be critiqued from a clearly postmodernist perspective.

16   Foucault offers a similar analysis of Nature in the Enlightenment, though he rightly underlines the important epistemic changes which occurred after this point (1966/1994: 128ff).

17   *Essais*, Book I, 31. Having described in detail the cannibalistic practices of the New World, he writes that 'it does not sadden me that we should note the horrible barbarity in a practice such as theirs: what does sadden me is that, while judging correctly of their wrong-doings we should be so blind to our own. I think there is more barbarity in eating a man alive than in eating him dead' (Tr. Screech, pp. 235–6; he is specifically referring to torture). The second half of the essay stresses repeatedly the inferiority of the European to Montaigne's imagined New World precisely because of, first, the similarity between the two, and second, the European's failure to see this similarity. It is finally in his own awareness of this identity, in the critical vision, that he locates his and his readers' salvation.

18   See Sahlins (1985), Obeyesekere (1992a), Sahlins (1995), and especially Obeyesekere (1992b), where he discusses Cook's positive conclusions for Hawaiian cannibalism, especially in the case of defeated enemies.

19   See Torgovnick (1997: 6–7) for a discussion of the links between sacrifice and cannibalism, suggesting that the sacrificial strategy used by the texts in this article is finally yet another, metaphorical form of Western cannibalism.

References

Adorno, Theodor (1981) *Prisms*, trans. Samuel and Shierry Weber, Cambridge, MA: MIT Press. (Originally published 1955.)

Arens, William (1979) *The Man-Eating Myth*, New York: Oxford University Press.

Boyer, David S. (1967) 'The Americanization of Eden', *National Geographic*, 131(5): 702–44.

Brooks, Peter (1993) *Body Works: Objects of Desire in Modern Narrative*, Cambridge: Harvard University Press.

Brown, Paula and Tuzin, Donald (eds) (1983) *The Ethnography of Cannibalism*, Washington DC: The Society for Psychological Anthropology.

Bryan, C. D. B (1987) *The National Geographic Society. 100 Years of Adventure and Discovery*, New York: Harry N. Abrams.

Cowell, Andrew (1995) 'Diderot's Tahiti and Enlightenment sexual economics', *Studies on Voltaire and the Eighteenth Century*, pp. 332, 349–64.

Daniken, Erich von (1969) *Chariots of the Gods? Unsolved Mysteries of the Past*, trans. Michael Herin, New York: Putnam.

Deitering, Cynthia (1996) 'The postnatural novel: toxic consciousness in fiction of the 1980s', in Cheryll Glotfelty and Harold Fromm (eds) *The Ecocriticism Reader. Landmarks in Literary Ecology*, Athens: University of Georgia Press.

Diderot, Dénis (1964) *Oeuvres philsophiques*, ed. Paul Vernière, Paris: Bordas.

Ellis, William S. (1986) 'A way of life lost: Bikini', *National Geographic*, 169(6): 810–34.

Foucault, Michel (1994) *The Order of Things*, New York: Vintage. (Originally published 1966.)

Griffith, Richard, Mayer, Arthur and Bowser, Eileen (1981) *The Movies*, New York: Simon & Schuster.

Harris, Marvin (1977) *Cannibals and Kings. The Origins of Cultures*, New York: Random House.

Heyerdahl, Thor (1950) *Kon-Tiki. Across the Pacific by Raft*, trans. F. H. Lynn, Chicago, IL: Rand McNally. (Originally published 1947.)

—— (1958) *Aku-Aku. The Secret of Easter Island*, Chicago, IL: Rand McNally.

Hochman, Jhan (1997) 'Green cultural studies: an introductory critique of an emerging discipline', *Mosaic*, 30(1): 81–96.

Jameson, Fredric (1991) *Postmodernism, or the Cultural Logic of Late Capitalism*, Durham, NC: Duke University Press.

Kilgour, Maggie (1990) *From Communion to Cannibalism. An Anatomy of Metaphors of Incorporation*, Princeton, NJ: Princeton University Press.

—— (1997) 'Cannibalism and its critics: an exploration of James de Mille's "Strange Manuscript"', *Mosaic*, 30(1): 19–38.

Kluge, P. F. (1991) *The Edge of Paradise. America in Micronesia*, New York: Random House.

Lasch, Christopher (1991) *The True and Only Heaven: Progress and its Critics*, New York: Norton.

Lough, John (1971) *The Encyclopédie*, London: Longman.

Lutz, Catherine and Collins, Jane L. (1993) *Reading National Geographic*, Chicago, IL: University of Chicago Press.

McKibben, Bill (1989) *The End of Nature*, New York: Random House.

Markwith, Carl (1946) 'Farewell to Bikini', *National Geographic*, 90(1): 97–116.

Maslin, Janet (1994) 'Review of *Rapa Nui*', *New York Times*, 9 September: C3.

Montaigne, Michel de (1991) The *Essays of Michel de Montaigne*, trans. M. A. Screech, London: Penguin Press. (Translation based on posthumous editions published 1595–1617.)

Obeyesekere, Gananath (1992a) *The Apotheosis of Captain Cook*, Princeton, NJ: Princeton University Press.

—— (1992b) '"British cannibals': contemplation of an event in the death and resurrection of James Cook, explorer', *Critical Inquiry*, 18(4): 630–54.

Osborne, Lawrence (1997) 'Does man eat man?', *Lingua Franca*, 7(4): 28–39.

Patterson, Carolyn Bennett (1986) 'New nations in the Pacific', *National Geographic*, 170(4): 460–500.

Rapa Nui (1994) Producer Kevin Costner, director Kevin Reynolds. Warner Brothers Pictures.

Ross, Andrew (1991) *Strange Weather*, London: Verso.

Sagan, Eli (1974) *Cannibalism: Human Aggression and Cultural Form*, New York: Harper Torchbooks.

Sahlins, Marshall (1983) 'Raw women, cooked men, and other "great things" of the Fiji Islands'. in Paula Brown and Donald Tuzin, *The Ethnography of Cannibalism*, Washington DC: The Society for Psychological Anthropology.

—— (1985) *Islands of History*, Chicago, IL: University of Chicago Press.

—— (1995) *How Natives Think. About Captain Cook for Example*. Chicago, IL: University of Chicago Press.

Sanday, Peggy Reeves (1986) *Divine Hunger. Cannibalism as a Cultural System*, Cambridge: Cambridge University Press.

Smith, Bernard (1985) *European Vision and the South Pacific*, 2nd edn, New Haven, CT: Yale University Press.

—— (1992) *Imagining the Pacific. In the Wake of the Cook Voyages*, New Haven, CT: Yale University Press.

Teaiwa, Teresa K. (1994) 'bikinis and other s\pacific n\oceans', *The Contemporary Pacific*, 6(1): 87–110.

Torgovnick, Marianna (1997) *Primitive Passions. Men, Women and the Quest for Eternity*, New York: Alfred A. Knopf.

Tuzin, Donald (1983) 'Cannibalism and Arapesh cosmology. A wartime incident with the Japanese', in Paula Brown and Donald Tuzin, *The Ethnography of Cannibalism*, Washington DC: The Society for Psychological Anthropology.

Wolf, Eric R. (1982) *Europe and the People Without History*, Berkeley, CA: University of California Press.

■ Book Reviews

Myra Macdonald
RETHINKING 'THE ORDINARY' IN TELEVISION NEWS

John Langer, *Tabloid Television: Popular Journalism and the 'Other News'* (London: Routledge, 1998), 192 pp., ISBN 0-415-06636-0 £45.00 Hbk; ISBN 0-415-06637-9 £14.99 Pbk.

John Langer challenges his readers to inspect their prejudices about everyday news items in mainstream bulletins. In the context of current hype about the novelty of docu-soaps, video diaries and 'reality' programming, a reminder that the televisual 'ordinary' also resides in prestigious and longer lasting genres is welcome and provocative. Decrying recent habit-forming 'laments' about declining seriousness in television journalism, Langer persuasively argues that 'the other' of television news (generally neglected by academics as trivial, people-centred and gossipy) is a significant form of 'cultural discourse' with a varied pedigree and a distinctive internal logic. In meticulous detail, he explores stories about 'especially remarkable' people and individual 'victims', alongside analysis of 'community at risk' narratives and celebrations of communal rituals or acts of social remembering.

Etched into this cultural genealogy, 'other news' is related to traditions of gossip, folklore, horror movies and wider constructions of social memory intrinsic to the formation of national identity. If this is an eclectic lineage, Langer prevents it from spinning out of control by looking consistently for clues to explain both these stories' continuing 'communicative power' and their ideological import. The trail brings him back repeatedly to two preoccupations: how the 'regimes of signification' in these differing forms of news construct or mask causality and agency; and how the ordinariness of everyday life, by being inscribed into the address to audiences, wins consent for ultimately conservative ideological positions. Comfortable with his debt to Gramsci and to the Althusserian concept of interpellation, Langer is more defensive about deploying a class analysis to theorize the textual positioning of the audience. He draws on Frank Parkin's 1970s' model of responses to social inequality to suggest that 'other news', by talking to us about a world that we recognize as ours, mobilizes the variety of reactions associated with the subordinated classes, including aspiration, deference and accommodation.

Using texts from late 1970s' and early 1990s' early evening news bulletins on Australian television, Langer highlights recurring systems of signification. The emergent pattern of hidden contradictions is reminiscent of earlier work on the human-interest story in the British popular press. If 'victim' and 'community at risk' stories emphasize the arbitrariness of sudden reversals of fortune, celebrations of forms of social remembering reassure us by reasserting continuity, order and permanence. If the 'especially remarkable' whet our aspirations, victim stories remind us of the pointlessness of trying to change our lot. Langer, however, rejects the common assumption that television has in these respects taken its cue from the tabloid press, arguing instead for longitudinal consistency within television's own conventions, and claiming productive formal links between television's 'other news' and its overtly political and social agenda. *Tabloid*

Television ends with a tantalizingly brief account of relations between the new generation of 'reality' television programming and the conventions of 'other news' stories.

Langer's book is an orderly and contained discussion of questions that continually threaten to break through the discipline of its approach. Some of its boundaries frustrate potentially productive lines of enquiry. Contending that there is remarkable consistency between stories from the 1970s and 1990s, Langer emphasizes diachronic stability in their underlying structure at the expense of investigating fluctuations in, for example, constructions of 'victimhood', 'fame' or 'community'. In a book whose title topically connotes a medium in the process of change, the sense of stasis is especially paradoxical. In the eyes of the media analyst, Langer underplays the effect of developments in televisual techniques over a period of twenty years: cultural analysts equally might wish for an acuter recognition of the evolving positioning of the audience. Langer makes a late attempt to outline recent realignments in its class composition, but ignores the altering relationship between an apparently stable 'cultural discourse' and an increasingly aware and sceptical audience. In a decade that has seen the rise of parodic talk shows, and tearful pleas from 'victims' speedily transformed into star performances from murderers, shifts in our relationship to television's 'ordinary' cry out for developmental analysis.

Langer's theoretical approach is also curiously fixed in a moment from the past, even though he rightly warns that theory can too easily and unthinkingly fall victim to our throw-away culture. The turn of his argument around the axis of the everyday, and his claim that 'we' are incorporated in news bulletins 'via our proxies in the "other news"' (p. 30), provoke unease about his decision to ignore the gender, ethnic or national subjectivities potentially inscribed or masked within those formations. While it is refreshing to have class recalled from its fashionable exile in many recent versions of cultural theory, there is something artificial about discussing victim stories (which, as Langer mentions, frequently centre on women) without reference to a gendering of audience positioning; or 'community at risk' or 'social memory' stories without exploring the ethnic or national inclusions and exclusions that might be part of their ideological construction.

The final chapter of *Tabloid Television* opens up several of the issues suppressed in the drive of its central argument. The counter-hegemonic potential of the variety of pleasures on offer in the 'other news' (including spectacle and a celebration of randomness); the relation between directions in tabloid television and consumerism; and the possibility that 'being on television' might create a new form of identity affirmation: all of these complicate notions of the 'ordinary' and propel further work. By identifying some of the gains that ensue from rethinking news as a form of cultural discourse, Langer pulls off the trick of opening up new possibilities in an apparently overworked genre. He also ensures more immediately that readers of his book will look again, and more critically, at 'other news' and their own relation to it.

Norman K. Denzin
CULTURAL STUDIES IN SEARCH OF A METHOD

Jim McGuigan (ed.) *Cultural Methodologies* (London: Sage Publications, 1997), 215 pp., ISBN 0-8039-7485 £28.95 Pbk.

With its title, *Cultural Methodologies* and this assertion 'it remains difficult to say quite what cultural studies amounts to methodologically' (p. 1), Jim McGuigan's book firmly but ambiguously locates itself in a long interpretive tradition. That formation named cultural studies has resolutely and historically refused to privilege discourse on research methodology. Indeed, Nelson *et al.* (1992: 2) assert that 'cultural studies has no distinct methodology, no unique statistical, ethnomethodological, or textual analysis to call its own'. They continue, suggesting that the methodologies of cultural studies are best regarded as 'a bricolage. Its choice of practice . . . is pragmatic, strategic, and self-reflective' (p. 2). And 'no methodology can be privileged . . . textual analysis, semiotics, deconstruction, ethnography, interviews, phonemic analysis, psychoanalysis, rhizomatics, content analysis, survey research – all can provide important insights and knowledge' (p. 2).

As this string of methodological examples indicates, within the humanities and social science branches of cultural studies two methodological strategies interact. That is semiotic, psychoanalytic, feminist, and poststructural-based textual studies inform close-up, naturalistic, ethnographic studies of lived cultures. Still, as Nelson *et al.* argue, cultural studies scholars have refused to put their interpretive stamp on either of these generic forms of enquiry.

This is regrettable, because anything can apparently pass as a form of cultural studies research if it is historically self-reflective, critical, interdisciplinary, conversant with high theory, focuses on the global and the local, takes account of historical, political, economic, cultural and everyday discourses, and focuses on 'questions of community, identity, agency and change' (Grossberg and Pollock, 1998). Several negative consequences follow from the absence of a reflective discourse on methodology. Cultural studies scholars stand outside the complex discourse that now defines the field of qualitative research (see Denzin and Lincoln, 1994). They remain unconversant with the complicated discourses surrounding theoretical paradigms, ethical traditions, strategies of enquiry, methods of collecting and analysing empirical materials, criteria for assessing interpretive authority, evaluation and policy research issues, and controversies surrounding poetics, first-person performance texts, and the art of politics of interpretation. Voyeuristic cultural studies scholars use a politics of resistance to justify their refusal to engage this discourse. This allows them to remain under the protective umbrella which the surveillance society has traditionally made available to the voyeur disguised as theorist, ethnographer or cultural critic.

And so McGuigan's book is received with delight. Here at last is a book that talks about cultural methodologies. But sadly, such is not the case. The title promises more than the book delivers. The book's eleven chapters, counting the editor's Introduction, are divided into three sections: Methodologies, Researches and Reflections. In Part 1 Kellner brilliantly reconnects British cultural studies with the critical theory of the Frankfurt School. Tony Bennett continues his important articulation of an Australian agenda for putting politics, pragmatics and policy back into cultural studies. Stevenson re-examines Habermas' concept of public sphere in an attempt to develop a more critically informed notion of a morally responsive cultural democracy that does not blindly endorse a universal modernist ethical code (p. 83). Gray and Steedman (in Part 2) revisit feminism and cultural studies, and recent discussions of race, class and sexuality. Gray offers important arguments for using interviews, autobiographies and life stories as sources of data for a critical feminist methodology. Steedman presents critical reflections on classic cultural studies models of the working-class autobiography. The other three chapters in Part 2 connect cultural studies to human geography (Lee), so-called Geertzian ethnography (Thomas), and a close reading of Joyce's *Ulysses* (Sharkey). The book ends with reflections by Murdock on the value of quantitative studies, statistical analysis and social surveys (p. 182). Green outlines four institutional paths for doing graduate work in cultural studies (full-time funded student, collaborative projects, postdoctoral study, and part-time work).

Saukko (1998) observes that empirical research in cultural studies is pulled in two directions at the same time: the textual and the ethnographic. She notes how multi-voiced textual enquiries inform multi-sited, travelling ethnographies. She contends that these two formations cannot be joined without friction. But both approaches are needed; neither alone can be simultaneously critical, poststructurally self-reflective, multi-voiced, dialogical, global and local (p. 272).

The essays in *Cultural Methodologies* can be read back through Saukko's observations. Each author seeks some version of the multi-sited, multi-voiced text. In many important ways McGuigan and his collaborators significantly advance the methodological discourses of cultural studies. But I wanted more. No author directly engages current controversies surrounding ethics, validity, textual authority, voice, audience, and the author's place in the text. These are hotly contested issues in qualitative research today (see Tierney and Lincoln, 1997: x). Students of cultural studies can ill afford to neglect this literature.

References

Denzin, Norman K. and Lincoln, Yvonna S. (eds) (1994) *Handbook of Qualitative Research*, Thousand Oaks: Sage.

Grossberg, Lawrence and Pollock, Della (1998) 'Editorial statement', *Cultural Studies*, 12(2): 114.

Nelson, Cary, Treichler, Paula A. and Grossberg, Lawrence (1992) 'Cultural studies: an introduction', in Lawrence Grossberg, Cary Nelson and Paula A. Treichler (eds) *Cultural Studies*, New York: Routledge.

Saukko, Paula (1998) 'Poetics of voice and maps of space: two trends within empirical research in cultural studies', *European Journal of Cultural Studies*, 1(2): 259–75.

Tierney, William G. and Lincoln, Yvonna S. (1997) 'Introduction: explorations and discoveries', in William G. Tierney and Yvonna S. Lincoln (eds) *Representation and the Text: Reframing the Narrative Voice*, Albany: SUNY Press.

Michael Green
IRRITANT AND/OR STIMULANT

Marjorie Ferguson and Peter Golding (eds), *Cultural Studies in Question* (London: Sage, 1997), 247 pp., ISBN 0-8039-7923-1 £40.00 Hbk; ISBN 0-8039-7924-X £13.95 Pbk.
Cary Nelson and Dilip Parameshwar Gaonkar (eds), *Disciplinarity and Dissent in Cultural Studies* (London: Routledge, 1996), 475 pp., ISBN 0-415-91371-3 £45 Hbk; ISBN 0-415-91372-1 £14.99 Pbk.

'I met a ghost that wasn't there. It wasn't there again today – I wish that it would go away.' Here are two collections exploring what cultural studies (to Robbins in *Disciplinarity and Dissent in Cultural Studies*, a community of 'reflective practitioners' for whom objectivity has been replaced, ambiguously, by self-consciousness) has been, is and might become.

Cultural Studies in Question had its origins in the editors' 'deep sense of unease' about the new dominance of a 'pedagogy of infinite plasticity' which has avoided 'economic, social or policy analysis'. Their introduction summarizing 'a substantial charge sheet' has a thoroughly awkward and uneasy tone. We read of the cultural studies 'whole earth intellectual catalogue', its 'Odyssey more Hollywood than Homeric', and the 'route march' of its 'toiling multitudes' whose hard-pressed institutional circumstances are quite ignored. Objecting to opaque writing, they allow a contributor to speak of 'klutzily articulated formulations' (p. 187). Here and in some (only) of the other essays a version of the field emerges which seemed to this reviewer to be a caricature, and a decidedly unfriendly one. But then, as Appadurai observes in *Disciplinarity and Dissent in Cultural Studies*, 'debates about cultural studies – seen variously as an area, a field, a program, a discipline or a conspiracy' reveal an 'overdetermined landscape of anxieties' which he sardonically charts as an 'omnibus characterization about its "theory" (too French), its topics (too popular), its style (too glitzy), its jargon (too hybrid), its politics (too post-colonial), its constituency (too multicultural)' (p. 30).

Despite interesting remarks in many of its chapters, *Cultural Studies in Question* is far too ready to generalize about the features and failures of cultural studies work, though it contains a very fine, exemplary essay by Carey charting the necessarily specific circumstances of its intellectual and political formation in the United States. Too often elsewhere, arguments are not made properly, punches are pulled, names are not named ('fancy epistemological footwork' and 'incredible lightness of practitioner being' are 'not without their critics': p. xvi). Cultural studies is reduced, in the main, to its interface with communication studies. Charges levelled, sometimes plausibly, are extremely familiar from previous statements of the same case. A generation of younger scholars' work is ignored, as when we are told of the 'curious absence' of 'any critical assessment of the epochal changes in Eastern Europe' without reference to Hilary Pilkington's wonderful *Russia's Youth and its Culture* (Routledge, 1994). Thoughtful sketches are weighed down by the prevailing sense of resentment and political disappointment (cogently registered from the older new left by Todd Gitlin). Much of this bears out Carey's despair ('intellectually and politically cultural studies is not very healthy . . . its days are numbered except as an irrelevant outpost in the academy': p. 15) that an intellectual project of the left (a new attitude, 'a reconciling tolerance') has been impoverished by factionalism ('competing for status within a constantly constricting and powerless intellectual orbit': p. 7), introversion and lack of generosity.

No such pessimism is found among the contributors to *Disciplinarity and Dissent in Cultural Studies*, also working in the United States, though not in the sociology of communications. This is a magnificent volume, with broad historical and intellectual horizons, many substantial and striking essays, and a persistent sense of adventure and excitement, though also with a sustained and careful eye on national differences, on the politics of universities and on the progress of the new right. The collection's division into parts (unlike the 'Questions and critique' followed by the more frail 'Answers and alternatives' of *Cultural Studies in Question*), is compelling. It opens with essays engaging with disciplines, moves on to a series of suggestive chapters on past and present public locations for cultural studies work, and ends with 'unhoused and unhousable' essays including work on the visual arts on US television (Spigel), fifty pages on the condom

(Treichler), thoughtful remarks on the 'new face of America' (Berlant) and an experiment in montage (Hirsch). The writing throughout is both dense and subtle, while many of these pieces will become invaluable reference points, not least in teaching.

Disciplinary encounters include those through history, literature, science, anthropology, communications and native studies, though not geography or (more surprisingly, read in Britain) sociology, given what we are told is the 'sometimes hopeless character' of present debates and the 'homicidal confrontation' between quantitative and qualitative methodologies (though the dominance of 'positive science' is well explored by Carey in *Cultural Studies in Question*, and Ross in the other collection has a clear, optimistic essay on the need for a sustained engagement with science and technoscience). The contributors seek to engage with disciplines rather than dismiss them, aware that cultural studies may have become 'inflated' (Gray) or that because 'living outside the law' can be 'subtly dishonest', dissent has to 'form its own kind of discipline' (Abbas). The essays are also attractive in their contrasting strategies including historical case studies, analysis of keyword and citation indices in anthropology (Dominguez) and historical meta-reflections ('like Durkheim's sociology a century ago, cultural studies today is perceived as dangerously inclusive in its subject matter and admissions policy and dangerously internationalist': p. 186 (Robbins)). Appadurai's essay is a sketch towards what should be an important book on the organization of American universities, seeking connections between a 'specifically American utopianism of the plural' and the management of universities, specifically the adequacy of disciplines to diversity defined as 'a particular organisation of difference'.

The anthology is sustained throughout by reflections on the politics of cultural studies work, sharing at times the *Cultural Studies in Question* sense that claims have been too grandiose, and in Grossberg's essay ('cultural studies offers a theoretically grounded basis for intervening into contexts and power . . . attempts, temporarily and locally, to place theory in-between in order to enable people to act more strategically': p. 143) perhaps exemplifying that. Other pieces are grounded in particular circumstances: in vivid thoughts all through about citizenship, in Denning's work on the origins of cultural studies in the Popular Front (Kenneth Burke aligned with Gramsci, C. L. R. James read for his sense of a 'popular desire' for 'the fulfilment of the promises of mass production in both the popular arts and the labor movement'), in Penley's witty narrative of brave encounters with NASA, pornography trials and Hollywood. She argues that public spheres, including the universities themselves, 'do not so much exist as have to be made' and that academics, the freelancers or 'deep journalists' (Molotch) of an earlier generation can try to 'travel the work of cultural studies into other public spheres . . . a messy, messy business': p. 249.

These essays are consistently sensitive to the constraints and possibilities of particular locations within which disciplinary negotiations and political engagements in wider spheres take place. The editors speak well about younger researchers entering a job market where 'many departments look first to protect their more traditional investments and object choices'. Hanchard carefully charts the very different conditions and challenges for black intellectuals in the Caribbean, Latin America and the United States. Abbas, working from Hong Kong, talks of a postculture which contains both the 'slippery dis-locations', the 'morphings of coloniality' and East/West boundaries which persist despite 'the deconstructions of binarism and the exposures of orientalism'. Lee argues that the transactions between the local and global are understood properly by neither area studies nor international studies but require 'the creation of a culturally sensitive international cultural studies' in which students on campus ('100,000 Chinese students from Mainland China, Hong Kong and Taiwan in North America who represents the future of a pan-Chinese cultural identity': p. 232) and local communities which 'may play a crucial role in the internationalization of their mother countries' may constitute a rich resource.

None of the above is 'almost terminally obscure' or suggestive of a 'loss of certainty as to directions and destinations' (*Cultural Studies in Question*, Preface). Nelson and Gaonkar should be greatly thanked for eliciting this rich collection.

Mike Gane
REGARDING BAUDRILLARD

N. Zurbrugg (ed.), *Jean Baudrillard: Art and Artefact* (London: Sage, 1998), 184 pp., ISBN 0-76195-580-1 £14.99 Pbk.

This collection of essays and photographs derives from the 'Baudrillard in the Nineties' conference and exhibition held in Brisbane, Australia in 1994. It was launched at another exhibition of Baudrillard's photographs, 'Strange World, Strange Theory' in Leicester, UK, in February 1998. The collection is a major addition to Baudrillard studies and interpretation, yet it raises more issues and problems than it solves. It contains three papers by Baudrillard on aesthetics and photography, two interviews on these themes, and essays on Baudrillard's ideas by Butler (on the real), Cholodenko (on Jurassic Park), Coulter-Smith (on Marx/Derrida), Genosko (on McLuhanism), Patton (on war), Willis (on photography), and Zurbrugg (on 'absolute' photography). The collection finishes with a bibliography of writings on Baudrillard, compiled by R. Smith. Many of the contributors have written either doctoral theses, studies or translations of Baudrillard's work.

What strikes the reader however is that Baudrillard seems to have been able to set puzzles and riddles for his interlocutors which enable him to remain at least two steps ahead of them. Commentators are forced to do their own thing and go their own way, trying either to capture, divert or even let go of Baudrillard's ideas. In the interviews it is curious that time and again Baudrillard says in effect 'no, that's not what I'm saying' in the face of relentless efforts to redirect his thought. Butler's essay, against all the evidence, sees Baudrillard as a platonic philosopher of the real. Cholodenko's ingenious essay sees Baudrillard in Jurassic Park, an exemplification of the 'principle of evil' and fourth order simulation (p. 65). Coulter-Smith, in the next essay, notes that Cholodenko's interpretation is 'at odds' with Baudrillard's remarks on cinema which are more pessimistic. Coulter-Smith prefers Derrida's 'sweet' and more positive alternative (p. 92). Genosko provides a scholarly discussion of Baudrillard's ambivalent relation to McLuhan's work. Patton writes on the Gulf War and comes to agree with Baudrillard that 'the Gulf war did not take place' (p. 134). Anne-Marie Willis discusses Baudrillard on photography and concludes that 'Baudrillard and I have grown apart, and we really are incompatible now' (p. 147). Zurbrugg's essay argues that against the apparent pessimism in Baudrillard's essays it is possible to find 'unexpected alternatives' to a vision of a world as irredeemably banal. Zurbrugg suggests that a 'reading against the lines – one finds traces – apparitions, perhaps – of a surprisingly affirmative "secret" logic' (p. 166).

This collection also includes eight colour prints of Baudrillard's photographs, and two further examples on the jacket. Baudrillard's contribution to the text are three brilliant papers. First, 'Objects, images and the possibility of aesthetic illusion'; second, 'Aesthetic illusion and virtual reality', and third, 'The art of disappearance'. He defends these papers in two interviews with great wit and agility. His basic thesis is that in the contemporary situation an important transformation has occurred, rendering the old idea of art as an aesthetic sanctuary obsolete. Artistic representation of the real world has become simply impossible since the 'image has become the real' (p. 12), and in 'virtual reality it's as if things had swallowed their mirrors, and then become transparent to themselves' (p. 13). Today the irony of this doubling 'breaks through at each moment' so that we have not a metaphysics but a 'pataphysics of objects'. The world, perhaps because of capitalism (p. 14), has become a world of self-publicizing objects. Objects and artefacts 'want to signify . . . to be photographed' (p. 14). Baudrillard understands this fundamental condition as follows: first, an anthropological thesis – that before the world becomes real it has first to be an illusion; second, the world of aesthetics attempts to control a secondary illusion of the world so as to exorcise the real (an order of simulacra) which has come to replace the initial illusion (or symbolic order). This creates, says Baudrillard, a dilemma. Either we are in 'absolute banality . . . a definitive nihilism . . . or, there is an art of simulation, an ironic quality that evokes the appearances of the world in order to let them vanish again' (p. 18). The aesthetic realm is therefore a conditional simulacrum, which may be giving way to what Baudrillard calls an 'unconditional simulacrum, that is, of the primitive scene of illusion, where we may join again with the rituals . . . of symbolic cultures, and with the fatality of the object' (p. 18).

Baudrillard's imaginative theorizing, and the counter-strategies of the interlocutors and critics, makes fascinating reading, even if everyone seems to be going off in different directions.

Simon Cottle
TOWARDS THE 'SOCIAL' IN SOCIAL CONSTRUCTIONISM

A. Anderson, *Media, Culture and the Environment* (London: University College London Press, 1997), 236 + x pp., ISBN 1-85728-383-X Hbk; ISBN 1-85728-384-8 £12.95 Pbk.

In recent years the turn to language, linguistics and theories of discourse has exerted a profound impact upon how we conceive and approach the study of social and cultural processes. Social constructionism, whether of the 'strong' (anti-realist) or 'soft' (epistemological) variety, has forefronted texts and textuality as the terrain on which the social is either constituted or played out. Small wonder, then, that the mass media should so often be singled out for discussion or that the nature of media representations, its 'pictures of reality', should be a focal point of enquiry. Not that researchers, for the most part, any longer assume that the media's 'pictures of reality' are either internally unfractured or uniformly 'read' by audiences but, with respect to the circuits of media consumption and production, it is true to say that 'representations' continue to command inordinate attention. Take studies of claims making, for instance, where studies of news representations have revealed how processes of discursive contest and the pursuit of legitimacy waged via the public stage often involve performative, rhetorical, symbolic and moral features, each simultaneously inscribed into the language of contending 'claims'. While undoubtedly this approach has won insights into the multi-layered complexities of language use and how each contributes to the production of meanings within *texts*, these findings none the less often appear to be at the expense of a more grounded appreciation of informing *contexts* of production and surrounding social forces. Forensic analysis of media texts, no matter how dazzling, even when complemented by 'deep' (though too often surface) audience 'ethnographies', simply cannot recover these contexts and processes. Such approaches remain, in consequence, of limited explanatory value and, despite their political intentions, unable to situate their findings in relation to the wider play of social power.

All this, of course, is by way of introducing what I consider to be one of the principal strengths of Alison Anderson's *Media, Culture and the Environment*. Here is a book that usefully reviews the burgeoning literature on the mass media and its representations of the environment and, importantly, in so doing begins to demonstrate how the explanatory gaps immanent to textualist approaches can be filled. In short, her review and discussion help to put the 'social' back into social constructionist approaches to the media while holding on to some of the gains of culturalist approaches to media texts. Written in a straightforward and unpretentious style, the book is eminently accessible to all those interested in the role of the mass media in 'mediating' the environment. Structured into six substantive chapters with an introduction and conclusion, the book first situates its approach in relation to social theory, social constructionism and environmentalism and the news media. Chapter 1 centres on the environment as a contested discourse and relates ideas of claims makers to research on other mediated 'social problems'. Principal findings from studies of news production and the professional ideologies of journalism are outlined in Chapter 2. This is followed by discussion of the competing explanations for the rise and fall and rise again of environmental consciousness in Chapter 3, and how ideas of risk and the environment are framed within the news media in Chapter 4. Chapter 5, drawing upon the author's own research findings, considers the increasingly important issue of vying news sources and the various strategies and differentials of power – whether financial, organizational or symbolic – deployed in their bid to access the news public stage. Chapter 6 then considers the role of audiences in sensemaking activity and appraises the current vogue for 'active audience' theory. The book concludes with an appreciation of the role of both the mass media and culture in the elaboration of contemporary social problems.

The discussion thus traverses considerable conceptual ground including media-relevant ideas of 'public arenas', 'issue entrepreneurs', 'claims makers' and 'claims making', 'agenda setting' and 'agenda building', 'framing', 'news thresholds', and 'cultural resonance' and 'symbols'. All this makes for a multifaceted appreciation of how and why the news media have contributed to the social construction of the environment in the ways they have – a relatively eclectic and open approach that can accommodate and recognize the importance of surrounding social forces as well as the discursive and cultural dimensions embedded within media representations of the environment.

For this reviewer, perhaps it is the book's discussion of the 'behind the scenes' struggle waged by competing environmental sources that proves most interesting. This dimension to news production helps open up an important, but too often overlooked vista on the dynamic interaction between the news media and wider social forces, a vista that is also currently being pursued by other researchers in empirical analyses of news source interactions in other fields. Collectively, this research points to a more complex under-standing of ideas of 'primary definers' and news mediated 'primary definitions'. A second area discussed, also potentially productive for future work, is the role played by cultural symbols in attracting the news media to the environment and, indeed, how these also inform media framing of environmental concerns. When discussing the media's contri-bution to the social construction of environment, therefore, both the play of social *and* cultural power are usefully brought into view. Arguably, differences of disciplinary outlook and approach have hindered the simultaneous pursuit of each for too long. Anderson's book, through review and discussion, helps to map the fast-developing field of risk and environmental communication and provides a necessary starting point for others contemplating research in this area. *Media, Culture and the Environment* indicates that no adequate understanding of the changing discourses of the environment and the role of the news media within these discourses is possible without also attending to the complexities (and contingencies) of social and cultural processes.

Notes on Contributors

Simon Cottle is Professor in Mass Communication at Bath Spa University College. His recent publications and research interests relate to media production and representations of social conflicts, the production of ethnic minority programmes, changing news technologies and journalist practices, and theories of news access.

Andrew Cowell is an Assistant Professor in the Department of French and Italian at the University of Colorado. One of his interests is the relations between literature and socio-economic developments, from the Middle Ages to the present. His book *At Play in the Tavern: Signs, Coins and Bodies in the Middle Ages* (Michigan, 1999) examines the connections between the concepts of profit and play as both economic and literary phenomena originating in the High Middle Ages. He is currently working on a book examining the uses of anthropological gift theory in both literary history and contemporary literary theory, as well as a paper on the poetics of advertising.

Norman K. Denzin is Professor of Sociology at the University of Illinois at Urbana-Champaign.

Paul Mason Fotsch will receive his Ph.D. in Communication from the University of California, San Diego in the spring of 1998. His dissertation, by considering objects ranging from a World's Fair diorama to popular movies, reads urban transportation forms as both the product of and sustenance for dominant narratives surrounding US cities.

Mike Gane studied sociology at Leicester University (1965–1968) and at the LSE (1968–1971). He teaches in the Department of Social Sciences at Loughborough University, UK. He has written studies of Durkheim, Baudrillard and other French thinkers, as well as a study of gender theory entitled *Harmless Lovers?* (Routledge, 1994).

Michael Green was Head of the Department of Cultural Studies in Birmingham for five years and is now a Senior Lecturer in the renamed Department of Cultural Studies and Sociology, University of Birmingham.

David Hesmondhalgh was Lecturer in Media and Communications at Goldsmiths College, London from 1995–1998 and is now Senior Lecturer in Communication, Culture and Media at Coventry University. He is author of *Democratizing Music: Majors, Independents and Alternatives* (Routledge/Comedia, forthcoming) and co-editor, with Georgina Born, of *Western Music and its Others:*

Difference, Appropriation and Representation in Music (University of California Press, forthcoming, 2000). He serves as Treasurer on the Executive Committee of the International Association for the Study of Popular Music (IASPM).

Myung Koo Kang is Professor of Communication at Seoul National University, Seoul, South Korea and has published four books of Korean popular culture and journalism in Korean.

Myra Macdonald teaches communication and media at Glasgow Caledonian University and is the author of *Representing Women: Myths of Femininity in the Popular Media* (London, Edward Arnold, 1995).

Stephen Muecke is Professor of Cultural Studies at the University of Technology, Sydney. His latest book is the ficto-critical *No Road (Bitumen all the Way)* (Freemantle Arts Centre Press, 1997).

Laurie Ouellette is an Assistant Professor in the Department of Journalism and Mass Media at Rutgers University.

Jacinth Samuels is a Ph.D. candidate in the Department of Sociology at York University, Ontario, Canada. She is presently writing a dissertation on sexual metaphor in the discourse of discovery.

Mark J. V. Olson: a note of thanks

The editors, staff and publishers of *Cultural Studies* would like to extend their deepest appreciation to Mark J. V. Olson for his four years of dedication and service to the journal.

His patience, guidance and attention to detail throughout his tenure have been nothing short of exemplary.

Mark has moved on to serve as interim director of UNC Chapel Hill's University Program in Cultural Studies. We wish him continued success in his new position.

The

UTS Review

CULTURAL STUDIES AND NEW WRITING

Vol 4 No. 1: On or Off the Beaten Track?

Articles

Klaus Neumann, "Remembering Victims and Perpetrators"
Gloria Davies, "Towards a Reflective Critical Practice in Chinese Literary Studies: The Example of Wang Hui"
Wang Hui, "Local Forms, Vernacular Dialects and the War of Resistance Against Japan: The National Forms Debate — Part 1"
Martin Thomas, "Morphic Echoes, Stony Silences: Reading an Australian Landscape"
Lisa Palmer, "On or Off The Beaten Track?: Tourist Trails in Thailand"
Teresia K. Teaiwa, "Yaqona/Yagoqu: Roots and Routes of a Displaced Native"
Justin Clemens, "A Report to an Academy"
Gay Hawkins, "TV Rules"
Laurie Duggan, "Grotesque, Mirthful, Cunning and Quaint: May Gibbs and Suburban Space"
Robyn Ferrell, "Motherhood Sentiments"
Mark Gibson, "Blood in the Water: Violence and the Deterritorialised Public"
Therese Davis, "Becoming Unrecognisable"

Review Article

Jodi Brooks, Fugitive Images

Reviews include Ross Chambers on The Academic Postmodern, Toby Miller on Out of Bounds, Gary Wickham on Sport in Australian History, Philip Hayward on Popular Music and Local Identity, Greg Seigworth on The Subcultures Reader, Gilbert Rodman on Ganglands, David Carter on The Virtual Republic

The UTS Review
Po Box 123 Broadway
NSW 2007 Australia
Ph: 61-[0]2-9514-2728
Email: S.Muecke@hum.uts.edu.au

ORDER FORM

Routledge titles are available from good booksellers, or can be ordered direct by any of the following methods:

- Return this form to: **Tracy Perry, Routledge, Freepost, Andover, Hants, SP10 5BR**
- Telephone our **Customer Hotline on 01264 342939 or Fax 01264 343005**
- Access our Internet site. Full details of all Routledge titles are available On-Line at:**www.routledge.com**

Qty	Title	HP/Pb	ISBN	Price	Total
	The Visual Culture Reader	Hb	0-415-14133-8	£50.00	
	The Visual Culture Reader	Pb	0-415-14134-6	£15.99	
				Grand Total £	

POSTAGE & PACKING

Prepaid and credit card orders are sent free in the UK, otherwise a charge will be made according to the weight of order. (Minimum charge £2.50) Overseas please add £6.50 per book air mail, £2.75 surface mail

METHOD OF PAYMENT

- ☐ I enclose a cheque made payable to **Routledge** for £
- ☐ Please invoice me, purchase order number:
- ☐ Please charge my credit card: Access/Visa/Diners Club/American Express

☐☐☐☐☐☐☐☐☐☐☐☐☐☐☐☐   Expiry Date __/__

NAME AND ADDRESS

c	Surname
First Name/Initial	Position
Department	Establishment
Address	
Postcode	Telephone
EU Member States VAT number	
Signature	Date

INSPECTION COPY REQUEST

The Visual Culture Reader in paperback is available on 60 days inspection to teaching staff considering adopting it for a course of 20 or more students. If you adopt the book and a comment form is returned to this effect, then you can keep the book free of charge. Otherwise you must pay the full price or return it.
Please note that inspection copies are not sent out before publication and are sent at our discretion.

Name of Course	No. of students

Send inspection Copy requests to: Aine Duffy Routledge, 11 New Fetter Lane, London, EC4P 4EE

- ☐ Please send me a free 1998 Media and Cultural Studies catalogue
- ☐ Please tick here if you do not want to receive any more information from Routledge.

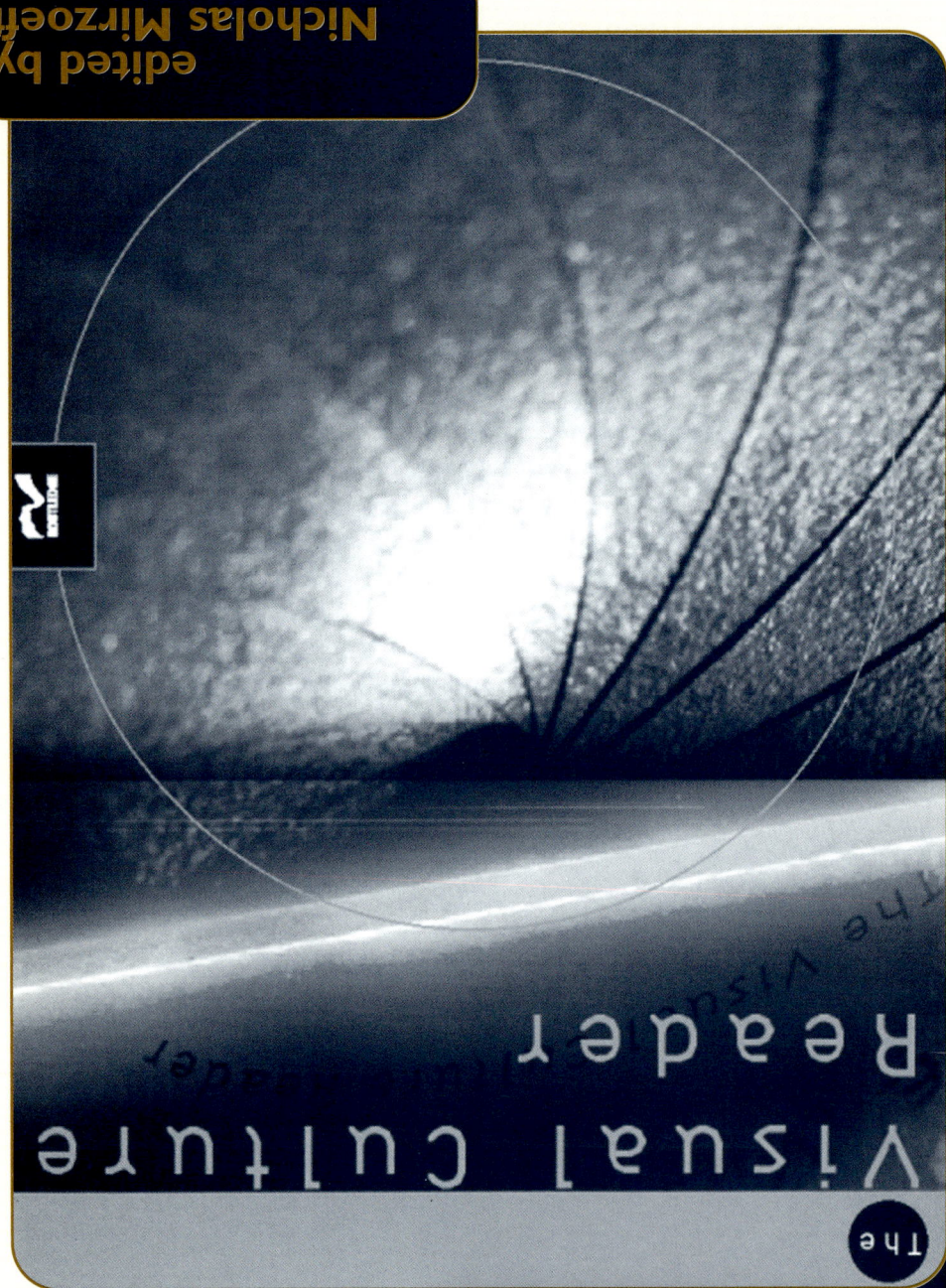

edited by
Nicholas Mirzoeff

The Visual Culture Reader

Visual Culture
Reader

The

New From Routledge